EVENTS MANAGEMENT

Edited by

Peter Robinson
University of Wolverhampton, UK

Debra Wale
University of Wolverhampton, UK

Geoff Dickson
Auckland University of Technology, New Zealand

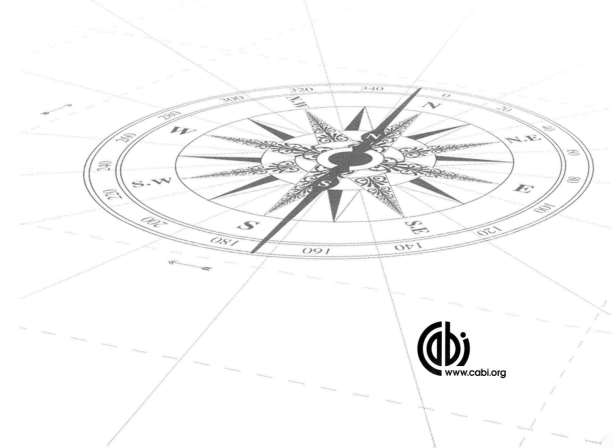

CABi
www.cabi.org

CABI is a trading name of CAB International

CABI Head Office
Nosworthy Way
Wallingford
Oxfordshire OX10 8DE
UK

CABI North American Office
875 Massachusetts Avenue
7th Floor
Cambridge, MA 02139
USA

Tel: +44 (0)1491 832111
Fax: +44 (0)1491 833508
E-mail: cabi@cabi.org
Website: www.cabi.org

Tel: +1 617 395 4056
Fax: +1 617 354 6875
E-mail: cabi-nao@cabi.org

A catalogue record for this book is available from the British Library, London, UK.

Library of Congress Cataloging-in-Publication Data

Events management / edited by Peter Robinson, Debra Wale, Geoff Dickson.
    p. cm.
  Includes bibliographical references and index.
   ISBN 978-1-84593-682-2 (alk. paper)
   1. Special events--Management. 2. Special events--Planning. I. Robinson, Peter, 1979--II. Wale, Debra. III. Dickson, Geoff. IV. Title.
  GT3405.E96 2010
  394.2--dc22

                                                              2010005505

ISBN-13: 978 1 84593 682 2

Commissioning editor: Sarah Hulbert
Production editor: Tracy Head

Typeset by SPi, Pondicherry, India.
Printed and bound in the UK by Cambridge University Press, Cambridge.

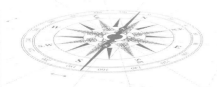

Contents

Contributors

Alison Booth, Auckland University of Technology, 55 Wellesley Street East, Auckland Central, Auckland City 1010, New Zealand. E-mail: alison.booth@aut.ac.nz

Crispin Dale, University of Wolverhampton, Leisure Industries, Walsall Campus, Gorway Road, Walsall WS1 3BD, UK. E-mail: c.dale@wlv.ac.uk

Lóránt Dávid, Department of Tourism and Regional Development, Károly Róbert College, 3200 Gyöngyös, Mátrai u. 36, Magyarország, Hungary. E-mail: davidlo@karolyrobert.hu

Geoff Dickson, Auckland University of Technology, 55 Wellesley Street East, Auckland Central, Auckland City 1010, New Zealand. E-mail: geoff.dickson@aut.ac.nz

Steve Gelder, University of Wolverhampton, Leisure Industries, Walsall Campus, Gorway Road, Walsall WS1 3BD, UK. E-mail: s.gelder@wlv.ac.uk

Sine Heitmann, University of Wolverhampton, Leisure Industries, Walsall Campus, Gorway Road, Walsall WS1 3BD, UK. E-mail: s.heitmann@wlv.ac.uk

Ade Oriade, University of Wolverhampton, Leisure Industries, Walsall Campus, Gorway Road, Walsall WS1 3BD, UK. E-mail: Ade.oriade@wlv.ac.uk

Ghislaine Povey, University of Wolverhampton, Leisure Industries, Walsall Campus, Gorway Road, Walsall WS1 3BD, UK. E-mail: g.povey@wlv.ac.uk

Andrew Ridal, The Arena Theatre and University of Wolverhampton, Leisure Industries, Walsall Campus, Gorway Road, Walsall WS1 3BD, UK. E-mail: aridal@wlv.ac.uk

Christine Roberts, University of Aberdeen, King's College, Aberdeen AB24 3FX, UK. E-mail: christine.roberts@abdn.ac.uk

Peter Robinson, University of Wolverhampton, Leisure Industries, Walsall Campus, Gorway Road, Walsall WS1 3BD, UK. E-mail: p.robinson@wlv.ac.uk

Dimitri Tassiopoulos, Walter Sisulu University, PO Box 1421, East London, 5200, Buffalo City, Eastern Cape Province, South Africa. E-mail: dtassio@wsu.ac.za

Jo-Ansie Van Wyk, University of South Africa, East PO Box 392, UniSA 0003, South Africa. E-mail: Vwykjak@unisa.ac.za

Debra Wale, University of Wolverhampton, Leisure Industries, Walsall Campus, Gorway Road, Walsall WS1 3BD, UK. E-mail: d.wale@wlv.ac.uk

Caroline Wiscombe, University of Wolverhampton, Leisure Industries, Walsall Campus, Gorway Road, Walsall WS1 3BD, UK. E-mail: c.wiscombe@wlv.ac.uk

About the Editors and Authors

THE EDITORS

Peter Robinson is a Senior Lecturer and Course Leader at the University of Wolverhampton, and a Member of the Tourism Society, Tourism Management Institute and Institute of Travel and Tourism. Previous experience in the public, private and voluntary sectors includes working in senior management teams in a range of roles including Tourism Development Officer, Visitor Services Manager and Tourism Projects Manager. Peter's research interests lie in the fields of community-led tourism development, events management and the sociology of leisure. Peter has published widely in these subject areas and in research around pedagogy, and believes in maintaining strong relationships with industry, ensuring that this complements his teaching and research.

Debra Wale is a Senior Lecturer in the School of Sport, Performing Arts and Leisure at the University of Wolverhampton. She is the Course Leader for the BA Event and Venue Management and BA Hospitality Management at the School of Hospitality and Resort Management in Singapore. She teaches Marketing on undergraduate and postgraduate programmes. Her industry experience includes Brand Management, Event Management and Sports Management, which have given her experience across the private, public and not-for-profit sectors and the disciplines of the leisure industries. She is currently studying towards her Professional Practice Doctorate in Education.

Geoff Dickson is the Associate Dean (Research) for the Faculty of Health and Environmental Sciences. As a member of the School of Sport and Recreation, Geoff leads the undergraduate and postgraduate programmes in sport and recreation management. His research interests centre on inter-organizational networks, sport governance and event-related tourism. He is an Associate Director of the New Zealand Tourism Research Institute, where he is responsible for the event tourism research programme area. Geoff is an editorial board member of the *Annals of Leisure Research, International Journal of Sport Marketing and Sponsorship, International Journal of Sport Marketing and Management*, and the *Sport Management Education Journal*. He initiated the establishment of the Research Advisory Board for the 2011 Rugby World Cup.

THE AUTHORS

Alison Booth is a lecturer in the BA and Diploma Event Management programme in the School of Hospitality and Tourism at Auckland University of Technology. She holds a Masters in Creative and Performing Arts (Arts Management) from the University of Auckland and is currently a PhD candidate at the New Zealand Tourism Research Institute. She has wide event management experience in the tertiary sector well as having a long career in world music as a producer and practitioner. She writes on world music and production management, and presents regularly at international conferences.

Crispin Dale is a Principal Lecturer and has taught strategic management for leisure industries at undergraduate and postgraduate level for a number of years. Crispin has published widely in peer-reviewed journals on strategic management for tourism businesses. His research has focused upon the competitive environment of travel businesses in the tour operating industry and the strategic networks of travel eMediaries. He has also researched the impact of contemporary strategic management issues on small tourism enterprises in the expanding European Union. As a consequence of Crispin's expertise in the field, he was invited to write a resource guide on strategic management for the Hospitality, Leisure, Sport and Tourism subject network of the Higher Education Academy.

Lóránt Dávid was born in Hungary, and graduated in History, Geography, European Studies and Tourism. He is the Jean Monnet Professor in Tourism at Károly Róbert College, Gyöngyös, and an Honorary Associate Professor at Szent István University, Gödöllő, in Hungary. He has longstanding teaching, publication and research interests in tourism, regional development and environmental studies. More recently, he has been undertaking research on tourism resources and management. He is the author and editor of over ten books as well as over 100 journal articles and book chapters, and has been active in a number of international research and teaching associations.

Steve Gelder is a Senior Lecturer at the University of Wolverhampton and has worked as a Principal Local Government Officer within the Leisure and Community Department. Steve has a Masters degree in Business Administration and focuses his teaching and research in policy, planning and operations management within the leisure and lifestyle industries. He cites the 'inclusion agenda' as close to his heart and of fundamental importance in ensuring equality of access to the service industry.

Sine Heitmann graduated with an MBA in Tourism and, since graduation, has been teaching tourism and leisure students at both undergraduate and postgraduate level. Work experience includes organizations within the public and private tourism and hospitality industries, from which her interest in human resource management derives. Current research areas include the sustainability of tourism, the relationship between tourism and media, tourism and accessibility, and cultural tourism – the latter has been subject of papers presented in conferences.

Ade Oriade is a senior lecturer in tourism and postgraduate programmes course leader at the University of Wolverhampton. Having worked in the industry in different capacities, Ade brought these experiences to bear in delivering customer service, quality management and operations modules. Ade specializes in Quality Management in Tourism; he also has special interest in Tourism/Hospitality education and career analysis and Transportation for Tourism.

Ade's interest in the travel industry was fuelled by his research findings when he was studying for a postgraduate diploma in Transport Studies. His current research works focus on quality perception and career development in travel and tourism.

Ghislaine Povey is a Senior Lecturer within the School of Sport, Performing Arts and Leisure. She holds an MSc in Tourism and Hospitality Education from the University of Surrey (1996). Ghislaine joined the University of Wolverhampton in 1992, and has been a member of SSPAL since its inception. Prior to that, she was a lecturer in tourism at Bourneville College of Further Education. Ghislaine has extensive international industrial experience, having worked in the travel industry in four continents, in both public and private sectors. She wrote a regular regional food recipe column in the *Express & Star* newspaper for 2 years, and has made numerous appearances on TV and radio discussing heritage, tourist experiences and regional food.

Andrew Ridal is Marketing Manager of the Arena Theatre, Wolverhampton, and a Visiting Lecturer in Marketing, PR and Sales for the Leisure Industries at the University of Wolverhampton. Andrew has over 10 years' experience working in the creative industries across the public and private sector, and in rural and urban settings. His specialism lies in Arts Marketing and Audience Development for theatre and performance venues, and he has written for industry journals including *Arts Professional* and the *Journal of Arts Marketing*.

Christine Roberts is a lecturer in Sport Management, having completed her MSc in Applied Sport and Exercise Science. Alongside maintaining an international athletic career and multi-regional coaching employment, Christine has established long-term work experience in the public, private and voluntary sport and leisure industries, whereby her interest in human relations and the management of human resources developed.

Dimitri Tassiopoulos is an Associate Director at the School of Tourism & Hospitality of Walter Sisulu University, South Africa. Since 1993, he has been involved in various national and international tourism research projects, of a multidisciplinary and multi-institutional nature, concerning agritourism, event, cultural and wine tourism, amongst others. Dimitri is the author and editor of the multiple edition books: *Events Management – a Developmental and Managerial Approach* (Juta). He is also the editor and author of *New Tourism Ventures – an Entrepreneurial and Managerial Approach* (Juta). In 2004, he was appointed a member of the South African Qualifications Authority's Standards Generating Body (SGB) for Travel, Tourism & Events, and was appointed the chairperson of the said SGB. He acts as the vice president of the Tourism and Hospitality Education Providers of South Africa (THEPSA). This federation represents further (FET) and higher education (HET) institutions offering the spectrum of qualifications related to the management of the tourism industry. He also acts as the chairperson of the Tourism and Events Educators' Chamber of South Africa (TEECSA), which is an association representing higher education travel, tourism and events-related programme providers.

Jo-Ansie van Wyk lectures on International Politics at the University of South Africa. She has obtained an MA (Political Science) from the University of Stellenbosch and is currently a doctoral candidate at the University of Pretoria, Pretoria, South Africa. She has published on political event management, international relations, foreign policy, space politics, environmental issues and international political economy. She is a Fulbright Alumna and a Member of the Suid-Afrikaanse Akademie vir Wetenskap en Kuns. She has served as the Review

Editor of *Politikon* (Routledge/Taylor & Francis) and the Editor of *Politeia* (UniSA Press). She regularly lectures at the South African National Intelligence Academy, the South African National Defence College, the South African War College and the South African Diplomatic Academy. She has completed consultancies for the World Bank, UNESCO, the Institute for Security Studies, the South African Department of Foreign Affairs and Consultancy Africa Intelligence.

Caroline Wiscombe has operated as an entrepreneur for some 20 years. An outstanding professional and current trustee of a major industry partner, she regularly makes decisions that have contributed to a £7.5m turnover. Recently negotiating capital assets of £1.5m, the business continues to strive for professional standards. A late blossomer in academic terms, Caroline has provided a unique insight in applying business to practice. Publications include: *But Why Do I Need Training? A Case Study Approach*; *On-licensed Retail Training Philosophies Amongst Tenants, Lessees and Free-house Operators*; *Foundation Degree (Arts) Professional Licensed Retailing: Innovations in Design and Delivery*; *Training for the Responsible Service of Alcohol: Guidelines for the Responsible Service of Alcohol* (Brussels: The Amsterdam Group: the European forum for sensible drinking).

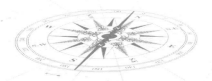

Events Management: an Introduction

Peter Robinson, Geoff Dickson and Debra Wale

THE MODERN EVENTS INDUSTRY

The scale and scope of the event industry have grown significantly in recent years, with increased professionalism, new innovations in event education, and a wider recognition of the event industry's political, social, cultural, economic and environmental impacts. Events today touch all our lives, and it is important to recognize the full range of organizations within the event industry, and move beyond its close affiliation with the tourism industry. Every business sector relies upon the events industry for meetings, conferences and product launches. The non-profit sector utilizes events for fundraising and awareness-raising purposes. The term 'events' covers a multitude of activities, including:

- Concerts
- Charity events
- Sports events
- Festivals
- Theatre performances
- Opera
- Dance and drama performances
- Fundraising activities

- Product launches
- Conferences
- Trade fairs and exhibitions
- Celebrations
- Weddings
- Arts events
- Family events
- Meetings

All of these events impact upon their host communities through additional visitor spend, with accommodation and food accounting for most of the expenditure. The economic impact of the Glastonbury music festival in England is almost £1 billion, with approximately one-quarter spent away from the festival site in the local community. The global size of the events industry makes it difficult to measure the true size of the sector and no formal research exists that explores the full breadth of the industry. However, evidence from the exhibitions sector provides some insight into the scale of its impacts:

> The exhibition/event industry ... generates considerable economic activity ... There are approximately 500 UK trade fairs and exhibitions each year attracting 17 million people annually. The UK exhibitions/events industry contributes £9.3 billion to the UK economy, and provides 137,000 jobs – 0.5% of total UK employment – generating £1 billion in tax revenue per annum ... (and) generating revenue relating to accommodation of £720m, the equivalent of 19m beds a year.
>
> (Association of Event Organisers, 2009)

The modern event industry is synonymous with innovation – new ideas to create increasingly impressive events using state-of-the-art production technologies. At the same time, events are often consumed by strong emotional attachments that are linked to the past through ritual, nostalgia and tradition. An event that does not have these is likely to be in search of them. At the same time, the event will be expected to provide a financial return on its investment and ensure that it is novel, that it retains its relevance to the market and that the production is of a contemporary standard. Event managers and marketers must understand these ambiguities and adopt a perspective that is consistent with the event's social, cultural and commercial context.

When considered together, it is evident that commercial logic and economic rationality are often at odds with the romantic visions, passion and emotion present in an event. This is the paradoxical nature of events and it is these paradoxes and points of difference that justify event management as a legitimate profession.

These tensions are placing more demands on the skill levels of those people who work in the industry. There are a number of entry points into the events sector and each has a corresponding level of qualification and/or skill. For example, someone involved in the implementation of sound and lighting at an event will have a different skill set and professional background from the person responsible for negotiating government/corporate sector support for the event. It is important that event organizations are not assumed less complex or that performance outcomes are more easily achievable when compared with other organizations.

The growth and development of the events industry worldwide has created opportunities for management professionals in a wide variety of settings. Boosted by advances in telecommunications, increased government and corporate sector investments, the industry continues to develop new products that provide quality experiences for consumers. Demand for competent managers in this area, underpinned by tertiary qualifications, has grown rapidly in recent years.

Because the events industry is perceived as an exciting and dynamic industry, it attracts people with a diverse array of experiences and qualifications, acquired outside of the events context. Students enrolled in events-specific qualifications should not perceive that they have a mortgage on positions in the events industry. Tertiary education in event management is best complemented by real-world involvement either in a paid or unpaid capacity.

Professional associations are another source of ongoing education and, in addition, they advance the standards governing the sector, provide a lobbying body for the industry, advocate policies and support their membership. In the events sector, there are numerous associations established on a regional, national or international basis.

THE ORIGINS OF THE EVENTS INDUSTRY

Events are a curious hybrid of old and new. Events can be traced back to early history, when communities would gather for religious worship and celebration. Of course, these were not considered events at the time. As society started to create towns and social systems, event venues became an intrinsic dimension of the town planning process. Roman cities often included arenas and amphitheatres for shows and events, forums or marketplaces for trading and community events, and shrines and churches for religious celebration were also evident. As these facilities became embedded in social structures, they became a key part of town planning and, in Europe and Asia at least, they are an essential aspect of the layout and structure of modern towns and cities.

Although this formal approach to events declined during the Dark Ages and early medieval history, by the 12th century events were gaining local identity and regionality, with famous annual events such as the Lord Mayor's Show and the Nottingham Goose Fair originating in the 13th century. Notwithstanding cancellations during the Bubonic Plague and other notable historic events, many of these continue today. The evolution of medieval town planning would create places for markets, religious activity and fairs – hence the term 'marketplace'. The location of these marketplaces in the city centres would assist in providing events with an element of centrality to daily lives, a theme that continues to this day.

In the 18th and 19th centuries, the Industrial Revolution produced a wider range of products and equipment. The commensurate growth in world trade led to the development of trade fairs and exhibitions. Enhanced transportation permitted people to travel further, facilitating growth of the hotel sector. Hotels soon built ballrooms and other facilities suitable for events.

Event venues added a new dimension in the 1970s with the introduction of a new generation of large-scale, multi-purpose venues. Cinemas and sport stadiums would seek a greater diversity of events to host, and new-generation cinemas and stadiums would be constructed with this diversity in mind. Today's event industry encompasses a wide range of event venues, including:

- exhibition centres;
- conference facilities;
- hotels with meeting facilities;
- open spaces, parks;
- historic properties;
- theatres;
- nightclubs;
- wedding venues;
- theme parks; and
- unusual venues (steam trains, themed attractions).

The evolution of the events sector reflects the social, political, economic, environmental and technological growth of society. For these same reasons, the events sector will also change in the future.

USING THIS BOOK

The book provides a detailed overview of the different aspects of events management. It is divided into three parts. The first part provides an introductory outline of the historical developments and current state of the industry, while also taking into account wider political and cultural issues. The second part of the book concentrates on practical operations management, including planning, project management, marketing, human resource management, health and safety, logistics and funding. Finally, the third part covers critical issues such as impacts, sustainability and legacy of events. Each chapter contains case studies from around the world and review questions, ensuring that the book is a useful learning tool and provides a current and up-to-date view of the industry in this increasingly popular field of study.

In the writing of this book, there has been considerable debate about the topic content, detail and coverage, and the need to ensure that it remains operational in its focus. The publication is designed for students and practitioners in the event sector and has been developed so that readers are able to understand theory and concepts presented through applied examples. To achieve this, each chapter ensures that theories and concepts are illustrated with case studies and debated within the text. All chapters have a mixture of tasks, activities and questions to support the factual content, and a set of review questions at the end, which can be used by lecturers or by the individual reader. A brief guide to additional sources and reading material is also provided at the end of each chapter. A comprehensive reference list provides the opportunity for particular quotes and ideas that are discussed and debated in each chapter to be explored in more detail.

The first part discusses the theoretical basis of events management under the heading context and concepts. Chapter 1 investigates cultural, political and societal influences that have shaped the events industry since the 1960s. Through the use of case studies and other industry examples, the chapter will highlight key trends and influences that have contributed to the high profile of today's event industry, aligned as it is to high-profile celebrations, celebrity culture and major public followings. Chapter 2 introduces key theories and ideas surrounding the design, development, delivery and analysis of events. The chapter provides definitions of key terms, explains underpinning models and illustrates the range and scope of the events industry. Through the use of short case studies the chapter also demonstrates the range of activities that are classed as 'events' and explores the relationship between events and tourism, hospitality, leisure, business, fundraising, charities and sport. Chapter 3 explores the scale and scope of the events industry, paying particular attention to the types of businesses involved in events management, the complex relationships between these organizations and their use of new technologies.

The second part of the book then explores the operational aspects of event management. Chapter 4 explores the financial challenges of managing and delivering events and considers the ways in which events are funded. Topics around sponsorship will be discussed as fundraising tools, and the different models needed for financing public, private and third sector events will be analysed. This leads into Chapter 5, which explains event management from an operational perspective and demonstrates, again through case studies, how effective logistics management is essential for events to be delivered on time and on budget. The chapter will discuss each stage of the event planning process, from initial concept to tidying up the site. This includes discussions around venue choices, site and facility design, quality and capacity management, yield management, performance and productivity management, and supply chain management.

Chapter 6 discusses human resource management (HRM) theories, processes and concepts in the context of the event management organizations. Key topics include theories of motivation and leadership, human resources planning, recruitment and selection, training and development, grievance and discipline, as well as key issues such as legislation and labour market realities. The ideas are analysed and discussed in the context of their application and usefulness in practice to show the importance of the key concepts for managers in an increasingly competitive and diverse working environment. Chapter 7 applies marketing concepts, principles and models to the events industry. The chapter provides explanation with case studies of strategies for marketing events with a particular focus on contemporary e-marketing communications. Chapter 8 evaluates the importance of quality management in the event sector, and examines the nature of quality and how this influences satisfaction and repeat visits to events. Concepts such as perceived quality, value and customer expectation are explored. In the same vein, theories such as cue utilization, gap analysis and Kano's theory of attractive quality are highlighted to provide frameworks to enhance student understanding and assist practitioners to evaluate and manage service quality in the industry. Chapter 9 begins by introducing concepts of ethics and social responsibility, and then takes an issues-based approach to consider the social, environmental and legal issues influencing the successful management of events. This chapter explores the impacts events can have on a destination and its community. Both negative and positive impacts on economies, environments (built and natural) and societies are included in the discussion. In order to minimize any negative impacts, the concept of sustainability and corporate social responsibility (CSR) is analysed, using principles of good practice and various case studies to highlight the issues surrounding impacts and the responsibility of event managers.

The final part of the book takes a long-term view of the events sector, starting with an overview of the themes in event planning that have grown exponentially in recent years. Chapter 10 explores strategic management concepts and theories within the context of the events industry. The chapter will acknowledge the interrelationships between the different management functions and analyse business situations and strategic options. The chapter will initially introduce the deliberate and emergent nature of strategic management and its impact upon event strategy and planning. Approaches to analysing the external macro- and microenvironment will be discussed with an understanding of the factors that may impact upon events and event operators. Consideration will then be given to concepts and theories that address the strategic options and methods of event operators. Approaches to understanding the implementation of strategies to events as part of the strategic management process will then be addressed. To enhance understanding of the material, the chapter will apply the theories and concepts to 'live' mini-case studies of events and event operators. Chapter 11 explores the potential for events to provide host communities with a legacy. The chapter helps to explain why cities and countries want to invest in hallmark and mega-events and demonstrates this through case studies of past events. The final section concludes with a summary and review of the key discussions from the book while also considering current and future developments within the event industry.

Events are a part of the fabric of society. Fundamentally, they bring people together. They create communities. These communities might only be together for a limited duration but, none the less, they create opportunities for celebration, commemoration, learning, understanding and contemplation.

In return for hard work and unfriendly work hours, event management is a career that offers excitement and the occasional opportunity for glamour. The knowledge that we share in this book is a starting point for a career in events. The knowledge needs to be complemented by personal attributes. These include: tenacity – things can and do go wrong; physical and emotional endurance – the hours can be long and criticism plentiful; attention to detail – the little things always count; and creativity – everyone expects next year's event to be bigger and better. An eventful career is all but guaranteed to those who acquire this knowledge and possess these skills.

chapter 1

Culture and the Event Experience

Ghislaine Povey and Jo-Ansie Van Wyk

OBJECTIVES OF THE CHAPTER

Culture is fundamental to our society. It shapes how we think, what we eat, how our families are formed, what work we do and how we spend our leisure time. This chapter addresses the nature of culture, societies and politics in the event context. The political, cultural and sociological impacts/consequences of participation for event attendees, organizers and host communities are explored, and the implications of these for the events industry are discussed. The nature of the relationships between events industry stakeholders is also examined. The character of the event experience is investigated from the viewpoints of the various participants, with issues including authenticity and the impacts of visitor behaviours. A diverse range of case studies is included as exemplars of the diversity of the event experience and the political climates, cultures and societies involved in the events industry.

The objectives of this chapter are to:

- analyse the importance of culture, societies and politics in relation to events;
- discuss aspects of the event experience and authenticity;
- explore the event attendee, organizer and host relationships and their socio-cultural aspects; and
- investigate political influences and impacts of events.

EVENTS AND POLITICS

Events, like every other aspect of everyday life in the 21st century, are influenced by political factors. From a political perspective, as well as a cultural perspective as discussed earlier, a society can be defined by what it celebrates. The determination of what is celebrated when, by whom, where and how is a political process with economic implications and vice versa. This political process involves decision makers, their supporters, some form of authority such as a government or a city council, and investors.

Politics shape the organization and staging of events in various ways. First, politics determines rights and obligations. In order for event managers to stage an event, cognizance should be taken of various local by-laws and national legislation – products of political processes – pertaining to rights (such as freedom of association) and responsibilities (such as environmental protection and tolerance to different cultures) related to events. Furthermore, event managers often have to apply for permission or a licence to stage an event, cooperate with authorities with regards to traffic and crowd control, as well as pay royalties. The role of authorities is to secure events' compliance with the norms and values of the society in which it takes place. More importantly, in a democratic society, their role is also to protect citizens' right to assembly, free speech and cultural expression. In undemocratic societies, these rights are severely compromised, often to the detriment of people's and ethnic groups' ability to practise their culture by, for example, staging an event.

Second, politics determines the allocation of and competition for power (and hence decision making and influence) and resources, and access to these resources (such as budgets or a political position) within host communities, cultural representation, socialization and the income of a particular community. Countries emerging from a violent past often have to re-interpret a war, battle, genocide, victimization, leaders and culture in order to achieve reconciliation. One way to overcome historical memories of victimization is to institute new national public holidays to promote nation building and to celebrate it by staging events countrywide, or at

---

Box 1.1. The Zulu Reed Dance.

The isiZulu is one of the largest ethnic groups in South Africa and was, historically, one of the largest empires in southern Africa. The annual Zulu Reed Dance attracts thousands of participants and tourists. The event is controversial because of its patriarchal and sexist nature. In post-apartheid South Africa, cultural rights are protected in the country's democratic constitution and the Zulu King is acknowledged as a traditional leader and a member of the House of Traditional Leaders. For the Zulu nation, it is a major event to showcase their unique culture. Every year in September, young girls converge in groups from the Zululand regions in South Africa's KwaZulu Natal Province for the Zulu King's Reed Dance (the *Umkhosi woMhlanga*), which takes place at eNyokeni Palace. The purpose of the Zulu Reed dance is an educational opportunity for young women to learn how to behave in front of the King and is a key element of keeping the young girls virgins until they are ready for marriage. Approximately 15,000 Zulu virgins gather in traditional outfits such as the *izigege* and the *izinculuba* that show their bottoms. On the day of the ceremony, the girls walk to the main hut of the King. When the King appears to watch the procession of girls, he is praised by his poets or praise singers (*isimbongi*). Next, the girls collect a reed from a huge pile and form a very long procession, led by the senior princess. As they pass the King, they put it down and go back, while men sing traditional songs and engage in mock fighting. After the ceremony, the King delivers a speech on the expected mores of the Zulu nation. The girls are now ready for marriage.

Source: Zululand EcoAdventures (2010)

historically relevant locations. This is illustrated by the Yakusuni Shrine in Japan. Since 1869, when Japanese Emperor Meiji established the Yasukuni Shrine, the Shrine has commemorated and, in terms of Japan's Shinto religion, worshipped the souls of Japanese who died in defence of their country. For outsiders and countries such as China, Korea and the USA, which have been attacked by Japan, the Shrine is controversial, as it includes 14 convicted Class A war criminals in terms of the Tokyo War Crimes Tribunal, which took place after the Second World War. Annually visited by hundreds of thousands of visitors, the Shrine is a symbol of patriotism and a symbol of foreign invasions. Japanese Prime Ministers often visit the Shrine during their terms. These visits often anger opposition parties and Japan's Asian neighbours, particularly China and Korea, which have been victims of the Japan's military aggression in the past (BBC News, 15 August 2008: Internet).

The wide range of benefits and disadvantages associated with staging an event are outlined in Table 1.1.

Table 1.1. Political impacts of hosting events.

Event	Positive	Negative
1984 Summer Olympics, Los Angeles, USA (Andranovich *et al.*, 2001)	US$145 million tax revenues; LA mayor's presence enhanced; inter-local cooperation; public art; infrastructure development	Anti-LA sentiment mobilized in surrounding areas, which prevented their development
2002 Winter Olympics, Salt Lake City, USA (Utah Office of Tourism, 2008)	Enhanced inter-governmental lobbying capacity; US$76 million tax revenues; infrastructure development	Conflict over paying for costs in venue communities
1996 Summer Olympics, Atlanta, USA (Andranovich *et al.*, 2001)	Affirmative action employment and purchasing policies; public art; Centennial Olympic Park infrastructure development	Local politics nationalized; federal empowerment zone; liquor store licences not renewed
Annual Guelaguetza Festival, Mexico (Whitford, 2009)	National prestige of the Oaxaca region; improved national and international profile of the Oaxaca region; presents means for the facilitation of indigenous capacity development; increases awareness of indigenous Mexican people; promotes tourism to Mexico	Exacerbates political corruption and/or exploitation; engenders political unrest; provides an opportunity to communicate propaganda; loss of local community ownership and control; promotes centralized, monopolized management; increases negative image of Oaxaca

THE EFFECTS OF TYPES OF POLITICAL GOVERNANCE ON EVENTS

In democratic societies, the freedom exists to commemorate events of cultural, historical and political relevance. Annually, countries that have participated in major political events such as the First (1914–1919) and Second (1939–1945) World Wars commemorate the end of these wars and major turning points in these wars. Examples include staging events relating to D-Day, and Armistice Day on 11 November. Other politically related events include a state's national day, independence day or the day of its establishment. National public holidays often celebrate or commemorate a political event that took place in the past and has significance for a particular country and its people. In France, for example, Bastille Day, the country's national day, is commemorated on 14 July. It commemorates the storming of the Bastille prison in 1789, which initiated the French Revolution. South Africa, for example, annually commemorates the end of apartheid on 27 April, the date of the country's first ever democratic elections in 1994 since it became a Dutch colony in April 1652.

In undemocratic countries, governments issue travel documents for their citizens to travel from one of its regions to another, as free movement of people is strictly regulated to, *inter alia*, prevent political events from taking place. Even democratic governments have placed some legal restrictions on the hosting of civic events. These restrictions are often enacted in legislation and local government policy papers and related to, *inter alia*, the time, location, scope and the details of the organizers of the event. Although most of the restrictions relate to political and government events, civic events such as protests and marches can very often result in violence, as they are a more direct mode of expressing grievances.

Governments are often instrumental in establishing a society's political rituals. Political rituals such as the collective celebration of national heroes, artists, literature and national public holidays are important for nation building and reconciliation in any state. The commemoration of a common past and culture, and political symbols ensures social cohesion, political inclusiveness and political stability, which, in turn, contribute to socio-economic development in a country.

THE IMPORTANCE OF POLITICS IN THE EVENTS SECTOR

A government's policies may enhance or hinder the events sector in a country. In democratic societies, greater tolerance for 'the other' and the celebration and commemoration of its cultural goods exists. Freedom of speech, association, assembly and the recognition of different cultural identities assist the events sector to initiate and stage events celebrating unique cultures and their practices. However, the corollary of this right is the responsibility to not stage an event that may infringe on the rights of other cultural groups.

Political elites often influence the citizenry in maintaining or innovating political rituals. When political rituals exclude 'the other' or vilify a different culture, it may result in controversy and even conflict in a society. The elite's use or denial of memory can be used to reinforce or destroy an identity. Both reinforcement and destruction determine the commemoration or the abolition of the commemoration of an event. Often, a hero is another's villain or terrorist.

Events are often targeted by political groups to attract publicity to their cause. Individuals of groups with grievances have in the past targeted events to either assassinate participants, murder, and kidnap or attack a high profile decision maker or celebrity. In 1996, a bomb exploded at the Olympic Games in Atlanta, USA. In 1972, Israeli athletes were murdered by members of a Palestinian opposition group at the Olympic Games in Munich, Germany. These and other similar events illustrate the risks associated with staging an event. In January 2010, a separatist group of the Angolan enclave Cabinda attacked a bus transporting the Togolese team participating in the African Cup of Nations soccer tournament hosted by Angola. The attack not only killed a player and wounded others, but its spill-over effect was significant; the government of Togo recalled their team. The attack illustrated the Angolan government's poor security arrangements pertaining to the soccer tournament, and raised questions about South Africa's ability to host the 2010 FIFA World Cup. Internationally, a perception has been reinforced that events cannot be staged in politically unstable countries and locations. For South Africa, the FIFA World Cup is of major economic importance. It is estimated that it will inject about ZAR55 billion into the country's contracting economy (GCIS, 2009).

As political actors, governments set the legal parameters within which events can be staged. These parameters can, for example, include the institution of a national public holiday. In December 2009, Philippine President Gloria Macapagal-Arroyo signed a law declaring the observance of Eidul Adha (the Feast of Sacrifice or Day of Sacrifice) – the tenth day in the month of Hajj or Islamic pilgrimage to Mecca in Saudi Arabia – a national holiday (*Philippine Daily Inquirer*, 2010).

Events significantly impact on a country or community's development through tourism and investment. From May to October 2010, China will be the first developing country to stage the World Expo, in Shanghai. For the government of China, the event is regarded as an opportunity to 'flaunt the [Chinese Communist] party's organisational power and the nation's engineering prowess and cultural greatness' (*The Economist*, 5 December 2009, p. 60). Some US$45 billion has been invested in Shanghai in preparation of the event. The US pavilion at the Expo is expected to cost at least US$61 million (*The Economist*, 5 December 2009, p. 60).

Poor planning by political decision makers can result in major event-related financial losses for taxpayers. The South African government, for example, had to pay a cancellation fee of ZAR11.7 million for the cancellation of an African Diaspora Summit in 2009 (Democratic Alliance, 2010).

POLITICAL IMPLICATIONS FOR EVENT ORGANIZERS

International

Mega-events are often an excellent example of true international cooperation, while working towards a common goal. International organizations such as the European Union, the United Nations and the International Olympic Committee all work transnationally to organize events for international participants. Conversely, they can cause international tension when there are clashes of national interests and cultures.

National

National governments can gain great political benefits from well run events. International events have many political benefits to the host nation, particularly in gaining prestige. It is an opportunity to market the best of the country to an international audience. If the event experience is good, it can generate 'brand ambassadors' for the country, who will provide influential, positive word-of-mouth feedback to their friends and relatives. It gets the country into the consciousness of the international community. A well managed event can give many benefits to the country economically (see Chapter 11), socially and culturally (as discussed later in the chapter). It can also bestow a political benefit, giving the opportunity to be heard on the world stage.

If the host nation has political stability, this can be very beneficial; international under-standing can be engendered by interactions at the event. A host lacking political stability can, however, put off visitors who are likely to opt for an event that was perceived to be safer. Many modern-day events are dedicated to the memorial of wars, and this can in fact act very posi-tively to build bridges between the participants, even when they are from opposing sides in the conflict. This can be seen in the popularity of visits to Second World War memorial events by participants from all countries involved.

Local aspects

Local government has perhaps the greatest challenge when considering the political aspects of event organization. They can lose much goodwill among local residents when this is not effec-tive. This was seen in the research into Bruges' European Capital of Culture experience, which led to the marginalization of locals from the city centre, as discussed later in the chapter. Local governments have the responsibility to ensure that the benefits are maximized while mini-mizing the costs to the local community. This is particularly challenging when dealing with powerful event owners and the demands of national or (in the case of Europe) international governments. Strong local government with clear and well-focused strategies regarding events management can ensure great benefits for their region. Not hosting events to avoid problems can prevent the area from developing effectively and deprive residents of infrastructure that can have lasting positive effects.

EVENTS AND CULTURE

Derived from the Latin word *cultura*, which means 'to cultivate', culture as we understand it is complex term that defies precise definition. Culture encompasses aspects of human life includ-ing language, dress codes, religious practices, behavioural codes and rituals. It is saturated with meanings and symbols. Our perceptions of what is beautiful or ugly, good or bad, or entertain-ing or boring are all a reflection of our culture. Similarly, the manner in which we celebrate marriages, the birth of a child or the death of a parent are all culturally ingrained. Culture influences behaviour, and thus has particular importance for the events industry, and this is especially pertinent when the host culture differs significantly from that of the guest. A further complicating variable is that culture is dynamic – what was once a norm and an accepted way of doing things might now be considered inappropriate and culturally insensitive.

Cultural capital

Culture is a vital part of the social and economic well-being of any community, town or city. The first person to introduce the concept of cultural capital was Bordieu (1984). Essentially, in this context culture is not just seen as having peripheral educational and entertainment value, but is seen to carry its own capital, with economic success coming to regions that adopt and create cultural events (Bourdieu, 1984). In the economic recession of the 1980s, when consumerism faltered, culture began to give people a sense of belonging and a different focus for their lives (Ali-Knight and Robertson, 2006). Cultural capital comprises acquired cultural knowledge that gives the owner both status and power. Cultural capital is a non-financial asset that is given to individuals who grow up in an educated, intellectually sophisticated family. Their families are often professionals who have comparatively low incomes such as teachers, lecturers, religious leaders and artists. They do, however, have a high level of social and educational attainment.

Cultural capital is distinctly different from:

- economic capital – which is related to economic resources (such as cash);
- social capital – where the assets are related to networks of influence, support based upon group memberships and relationships (such as discounted tickets to events for certain groups); and
- symbolic capital – where assets are available to the individual because of honour, recognition or prestige (as for example in the case of celebrities getting priority access to events).

Cultural events have become an economic necessity in many towns and cities, for example the Edinburgh Festival of performing arts, and the building of the International Convention Centre in Birmingham, UK. Cultural events are now vital to these cities' cultural economies.

Experiencing 'the other'

The interaction between visitors and the hosts of the event is central to the visitor experience. Much of the attraction of attending an event lies in the fact that this is outside the daily life of the participant, and thus meeting the host community is 'the other'. Hosting an event leads to a meeting of different societies. The consequences of this meeting differ depending upon the management of the event. Events have impacts upon their participants, and the community that hosts the event. According to Ali-Knight and Robertson (2006), there is little agreement regarding the definition of culture in the context of the events industry. They suggest that it is the 'process' or product of a group of activities that create a culture.

Questions

- Think about an event that you are familiar with; it could be a sporting event or a wedding, for example. How would a visitor from a different country, who comes from a different culture, experience the event?
- What aspects of the event may present challenges for them? (Consider food, drinks, religious ceremonies, how people dance, etc.)
- How can event organizers make their events accessible to visitors from different cultures?
- If these changes are made, will the nature of the event be changed?

It should also be remembered that some change in culture is normal and often events do change in their nature as culture changes. It is as detrimental to an event's content and culture to condemn it to being preserved at a point in time, never changing, as it is to change its nature to just to suit the needs of external visitors.

SOCIO-CULTURAL IMPACTS OF EVENTS

This part of the chapter explores some of the concepts that are used to analyse the extent of socio-cultural impacts and the character of the host–guest relationship. Socio-cultural impacts studies are concerned with changes that occur in the society and culture of local communities as a result of visitors (Table 1.2). These could be changes in collective and individual value systems (i.e. moral conduct), changes in behaviour patterns (i.e. dress, food, social relationships, individual behaviour), changes in community structures (i.e. family relationships, gender roles), changes in lifestyle (i.e. religion, traditional ceremonies, changes in production of cultural practices and artefacts), or changes in the quality of life (i.e. crime, safety levels).

The relationship between visitors and residents: not guests any more

To understand the viewpoint of the host communities to visitors to their events, it is useful to look at tourism research. Essentially those visitors who are not local are in fact acting as tourists to the area. Much research in the tourism field examines this relationship between hosts and guests, and this is increasingly applicable to event attendees, especially those who stay in the area for a few days such as at a big event.

In many English-speaking cultures, there is a clear distinction between: (i) friends, to whom hospitality would be offered; (ii) strangers, who would probably be treated with suspicion and who would be treated courteously, but not offered hospitality; and (iii) enemies.

By contrast, in other cultures, such as that of Greece, strangers to the host community are considered special. In traditional Greek culture, a visitor could be a messenger from the gods, or even a god themselves, sent to test the individual; thus helping a stranger could quite possibly bestow significant rewards in later life or in heaven. This traditional host–guest relationship, however, has a set of strict rules and codes. The power in the relationship is in the hands of the host, who is in control. The guest has no rights as such and should accept with grace whatever the host chooses to offer to them. Traditionally this would be the best that the host had anyway. The guest could not make any specific demands. The host had a moral obligation to make the guest feel at home, which was not for monetary reward (Benveniste, 1969).

Table 1.2. Social consequences of events. Source: adapted from Reid (2007).

Positive	Negative
Showcase effect	Environmental damage and litter
Tool for urban regeneration	Loss of amenities
Encourages tourism	Antisocial behaviour
Provides leisure and recreation opportunities	Creates very few job opportunities
Promotes a civic boost	Financial burdens
Provides educational and cultural understanding	Exploitation and manipulation of event themes for commercial activities
Enhances community spirit and improves quality of life	Degradation of positive tourism and promotional imagery
	Causes social dislocation and increases housing costs
	Loss of traditions
	Changes in community values and patterns

This relationship has significantly changed, however, as the visitor is now a client and not a guest in the true sense. The host is selling a service to the person attending the event and not gaining moral merit. The relationship between the host and the visitor is a commercial transaction and thus governed by laws of commerce. The visitor holds the power, and is in the superior position, as they are the ones who are paying. It is now a transaction, not an interaction. The gain for the hosts is monetary, and neither spiritual nor moral.

Visitors to Greece in the 1950s and early 1960s often reported that they were not allowed to pay for services such as the use of local boats for trips. They had to leave the money for rooms surreptitiously, as hosts did not want to charge them for their stay. Sardine barbecues with local fishermen and their families on the beach were often free. This was even true in the 1980s in less travelled parts of the world. However, time has gone by and, 50 years later, this has all changed; visitors to Greece and other parts of the world find their hosts running very professional, profit-oriented businesses.

Host societies, however, are still sometimes shocked by visitors' behaviour. Traditionally churches were never locked, despite often being crammed with offerings of gold and silver. Thefts from these churches were unheard of until visitor numbers increased. Host societies have developed strategies to deal with this. Churches are now locked. Another area of great concern for many of the host communities has been the influence of visitor behaviour on their own community, particularly the demonstration effect (see below).

For many host communities, their reality is that significant parts of their lives are lived out on a stage created by the observations of the culture-seeking visitors. Imagine going to your local club for a night out, and finding busloads of people standing around looking at you and taking pictures while you dance. Imagine going to your local supermarket just as three coaches of visitors who are attending a local sporting event arrive. They walk around very slowly, looking at everything but only buying one or two small items, while they block all the aisles and create a shortage of trolleys. Long queues form at the toilets, so you cannot use the amenities. In these circumstances, communities tend to retreat from the main visitor areas and often develop recreational facilities for themselves that are not easily accessible to the visitors.

Box 1.2. The visitors are not guests any more.

Zarkia cites the case of Skyros, where festival feasting at their monastery takes place after the last bus of tourists leaves at night. If the tourists remained, they would be treated as guests and would be served first, with the best food and drink. The monks for whom the feast is prepared would get none (Zarkia, 1996).

For those communities that rarely host an event, this is less of a problem. However, for those communities that have an economic dependence on event visitors, the impacts are more profound. Event visitors are transitory, spending just one or even part of one day in the community, and only a portion of their economic expenditure may reach the host community that must cope with this influx of visitors. Residents of Bruges were disappointed by the impact of their city hosting the European Capital of Culture event in 2002, finding that they were marginalized from the city centre, where the majority of the cultural activities took place (Boyko, 2008). It is vital that the socio-cultural aspects of the host community are considered over the largely economic and political advantages of locating an event venue or convention centre in any area.

Box 1.3. Dolgellau Sesiwn Fawr.

Since 1992, Dolgellau has hosted a Sesiwn Fawr ('Big Session') music festival annually. This was originally a free festival based in the streets and hostelries of the town centre. From 2002 to 2008, it was held in the outskirts of the town and attracted up to 5000 visitors each year. It was broadcast live on BBC Radio Cymru. However, it was unable to run in that format in 2009, as the event had amassed debts of over £50,000 because of a low turnout in 2007 when wet weather put visitors off. The event returned to its roots with small musical events taking place in the town again.

The festival evoked significant emotions in the local community, with opinions being varied. Some locals supported and welcomed the festival, and felt it contributed greatly to the cultural life of the area, giving them an opportunity to see performers and enjoy a festival that they would not do if it were not held in their area. Others, however, saw it as an imposition, causing congestion, crime and violence in their home town, just bringing them problems and making no positive contribution to their lives. These residents had witnessed drunkenness, drug taking and fighting, and experienced difficulties in accessing their town centre facilities. For some, great benefit has been lost by the festival returning to a town-based smaller format; for others, there has been economic and cultural gain.

Visitor–host encounters

There are three key types of visitor–host encounters:

1. When visitors buy goods and services from locals.
2. When visitors are using facilities and visiting attractions at the same time as locals and find themselves side-by-side.
3. When visitors and locals exchange information face-to-face.

The visitor–host interaction has some specific characteristics that distinguish it from other encounters in daily life. First, the relationship is intrinsically temporal and transitory in nature. While being extraordinary to the visitor, it is often very ordinary to the host. The two have different perceptions and expectations of the interaction. The visitor is at the event for a very short time only and thus the encounter is shallow and superficial, and he or she will be soon replaced by another visitor. The hotelier or shopkeeper will meet hundreds of visitors, while for the visitor, meeting the local person holds disproportionate emphasis and importance. A short chat with a local waitress or barman is remembered for years by the visitor, while it is immediately forgotten by the local. Secondly, these encounters have spatial characteristics, as at most events by their very nature the encounter is controlled through the creation of the event venue.

Thirdly, visitors and hosts usually have very different cultural backgrounds and consequently have differing values and attitudes. These have a very significant influence on the interaction and relationship between the two parties. Both verbal and non-verbal communication can be a deciding factor on whether the encounter is a positive or negative one for the two parties. Linguistic differences can lead to difficulties in communication; however, other factors such as body language, facial expression, whether there is eye contact, physical touching or even just how close people stand can be significant to either the host or the visitor. In some cultures, for example, meeting someone's gaze can be considered rude, especially for a woman, while others think that not meeting a gaze is an indication of poor character. In some areas of the

Middle East, it is considered rude to blow your nose in public, while in Western Europe, it is considered worse to sniff and not blow your nose. Further examples include rules and patterns of personal interaction, such as how greetings are made and to whom. Making or refusing a request is similarly viewed differently within different cultures. Finally, except when visitors and hosts are attending events side-by-side, staging an event is usually an economic activity; thus the visitor–host encounter is primarily a commercialized relationship.

Doxey's Irritation Index

Doxey's Irritation Index is a good tool for assessing the socio-cultural impact of any event (Doxey, 1975). This framework illustrates well the positive and negative implications for host communities. Doxey's Irritation Index identifies four different stages that happen alongside tourism and event development in any area. Throughout the exploration stage of development in the early years, tourists and investors are very welcome and encouraged to visit, as they present new interactions and new revenue sources. Doxey calls this euphoria. It is followed by the apathy phase, which occurs when the visitors have started to be taken for granted and the encounters between visitors and residents have become significantly commercialized. Saturation takes place and residents stop seeing the visitors as a positive influence any longer. When the visitors are perceived to interrupt the locals' daily lives, and the benefits derived from the economic input are no longer thought to outweigh the inconvenience of their presence, the annoyance stage has been reached. This becomes antagonism when residents have little control over the situation and become openly hostile to visitors, who become scapegoats for all the ills experienced by the host community and their irritations are openly expressed. This is shown in Fig. 1.1.

While this model has been criticized for being somewhat simplistic, because it does not illustrate the differences in perceptions between different segments of the host community, it still offers a pertinent insight into the host communities' perceptions and experiences. Those who earn their livelihood from the event will not be antagonistic, nor forget the benefits that hosting the event bring to the area. Hosting events can create ongoing problems for host communities, as can be seen by the example in the box below. Phenomena such as the 'hoon effect' and the demonstration effect have been identified. This is discussed in more detail later in the chapter.

The demonstration effect

The demonstration effect is the name given to the phenomenon occurring when outside cultural values and lifestyles are introduced to a host community, as happens when it is host to an event. This is often seen in the tourism setting, and is particularly relevant to events held in less developed countries, which are attended by visitors from richer developed nations, for example the Football World Cup held in some parts of South Africa in 2010. While the visitor is at the event (or on holiday), he or she is acting outside the rules of normality and the monetary constraints of normal life. A visitor enjoys the duration of their leisure time as much as possible, spending money that has been saved specifically for that holiday. Similarly, a person attending an event will have saved for the occasion and will spend disproportionately. Locals observing this behaviour often aspire to emulate it, and this can cause friction. Another example is young people in communities who see visitors to events wearing clothing that is culturally inappropriate to local custom, and who consequently wish to emulate them. This can lead to the host experiencing an acculturation process because of the visitor's demonstration, resulting in young people wearing clothes inappropriate to their

Time		Phase	Resident viewpoint
Introduction and first running of the event		Euphoria	Residents are delighted at the prospect of the event and the investment it will bring. They welcome the event into their area.
Event becomes commercialized		Apathy	Visitors start to be taken for granted. They are no longer actively welcomed.
Event becomes more detached from local culture		Irritation/ annoyance	The saturation point of the area has been reached and the host community has worries about the event being held in their area.
Locals start to avoid the event		Antagonism	Residents actively resent the visitors and irritation with their presence is not concealed. Visitors are seen as the cause of all the area's problems.
Event is very commercialized and lacks authenticity and unique character		Forgetfulness	The hosts can no longer remember why they wanted to host the event, it has consequently lost its distinctiveness and character.

Fig. 1.1. Doxey's Irritation Index.

Box 1.4. The hoon effect.

The 'hoon effect' was identified by Arnold *et al.* (1989, in Allen *et al.*, 2008), when the hosts of the Australian Grand Prix in 1985 suffered a 35% increase in road traffic accidents compared with the previous 5 years, with visitors and locals alike attempting to emulate the style adopted by the racing drivers (Allen *et al.*, 2008). The brunt of these accidents was borne by the host community, who found their emergency services stretched, which had a consequential economic implication for the cost of their provision. There was a decrease in the quality of their lives because of a reduced sense of security and a higher danger level for them and their families.

---

local culture. As discussed earlier in the chapter, it is wrong to blame visitors for all cultural change, as there are other influences such as the Internet and television. The demonstration effect is, however, likely to have a catalytic effect on changes that would eventually happen anyway.

> **Activity**
>
> Discuss whether you think that the demonstration effect is a benefit or a problem. Is it destroying culture or helping to speed up development in remote areas? Give examples of where it can be beneficial to sections of societies and where it can create problems.

AUTHENTICITY

There has been considerable academic discussion among scholars regarding authenticity in the events context, and much of the discussion in tourism literature is being applied effectively to events and their visitors. It is very important to understand the meaning of 'authentic' in the event framework. In the Greco-Roman meaning of the concept, it implies a factual, honest or genuine element in an historical context, the 'real thing', unadulterated and truthfully presented. It was originally used in the context of museums and referred to the authenticity of an artefact or exhibit. It is now used in reference to cultural and heritage elements of events. If the factor is material, a tangible product, such as a work of art or a building, the authenticity is simply verified by documentation (such as certificates of origin or authenticity) or the opinions of experts, to assess whether the object has been changed since it was originally made.

The judgement of authenticity in the context of events is considerably more difficult, as it includes factors such as rituals, language use, traditions and the event experience. Authenticity can be based on the participation of local people in the event, for example in the case of an historical re-enactment, or the making of foods or handicrafts in a traditional way, according to customs. Authenticity in this context infers a traditional culture and origin, a genuine, honestly produced item, made locally by residents.

Within academic literature, the subject of authenticity, particularly in the context of visitors, has inspired much debate. Boorstin and MacCannell are key participants who have done much to progress understanding in this area. Both of these authors assert that our current day society is inauthentic. They propose that people nowadays are alienated by the fast pace of life and developments in modern times, to the point that reality is no longer endurable and causes individuals to dissociate from their everyday reality. Boorstin develops the viewpoint that this means that individuals cannot experience reality directly but flourish on pseudo-events. Accustomed to the thrills and spills of modern life, the participant in any event needs to keep up the level of stimulation with thrills in their leisure life. Events held at Disney theme parks are an excellent example of this, as they put the visitor into a fabricated reality that is a hyper-reality, where every aspect of their experience is enhanced, designed and managed to ensure that they will be stimulated to experience thrills and excitement. The intrinsically false nature of this artificially engineered experience is irrelevant to the visitors who enjoy it anyway; this is discussed further below.

MacCannell and many other scholars argue that alienation from modern life leads people into a constant quest for authenticity. This leads to their becoming a kind of contemporary pilgrim, constantly seeking authenticity in other times and places, divorced from the individual's normal daily life and the modern day-to-day reality. This engenders the belief that authenticity is hidden away from modernity in historical periods and purer, less complicated cultures and simpler lifestyles. Authenticity infers historical and traditional, away from the modern, either in historical or other cultural settings. Cultures considered less developed are thus deemed to be imbued with greater cultural values. There is an implication for the events industry that authenticity is a motivation to attend.

The visitor's constant search for authenticity leads host communities to sell their culture and themselves to create products with market appeal. The event or festival taking place is changed to make it an affordable and acceptable commodity for the visitors, which sometimes alters the nature of the occasion itself. As in the case of Disney, the event or product that the visitor buys is 'staged' for their benefit. MacCannell proposes that this 'staged authenticity' is an illusion of authenticity to satisfy the desire of the visitor, and it is performed not because it is part of the local culture, but because it has a value and can be sold. Ironically, it is put on stage in this way to provide the resources to protect local culture, values and meanings.

Authenticity is widely considered by academic scholars to be a crucial factor in visitors' motivation to attend any event. In the heritage event, arena authenticity is a widely used marketing tool. If an event is authentic, then the attendee gains both in self-fulfilment because it is perceived to be a more valuable experience but also because it proffers greater status and prestige to them when discussing the visit with friends. However, it is important to remember that the degree of authenticity ascribed to the event is often different to different people. A visitor's perception of authenticity depends, however, upon their own understanding of culture and appreciation of art forms, such as dance or music, as well as their taste and educational level. It is also affected by external factors such as overcrowding, weather and traffic on the journey there. Similarly to motivation, each individual's perception of authenticity will be different. Visitors accept, and even expect, a certain level of staging and inauthenticity in events, which do not necessarily detract from the value of that experience, but are seen as intrinsic. Authenticity can be existential, in visitors' minds rather than an actual reality (Feifan Xie, 2004).

An example of this was found when researching attitudes to traditional local food when attending festivals in North Wales. It clearly emerged that as long as the consumer perceived that the food was local and traditional, then it was thought to be good. Often, such as in the case of eating fish and chips, visitors assumed products were local. They thought that the fish had been caught locally and commented that it tasted better for being fresh. The reality of the situation was that the fish they had eaten had been driven across the country from the town of Grimsby, on the east coast of England.

Activity

Discuss how event organizers can ensure that events they are organizing are thought to be authentic by the participants in the following cases:

- a battle re-enactment;
- a music festival;
- a food festival.

EFFECT OF COMMERCIALIZATION ON AN EVENT'S CULTURAL AUTHENTICITY

Participation in events by those outside the host community, particularly when those attending have paid a tour operator or events organizer for this privilege is generally considered by residents to devalue and commercialize that event. Ironically, the more events modernize and cater for the needs of external participants, the greater the likelihood that they will be considered staged and not authentic. It is also possible that government and event organizers can attempt to make the event a marketing tool for the area and cause some social exclusion. Often visitors wish to experience a sanitized version of culture, and they would not be able to cope with the festival's true reality. An excellent example of this is the nightly Mayan culture performance at Xcaret Theme Park in Mexico. Mayan culture was based upon a belief in human and, in more recent times animal, sacrifice. This, however, is not part of the performance presented to tourists, and is barely mentioned. This is because the vast majority of visitors are likely to find this aspect of local culture very offensive.

Different stakeholders view culture and authenticity differently. Producers have a vested interest in traditions as they can be used to attract visitors to their event. Some new traditions have been created, such the annual sausage trail around the Food Festival in Ludlow, and can add to local culture. Others, however, are recreations of existing culture, performed at a time and place convenient for the event organizers. This is commonly known as the cultural 'disneyfication'. It is considered that this devalues the event for the locals, who see their culture sold to the visitor. Conversely, this is sometimes perceived as a valuable way of preserving culture, although in a staged and sanitized way.

Some event visitors specialize in visiting a certain type of event such as historical re-enactments, and are very conscious of aspects of authenticity. They have numerous experiences by which to compare their visit and can make judgements based on a range of geographic event settings over a period of time. Other visitors focus on one type of event or location, often making repeat visits to festivals and events. Regular visitors to an event are more likely to have an understanding of local food, for example.

STAKEHOLDER RELATIONSHIPS

The relationship between the residents in the area where the event is being held, the organizers and attendees is complex. The impact of an event on the host community can be profound, and varies between being seen as very beneficial to being damaging. Various factors influence the relationship between the different stakeholders in the process of the event's planning, being held and legacy. Key stakeholders include organizers, residents and local traders, visiting traders, support staff and visitors to the event alongside institutions, interest groups and government at local, national and international levels, depending upon the event. In some cases, performers are involved too. The effectiveness with which the relationships between these stakeholders are managed is crucial to the ongoing success of the events. It is particularly important to minimize potential conflicts between stakeholders (Derrett, 2006).

The culture of the host community and the values and beliefs held by them are intrinsically linked to any event taking place in the area. It is likely that any area hosting a major event will be changed by this experience. With good management of the key relationships involved, this can be a very beneficial change, with host communities gaining resources for their use after the visitors go home. An event can offer an opportunity for a community to share its culture, which helps to engender pride in the area, and a very positive sense of self. This is sometimes referred to as the 'feel-good factor' and research has found that resident communities are willing to put up with considerable short-term inconvenience because of the entertainment factor and the hope of a permanent improvement in local facilities that they can use (Allen *et al.*, 2008). In some cases, while acknowledging that tourists are attending an event in greater numbers and commenting that there is crowding, less than 10% of residents were unhappy to see so many visitors (Richards, 2007). Events can unite communities engendering distinct cultural identities and civic pride (Derrett,

2006). They can help enhance residents' lives in rural areas by offering the opportunity for a quality recreational activity to locals as well as visitors.

Box 1.5. Ludlow Food Festival.

In 1995, a group of residents in Ludlow (Shropshire, UK), decided to hold a small food festival featuring local foods and drinks. This was done as an experiment 'to see what would happen'. Since that point, the Ludlow Food Festival has blossomed and become a celebration of artisan food and drink producers, which attracts visitors from all over the world. The Festival takes over the town for a weekend in September and, largely because of good management, it remains popular with residents of the area. A key element of the festival is the involvement of local shops, restaurant and food producers, including for example a Sausage Trail, which leads visitors to numerous butchers around the town, and a Real Ale Trail, where participants sample locally brewed beers and ales. The trails were designed to get visitors to explore the town, and not just visit the festival site. The advantage of this is that the whole town benefits, even those shops that are not involved in food and drink retail are passed by visitors on their way around the town, and thus they benefit from increased trade. Impacts on the town are minimized by extensive use of Park and Ride, with buses bringing the visitors into the town centre from car parks well outside. There has even been the development of the 'Ludlow Fringe Festival', which is free to visit and runs alongside the main event. Many locals enjoy supporting the festival and many of the support functions are performed by volunteers who just want to be part of the event.

In other circumstances, however, where events management is not effective, this experience can be problematic, and damaging to the host community and their culture. Communities can be alienated, or manipulated by outside bodies such as regional governments or powerful international companies (Allen *et al.*, 2008). Environments can be damaged, and resources lost from the community. Derrett notes that the relationship between the actual place where the event is held and the host community is very important, because it is central to their identity. The geography, climate and natural resources intrinsically shape the residents' culture. Similarly, there is a relationship between the visitors and both the host community and the place itself (Derrett, 2006). This local distinctiveness adds greatly to the attendee's experience, giving the event its individual identity.

THE EVENT EXPERIENCE

Analysis of consumers' experiences during an event is always challenging, but is a vital element in really understanding this phenomenon. An interesting approach is that used by Morgan, when he uses a 'Prism of Event Experience' model (Fig. 1.2), an adaptation of Kapferer's 'prism of brand identity'. As shown in the diagram, the model enables an analysis of the 'push' and 'pull' factors and their relationship to internal and external perceptions. He applies this model to the 2005 Sidmouth Folk Festival (Morgan, 2008).

Morgan concludes that a key aspect of good organization is to enable visitors' flexibility, and abundant opportunities for social interaction with hosts and other festival-goers. The development of fringe events is also very popular, as is the case at the Ludlow Food Festival, and the famous annual Edinburgh Fringe Festival.

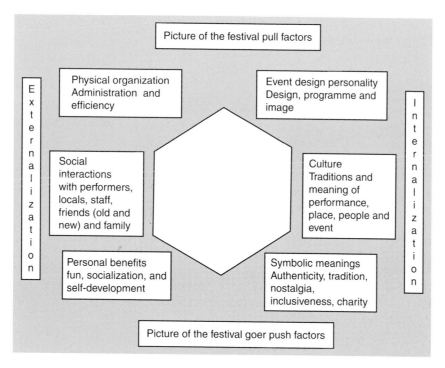

Fig. 1.2. The event experience prism. Source: adapted from Morgan (2008).

FURTHER RESEARCH

General reading:

Agrusa, J.F., Maples, G., Kitterlin, M. and Tanner, J. (2008) Sensation seeking, culture, and the valuation of experiential services. *Events Management* 11, 121–128.

Nurse, K. (2004) Trinidad Carnival: festival tourism and cultural industry. *Events Management* 8, 223–230.

Van Zyl, C. and Botha, C. (2004) Motivational factors of local residents to attend the Aardklop National Arts Festival. *Events Management* 8, 213–222.

For general examples of events see www.youtube.com, for films of the aftermath of events such as Glastonbury Festival.

REVIEW QUESTIONS

- Why is it important to understand the socio-cultural impacts of events?
- Who are key stakeholders in a music festival?
- Is the demonstration effect likely to cause significant problems for local residents during and after the London 2012 Olympics?
- Discuss whether a rock music festival is likely to have a positive or negative impact on the lives of the following local residents:
  - a 57-year-old supermarket manager;
  - a 75-year-old woman who lives 500 yards from the event site;

- ⟩ a 17-year-old boy;
- ⟩ a couple in their 30s with two young children.
- In what ways does politics influence events?

REFERENCES

Ali-Knight, J. and Robertson, M. (2006) Introduction to arts, culture and leisure. In: Yeoman, I., Robertson, M., Ali-Knight, J., Drummond, S. and McMahon-Beattie, U. (eds) *Festival and Event Management: an International Arts and Culture Perspective*. Elsevier Butterworth-Heinemann, Oxford, pp. 3–13.

Allen, J., O'Toole, W., Harris, R. and McDonnell, I. (2008) *Festival & Special Event Management*, 4th edn. John Wiley & Sons, Chichester, UK.

Andranovich, G., Burbank, M.J. and Heying, C.H. (2001) Olympic cities: lessons learned from mega-event politics. *Journal of Urban Affairs* 23, 113–131.

BBC News (2008) Japan's controversial shrine. 15 August. Available at: http://news.bbc.co.uk/go/pr/fr/-/2/hi/asia-pacific/1330223.stm (accessed 24 January 2010).

Benveniste, E. (1969) *Le vocabulaire des institutions indo-européennes*. Les Editions de Minuit, Paris.

Bourdieu, P. (1984) *Distinction*. Harvard University Press, Cambridge, Massachusetts.

Boyko, C.T. (2008) Are you being served? The impacts of a tourist hallmark event on the place meanings of residents. *Event Management* 11, 161–177.

Democratic Alliance (2010) Govt spending R 11.7m on non existent event – DA. 13 January. Available at: http://www.politicsweb.co.za (accessed 14 January 2010).

Derrett, R. (2006) Festivals, events and the destination. In: Yeoman, I., Robertson, M., Ali-Knight, J., Drummond, S. and McMahon-Beattie, U. (eds) *Festival and Events Management: an International Arts and Culture Perspective*. Elsevier Butterworth-Heinemann, Oxford, pp. 32–50.

Doxey, G.V. (1975) A causation theory of visitor–resident irritants, methodology and research inferences. *The Impacts of Tourism 6th Annual Conference Proceedings*. Available from the Travel and Tourism Research Association.

Feifan Xie, P. (2004) Visitors' perceptions of authenticity at a rural heritage festival: a case study. *Events Management* 8, 151–160.

GCIS (Government Communication and Information System) (2009) World Cup to inject R55bil into economy. 26 November. BuaNews Online. Available at: http://www.buanews.gov.za (accessed 27 November 2009).

Morgan, M. (2008) What makes a good festival? Understanding the event experience. *Event Management* 12, 81–93.

Philippine Daily Inquirer (2010) Muslim holiday declared. 22 January. Available at: http://www.inquirer.net/mindandbody/newyou/view.php?db=1&article=20100122-248765 (accessed 24 January 2010).

Reid, S. (2007) Identifying social consequences of rural events. *Event Management* 11, 89–98.

Richards, G. (2007) Culture and authenticity in a traditional event: the views of producers, residents and visitors in Barcelona. *Events management* 11, 33–44.

The Economist (2009) The world's forgotten fair. 5 December, p. 60.

Utah Office of Tourism (2008) Olympic Legacy. Available at: http://travel.utah.gov/publications/documents/OlympicLegacy_web_000.pdf (accessed 5 July 2010).

Whitford, M. (2009) Oaxaca's indigenous Guelaguetza Festival: not all that glistens is gold. *Event Management* 12, 143–161.

Zarkia, C. (1996) Philoxenia: receiving tourists – but not guests – on a Greek Island. In: Boissevain, J. (ed.) *Coping with Tourists: European Reactions to Mass Tourism*. Berghahn Books, Oxford.

Zululand EcoAdventures (2010) The Zulu Reed Dance. Available at: http://www.eshowe.com/article/articlestatic/24/1/13/ (accessed 25 January 2010).

chapter 2

Developing the Event Concept

Alison Booth

OBJECTIVES OF THE CHAPTER

This chapter introduces the key theories and ideas surrounding the design, development, delivery and analysis of events, identifying key definitions, and explaining underpinning models and the range and scope of the events industry. Through the use of short case studies, the chapter will demonstrate the range of activities that are classed as 'events' and explore the relationship between events and tourism, hospitality, leisure and sport.

The chapter will:

- define and apply important key words including: event idea, event concept, event context, client, stakeholders, marketing mix, event design and evaluation;
- demonstrate through case studies how event ideas are developed into concepts and put into the wider context of stakeholder relationships and event marketing; and
- demonstrate how theoretical models are applied to events across the events industry.

INTRODUCTION

This chapter will demonstrate through case studies and events management theories how an event idea is developed into an event concept and placed into the wider event environment, through the way in which the event is structured and designed. A key to designing successful events is creating a clear sense of purpose and concept. The event design process includes event environments that are internal as well as external to the events management team. The wide scope of interactions with stakeholders as well as suppliers creates communication and supply chains. The event scope identifies the goals and objectives of the project and the agreed work allocation between the events management team and stakeholders. The event evaluation process involves a continuous loop of questioning as to how well the event meets the needs of everyone who has been involved in the events management process.

This chapter will also introduce key theories and ideas surrounding:

Design: the idea, purpose and strategic needs of the client. Defining the event concept (WHO, WHAT, WHY, WHEN and WHERE) and creating a memorable experience.

Development: developing the design of an event concept, considering the viability and fit of event components, stakeholders, marketing and resources.

Delivery: the production and technical requirements necessary in taking an event concept live including staging, audiovisual requirements, exhibition installations, communication networks, logistics and event and stage management.

Evaluation: development design of an event concept, considering the viability and fit of event components, stakeholders, marketing and resources. Evaluation is a multifaceted process that involves feedback from all those individuals, businesses and organizations that have an interest in or are affected by an event.

EVENT DESIGN

Events never work in isolation. Events involve teams that create relationships with other people, whether business, social, corporate or institutional. For the life of the event and often beyond, event relationships foster commercial, social and communication networks.

Successful events involve the event production team orchestrating a series of complex teams involved in interacting in stakeholder relationships. Events create positive or negative memorable experiences for all those participating in the event at all levels.

All events start with an idea. A good idea can create a spark that opens a complex field of creative activities that involve teams of people. How an idea is conceived and designed determines the success of an event. The event concept develops the initial idea to include the purpose, aims and desired event outcomes – understanding from the initial planning stage, for whom is the event being planned (including client as well as audience) and whether the financial and stakeholder expectations can be met. The event concept is a critical component of feasibility studies and is the initial building block on which successful events are created (see Chapter 5).

THE EVENT CONCEPT

Concepts are different from ideas. Concepts are clear statements that shape an event into a clearly laid out design. Concepts involve developing clear statements that give meaning and parameters to the event idea. Defining the event concept is a creative process that may be simple or complex depending on the scope of the event. The basic steps are the same for all events across all areas of the events industry including the tourism, hospitality, leisure and sport sectors.

THE EVENT ENVIRONMENT

Events have economic and social impacts on the local economy. Events have the potential to create positive as well as negative impact on the economic, social and environmental sectors of the event environment. The hypothetical model (Fig. 2.1) indicates the interdependent relationships between the leisure, tourism, sport and hospitality industries, and large events will have impact on all sectors. The other major events management sector includes meetings, conferences and conventions, and industry trade shows.

Events attract local as well as international visitors, either actively involved in the production of the event or as a passive participant such as a spectator. In the process of attending an event, visitors may support all four industry sectors and have significant financial impact on the local as well as the national economy. Visitors will support the hospitality industry by staying in hotels, eating in restaurants and frequenting bars and clubs. They may support the leisure industry by attending a concert, museum, park or local festival. While in town, they may attend a sport event or participate in one. They may book a package tour, rent a car or visit a tourist destination. All of these activities will have a direct and indirect impact upon the local economy. This is known as the multiplier effect (see Chapter 4). The impact is in proportion to the size of the event. Income generated can be internal as well as external to the event organization.

Box 2.1 illustrates how the 2009 Ellerslie International Flower Show generated over NZ\$19.7 million into a local economy, making positive economic impacts across the sport, hospitality, leisure and tourism sectors.

Activities may be part of pre-planned travel schedules or by casual encounters. A visitor from Christchurch attending a convention in New York City might participate in additional activities besides the core convention programme (Fig. 2.2).

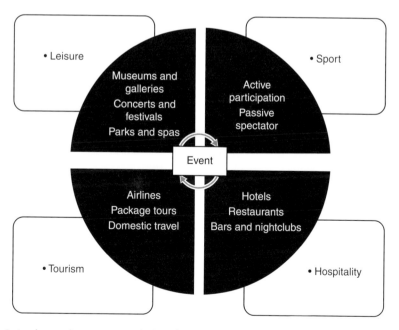

Fig. 2.1. Interdependent sector relationships.

	Spectator	Participant
Pre-planned	New York Knicks basketball game with friends who live in New York City	Optional delegate dinner and dancing purchased at the same time as registering for the convention
Casual	Broadway show ticket purchased from box office at Times Square	Ice skating at Rockefeller Plaza was not a planned activity but looked fun; took time during lunch break

Fig. 2.2. Event participants.

Box 2.1. Economic impacts of the 2009 Ellerslie International Flower Show.

The economic impact of the 2009 Ellerslie International Flower Show in Christchurch, New Zealand, was spread across the hospitality, tourism and retail sectors. The show generated more than NZ$19.7 million in direct expenditure for Christchurch's economy in its first year. Eighty thousand visitors came from outside the city to attend the event, representing 40% of all event attendees. International visitors represented 33% of the 80,000 visitors. The most significant level of expenditure was NZ$5.5 million in the retail sector, followed closely by NZ$5 million in the accommodation sector, including visitors requiring more than 33,220 bed nights. International visitors to Ellerslie contributed NZ$6.55 million to the economy, followed closely by South Island visitors with NZ$6.28 million and North Island visitors with NZ$3.2 million. The highest average daily spend for overnight stays was international visitors at NZ$382.82, followed by South Island visitors at NZ$231.34. More than 75% of visitors to the Show rated Ellerslie as good to excellent, spending on average 5.2 h at the event.

Source: NZAEP (2009)

Questions

Consider these questions in relation to an event being staged in your home town:
- How does the location of an event impact upon other event industries?
- What additional activities add value to the visitor experience in an event location?
- How do events impact upon local as well as international economies?

THE PROCESS: EVENT IDEA TO EVENT CONCEPT

The event idea, when expanded into larger contexts, becomes the focal point in the comprehensive event design and coordination process. The concept must align with the event purpose and expectations of the client and stakeholders. The event concept development process involves conceptualizing an event idea and then exploring how the idea intersects with the needs of the internal and external event environments. The following steps demonstrate the process in which an event concept is designed to fit into the wider scope of an event environment.

Event idea: describe the event in the simplest of terms defining what the event is planned to achieve, for example an outdoor summer blues festival at a local winery.

Event title: give the idea a name. This is a building block to assist you in the event design process. A good title creates a theme as well as adding promotional strength to an event.

The event concept – the 5 'W's: WHO, WHAT, WHY, WHEN and WHERE? The 5 'W's are a tool for transforming an idea into a concept. Joe Goldblatt explains the importance of the 5 'W's, as they help to determine whether an event idea is feasible, viable and sustainable (Goldblatt, 2001). These questions are crucial to focus on from the beginning; they shape the event design and reflect the event purpose. This is sometimes referred to as a needs analysis. Needs assessments are a critical component when considering the direction and way an idea is developed. Not all ideas are developed into a concept. Not all concepts become produced events.

Who: events bring people together to deliver an event experience; the people who will support an event include types of audience, suppliers, venues, colleagues, industry links and other internal as well as external stakeholders. How the event concept is imagined and designed from the start determines how the stakeholder relationships interact. This is true of events of all sizes across all industries. Event stakeholders are any groups or individuals who can affect or are affected by the impact of an event.

For the success of an event, it is important that communication channels are open between all stakeholders, as events have impacts on wider communities. It is important to remember that stakeholders are the people or organizations who have an invested interest in the event. Stakeholders add a larger 'WHO' dimension to an event concept.

What: the event experience includes an organizational team that creates what the event content or product is. This process can take time to develop. By creating a mission statement, specific goals and needs are established. The mission statements define the event's overall objectives and assist in establishing the event in the wider external contexts.

Why: make a simple statement as to why the event is happening in the first place. What lies at the heart of the idea? What is the reason or purpose for the event being produced? All events have a purpose, whether a book launch, music festival, sailing regatta or political convention.

When: event timing is a critical factor to the success of an event. In the design and development process, timescales for planning, including research, funding, promotion and design, will be considered. In the event delivery process, venue availability, production timelines, performers, client and participant requirements, competing events and supplier availability need to be considered.

The purpose of an event is carefully chosen as the stated purpose remains constant throughout the entire event production process. The event purpose places the event idea into the wider external environment that establishes the viability of events and essential stakeholder relationships.

Where: the location of an event (global, local and venue choices) places the event in the public context. With the exception of virtual events, all events include a site that is chosen to meet the event requirements including purpose, stakeholders and event design elements. The choice of venue is often a compromise between organizational needs and attracting an audience. The location chosen will require the capability to deliver specific production and technical needs within budget expectations.

Questions
- What is an event concept?
- What are stakeholders and how do they add value to an event?
- Identify three possible venue choices that would suit an event idea. How do different sizes, prices and potential audiences affect the event concept?

Activity
Develop an event idea, describing an event in the simplest of terms.
- Give your idea a name, state its purpose and apply the 5 'W's.
- Consider how your event concept is positioned in the wider event environment.

EVENT DEVELOPMENT

The event concept is further developed by considering how events are placed into the wider internal and external environments. Successful events create a complex combination of interacting relationships that access a variety of skills and resources. This is a creative process involving problem solving and places events into the wider contexts including meeting stakeholder requirements, resource management and the marketing mix.

THE MARKETING MIX

Marketing theory typically identifies the marketing mix as the 4 'P's: product, price, place and promotion. Some events can be successful by initiating a few phone calls and e-mails; a word-of-mouth campaign is begun. Other events require advertising, media releases and complex public relation strategies. Event marketing places events into the public arena or marketplace. As events have unique qualities as commodities, Hoyle (2002) extends the marketing mix concept to: product, price, place, public relations and positioning. The way in which an event is marketed is a critical component of putting an event concept in the wider external environment context. 'Only when the product is clearly defined can decisions be made as to strategies to be used in attracting audiences through price, place, positioning, and public relations' (Hoyle, 2002, p. 20).

Product: events are in fact products and entities that are bought and sold. They may have a strong valuable brand for example the Edinburgh Festival or the Grand Prix. Events are tangible assets.

Price: the price to attend an event is determined by who is most likely to attend, the venue, the number of expected audience and how much they are willing to pay for a ticket.

Place: the event purpose matches the event location taking into consideration venue price, audience, location, capacity and venue amenities. Selection of venue needs to be made with the audience and stakeholders in mind.

Public relations: the role of public relations in strategic marketing campaigns is to research and design tools that add value to the marketing mix by developing media including press releases, publicity strategies, media kits, tickets and invitation lists, radio and media spots, etc.

Positioning: an event is a product that requires careful positioning in the marketplace. The target audience must know about the event and see value in supporting it. Developing a promotional timeline as well as ticketing strategy is a key to the success of an event and adding value to the event product.

For further information about the marketing of events, see Chapter 7.

Box 2.2 demonstrates how an idea is brought to concept and how the event product is positioned or placed in the marketplace. Events create unique experiences that have potential to unite, bind and empower communities.

Box 2.2. I Love the Islands: Samoa Relief Concert.

- **Event idea**: urgent – organize as fast as possible. Concert to raise funds for the immediate community affected in Samoa.
- **Purpose**: raise funds for tsunami victims in Samoa through volunteer networks in the local music and events industry.
- **Title**: I Love the Islands: Samoa Relief Concert.
- **What**: benefit concert to fill a 14,000-seat donated arena organized through donated time and resources by local musicians, sponsors, ticketing, media and events management team. Tickets must be inexpensive so that the concert is accessed by youth and Pacific Island community. Promotion limited to word-of-mouth, text, Facebook and other viral marketing channels. Media promotion through radio, TV and newspaper.
- **Where**: Vector Arena, Auckland City.
- **When**: Monday, 19 November 2009.
- **Why**: Auckland, New Zealand hosts the largest Pacific Island population in the world. The Samoan represents the largest Pacific Island community in Auckland. Naturally occurring disasters can pull together wide communities to support, nurture and empower those who have been affected.
- **The outcome**: the I Love the Islands: Samoa Relief Concert was organized and produced in a couple of weeks by a team of committed volunteers. All involved in the production of this event donated their skills and services including performers, sponsors, government agencies, marketeers, businesses, venues and media. This benefit event in one evening donated NZ$300,000 to the people of Samoa.

Questions
- What external relationships place events in larger event environment contexts?
- Why is it important to understand clearly the purpose of an event?

STAKEHOLDERS AND EVENTS

The event concept and relationships that access the critical resources can become quite complex. The clearer the purpose is incorporated into the event concept from the initial planning stages the better chance of a successful event outcome. Without stakeholder support, creating a successful event may be problematic. Stakeholders add life and value to events. This can seem a simplistic statement until considering the wider context in which an event happens (Table 2.1).

Table 2.1. Stakeholder relationships (adapted from Bowdin *et al.*, 2006, p. 98).

Stakeholder	Value to stakeholder	Value to event
Host organization	Participation	Participation
Host community	Impact	Content
Media	Promotion	Editorials and advertising
Audience and participants	Entertainment/reward new experience	Participation/support
Co-workers including volunteers	Payment/reward	Labour support
Sponsors and funding agents	Acknowledgement	Money/in kind

Event stakeholders are divided into six general relationship categories: host organization, host community, sponsor, media, co-worker, participant and audience. A strong relationship between stakeholders adds event value and will impact on the success of an event. For example, if the host organization has a strong relationship within the community in which the event is located, the organizers will find it easy to attract participants, sponsorship and media attention. If the media and host community and participant do not support an event, it would be pointless to spend money on advertising, as this would not attract an audience. The event location may create a major traffic impact on the local community. The event may require city council approval as well as notifying the local police department. Notifying local residents may be required. Individual invitations may be designed as part of a public relations campaign that is intended to get local residents aware of the positive benefits of the event. Notifying local residents individually with a flier inviting them to the event may encourage local support. Local community awareness may increase participants, media awareness, volunteers, sponsors as well as other elements that add value to events.

Box 2.3. Sir Peter Blake Torbay Regatta – Theme: Good Water, Good Life.

The Sir Peter Blake Torbay Regatta is the largest 2-day sailing regatta in New Zealand, with more than 400 sailors involved since 2001. This annual event consists of youth and senior dinghy classes and keel boats, and is managed solely by volunteers from the Torbay Sailing Club. Competitors hail from all over New Zealand, as well as a few overseas entrants. The event has the support of the local city council as a major sponsor, offering venue support, promotion and permits for road closures, park access and water use. The Regatta maintains a youth focus and the Sir Peter Blake Trust supports the event to encourage participants to learn about the environment. Presentations take place over the weekend, with the most outstanding sailor at the event receiving the prestigious Sir Peter Blake Memorial Trophy.

Source: Team Site Torbay Sailing Club (2009)

Table 2.2 demonstrates how the major event stakeholders contributed to the success of the Sir Peter Blake Torbay 2009 Regatta (Fig. 2.3). The Sir Peter Blake Regatta has a long history of strong, interactive teams of stakeholder relationships. The Torbay Sailing Club has the Sir Peter Blake naming rights as part of their sponsorship agreement with the Sir Peter Blake Trust. Sir Peter Blake was one of New Zealand's most loved sports heroes. The emotive cultural significance for this event works as market leveraging.

With stakeholder relationships, if any element lessens or increases their event involvement, the balance in the stakeholder relationships will change. Community involvement comes with the added value of word-of-mouth, as this traditional medium of communication remains the most powerful medium for event promotion. For example, if the event receives bad press through the local community, the prestige of the event may falter. On the other hand, if the event attracts a major celebrity at the Regatta prize giving, the community will know through word-of-mouth as well as having potential to attract the media. This has the potential to change the balance in the existing stakeholder relationships.

Table 2.2. Sir Peter Blake Regatta stakeholders.

Stakeholder	Value to stakeholder	Value to event
Host organization: Torbay Sailing Club	Membership recruitment; brand awareness	Event organizers for event to happen
Host community: NZ Yachting Clubs	Raise profile of the NZ sailing industry; Torbay residents	Promote New Zealand sailing industry; community support
Media: primetime news, major radio, yachting industry magazines, sailing club websites, community newspaper free listings	Build brand awareness and advertising clients with specialized target market	Event promotion
Audience and participants	Sailing competitors, local and national clubs; friends and family of competitors; community residents	Registration fees for event; banquet; merchandise and food
Co-workers	Volunteers (administration, marketing, risk management and operations); vendors (corporate)	Production team; food and product % profit
Sponsors and funding agents	Trust: Sir Peter Blake Torbay Regatta; corporate: money as well as in kind support; local government: in kind	Naming rights; promotion items including T-shirts and banners, prizes, marquees; venue, permits, waste management, rubbish, power

Fig. 2.3. Sir Peter Blake 2009 Torbay Regatta (Alison Booth).

Questions

Consider the following questions in relation to the event concept that you developed earlier in this chapter.

- Create a chart that identifies the event concept stakeholders.
- What additional sport, leisure, hospitality and/or tourism activities would the audience/participants probably support? What advantages does the event venue offer?
- What further technical requirements might be required?
- What additional participant activities might add value to the event?
- How do additional activities make an event attractive to sponsors and media?

DELIVERY

The production and technical requirements will include staging, audiovisual equipment, exhibition installations, communication networks, logistics and stage management. Production and technical requirements needed to deliver the event design must reflect the choice of venue as well as budget considerations. For an outdoor venue as in the sailing regatta, access to electricity for the marquees as well as walkie-talkies for communication between land and sea are vital. If you are planning a jazz quintet that requires a grand piano, the venue that you choose will need to be able to supply a tuned piano on stage for the performance, at an acceptable quality to the musicians and within the budget. You may need to select and contract caterers, personnel including volunteers, road closures and a myriad of details that an event concept demands for a successful event experience. Julia Rutherford Silvers discusses that what is important is understanding the integrated process. An event is about people that come together to create, operate and participate in an experience (Silvers, 2004).

EVALUATION

Evaluation should be a reflection throughout the idea to concept process. It is the process by which the events management team reflects on each stage of the event development process. By stating from the beginning of the event idea to concept the event purpose and objectives, a feedback loop is put into place. This continuous process culminates with the event shutdown. The event shutdown is the process when all management details are signed off with suppliers, stakeholders and the management team. Event evaluation documents the activities that happened, and has the ability to give observations and feedback value.

The primary focus of event evaluation is to determine how well the event met the stated purpose. All stakeholders including vendors should be involved in the evaluation process. Formal reports will be required for stakeholders; including funding agents, sponsors and government agencies. A typical report will include the following details:

1. Event concept
2. Event contact information
3. Successes, pitfalls and outcomes
4. Stakeholders
5. Budget
6. Media analysis
7. Event observations and comments including participant observation – if the event involved a questionnaire, survey or other quantitative or qualitative data, this is also included.

Evaluating an event is a benchmark for the future as well as in the debrief process of closing down an event. When evaluating an event, it is important to capture the wider event impacts on the local and wider business, government and creative industries. The ability for an event to be replicated and be sustainable over time creates event legacies including the Rose Bowl Parade, New York Marathon, WOMAD (World of Music, Arts and Dance) and the many local festivals that are successfully delivered on a regular basis around the world.

SUMMARY

When designing successful events, it is important to have a clear idea as to the purpose of the event. The idea and purpose are the focal points from which the event concept is expanded and put into context. The event context is often a complex network that includes a wide range of stakeholders, intersecting industries and supply chains. Event contexts include internal as well as external relationships to the management team. These relationships are identified in the design, development and delivery process, and are continuously being evaluated. The evaluation process is a continuous practice involving feedback from all individuals affected by management decisions.

From the initial spark of an event idea, the event planning stage begins. Events are tangible products that create financial and social impacts across events industry sectors as well as the event stakeholders and suppliers delivering the production requirements. Successful events build relationships that create the contexts in which successful events are designed, delivered and evaluated.

FURTHER RESEARCH

For a detailed discussion on events industry management structures:
Goldblatt, J. (2005) *Special Events: Event Leadership for a New World*. John Wiley & Sons, Hoboken, New Jersey.
Tum, J., Norton, P. and Wright, J.N. (2006) *Management of Event Operations*. Elsevier, Oxford.

For a detailed discussion on event design and concepts:
Bowdin, G., Allen, J., O'Toole, W., Harris, R. and McDonnel, I. (2006) *Events Management*, 2nd edn. Elsevier, Oxford.
Hoyle Jr, L.H. (2002) *Event Marketing*. John Wiley & Sons, New York.
Goldblatt, J. (2001) *Twenty-First Century Global Event Management*. John Wiley & Sons, New York.

For a detailed discussion on stakeholder relationships:
Getz, D. (1997) *Event Management & Event Tourism*. Cognizant Communication Corp., New York.
Getz, D., Anderson, T. and Larson, M. (2007) Festival stakeholder roles: concepts and case studies. *Event Management* 10, 103–122.

For a detailed discussion on production requirements and event delivery:
Silvers, J.R. (2004) *Professional Event Coordination*. John Wiley & Sons, Hoboken, New Jersey.

For a detailed discussion on event evaluation:
Mikolaitis, P. and O'Toole, W. (2002) *Corporate Event Project Management*. John Wiley & Sons, New York.

Market segmentation and target markets:
Geodemographic Neighbourhood Classification: www.mosaicnz.co.nz

REVIEW QUESTIONS

1. How do industry sectors (sport, leisure, hospitality and/or tourism) add marketing leverage and value to events?
2. How do event concepts fit into wider event contexts?
3. What are potential financial benefits for the local economy?

REFERENCES

Bowdin, G., Allen, J., O'Toole, W., Harris, R. and McDonnel, I. (2006) *Events Management*, 2nd edn. Elsevier, Oxford.

Goldblatt, J. (2001) *Twenty-First Century Global Event Management*. John Wiley & Sons, New York.

Hoyle Jr, L.H. (2002) *Event Marketing*. John Wiley & Sons, New York.

NZAEP (October 2009) New Zealand Association of Event Professionals Monthly Update. Christchurch.

Silvers, J.R. (2004) *Professional Event Coordination*. John Wiley & Sons, Hoboken, New Jersey.

Team Site Torbay Sailing Club (2009) Available at: http://www.sportsground.co.nz/TeamSite.asp?SiteID=12323 (accessed 17 March 2010).

chapter 3

Event Networks
and Supply Chains

Geoff Dickson

OBJECTIVES OF THE CHAPTER

This chapter considers the scale and scope of organizations that combine to create the events industry. Particular attention is devoted to complex relationships that exist within an organization's supply chain.

This chapter will:

- conceptualize events as inter-organizational networks;
- apply basic supply chain management concepts to events;
- consider criteria for the 'make or buy' decision and outsourcing; and
- discuss the contribution of event networks to innovative events.

INTRODUCTION

It is very rare for a single organization to produce an event. Events will nearly always be a collaborative effort between organizations. Events are temporal – they do not exist forever and they may only be offered occasionally. For example, the Olympics are a 17-day event staged every 2 years (alternating Summer and Winter Games) and the Glastonbury Festival of Contemporary Performing Arts is an annual 5-day event. Consequently, event organizations need to be flexible insofar as they spend much of their time in preparation mode, and then experience a rapid and significant build-up as the event approaches and then again when the event 'goes live'. Event organizations have finite resources and will rarely have the luxury of having all of their tangible and intangible production technologies available in-house. This is true for all organizations – but is exacerbated with events because of their temporal nature.

Establishing inter-organizational relationships can be both effective and efficient in coping with the temporal features of an event. Event managers, therefore, will take on a coordination and quality control role. This ensures that each part of the event jigsaw reflects the bigger picture and is in the appropriate place at the appropriate time.

Box 3.1. Melbourne Fashion Festival.

The Melbourne Fashion Festival (MFF) is owned by a non-profit organization of the same name. The Festival is the largest and most successful consumer fashion event in Australia. The programme consists of events that the public can attend together with invitation-only events for industry representatives.

The 2009 event attracted over 370,000 attendees, injecting an estimated AUS$69.9 million into the economy, an increase from AUS$50 million in 2007 and AUS$62.5 million in 2008. The organization employs 17 people across seven departments: programming and creative direction, event, sponsorship, ticketing, marketing and communications, administration and accounts, and strategy. In addition to this internal capacity, the organization established formal relationships with a variety of other organizations to ensure that a world-class event is created. These relationships are detailed in Table 3.1.

Table 3.1. Melbourne Fashion Festival's immediate inter-organizational network.

Function	Dimension	Company
Events management		Arts Events Management Australasia
Major sponsors		L'Oreal, Victorian Government
Publicity		Ann Morrison PR
Festival creative	Theming Website Image photographer Stylist Printing	Paper Stone Scissors Flint Interactive Steven Chee Photographer Brittany Singleton Mckellar Renown Printing
Festival television commercial	Soundtrack Motion graphics Mastering	Lalala Music Paper Stone Scissors Network Ten

Production and event support	Technical production
	Catering
	
	Set construction
	Equipment hire
	Place settings
	Lighting supplies
	Central pier
	  technical support
	Set and interior
	  design
	Sidewalk structure
	Staging Supplies
		Austage
		The Big Group, The Atlantic Group,
		  food & desire
		Animation & Display
		Harry the Hirer
		Place Settings for Hire
		Resolution X
		Advantage Presentation Services
		
		Moth Design
		
		Inflate Products Australasia
		The Staging Company

(Continued)

Box 3.1. Continued.

Table 3.1. Continued.

Function	Dimension	Company
Suppliers	Accountant	KPMG
	Auditor	Deloitte
	Copying	Brandprint
	Gift bag management	Ability Works Australia
	Official filming	Orangetoast Productions
	Official photography	Lucas Dawson Photography
	Programme distribution	Avant Card
	Risk assessment	Coleby Consulting
	Security	Andrew Wolveridge Security
	Ticketing	Ticketmaster
Market research		Russ Knight Research, Saturn Corporate Resources
Model agencies		Cameron's Models, Chadwick Management, FRM Model Management, Giant Management, Scene Models, Vivien's Model Management
Venues		Central Pier, Sofitel Melbourne On Collins, Malvern Town Hall, Federation Square

Questions

- With what organizations would you expect the Festival to have the closest working relationships?
- What organizations is the Festival most dependent upon?

Just as people within organizations have specialized roles, organizations within an industry are also specialized. The net result is the creation of niche organizations that segment the market creatively, focus efforts only on their especially valuable strengths that, in this case are to think and act small by offering small production volumes, focusing on a few customers and avoiding markets with many competitors or a dominant competitor, allowing them to establish strong, long-term relationships with a focus on customer needs, placing high value on firm reputation and using word-of-mouth references, specializing and differentiating, and charging a premium price (Toften and Hammervoll, 2009). A completely 'in house' production is very rare – a 'one stop shop' event organization would only be found organizing the smallest of events.

EVENTS AS INTER-ORGANIZATIONAL NETWORKS

'An inter-organizational relationship occurs when two or more organizations transact resources (money, physical facilities and materials, customer or client referrals, technical staff services) among each other' (Van De Ven, 1976, p. 25). More recent definitions place emphasis on the tenure of the relationship and the pursuit of joint interests. For example, Babiak and Thibault (2008) define an inter-organizational relationship as a 'voluntary, close, long-term, planned strategic action between two or more organizations with the objective of serving mutually beneficial purposes in a problem domain'. Inter-organizational networks take a number of forms: alliances, consortia, subcontracting, outsourcing or other cooperative arrangements (Ebers, 1997).

These inter-organizational networks are a common feature of the contemporary corporate landscape. In earlier times, the mindset was that organizations should collaborate only when necessary and that business was all about competition. Over time, however, there was a realization that greater efficiencies (and ultimately profits) could be achieved if organizations became more specialized in what they produced and established exchange relationships to supply each other with services and products. The events industry relies heavily on these relationships with most equipment and services being supplied by external specialists. This is discussed in greater detail in Chapter 5. Exchange relations between organizations are characterized by the voluntary transfer of resources between two or more organizations for mutual benefit. The premise of exchange within the context of inter-organizational relations is that organizations will interact voluntarily with other organizations in order to achieve independent and mutual goals. The members of both organizations share a realization that goal attainment is more likely to occur through a process of interaction rather than engaging in independent strategies.

Events are produced through partnerships between and among organizations. Partnerships promise a lot in terms of cooperation and goodwill, but they may be characterized by conflict, negotiation and tension at some time. Brinkerhoff (2002, p. 216) captures this sentiment when he writes, 'Partnership encompasses mutual influence, with a careful balance between synergy and respective autonomy, which incorporates mutual respect, equal participation in decision making, mutual accountability and transparency'.

SUPPLY CHAIN MANAGEMENT

Effective supply chain management enhances competitive performance by integrating the internal functions of an organization and linking them with the external operations of suppliers and channel members. A *supply chain* is defined as 'a set of three or more entities (i.e. organizations or individuals) directly involved in the upstream and downstream flows of products, services, finances, and/or information from a source to a customer' (Mentzer *et al.*, 2001, p. 4). The scope of a supply chain is a reflection of the number of firms in the chain and the diversity of the activities and functions involved. The larger and more complex the event, the more organizers can reasonably expect the number and diversity of organizations in the supply chain network to also increase. The London 2012 Olympic Delivery Authority (ODA) estimates that it will procure and manage 7000 direct contracts with businesses that will in turn manage up to 75,000 agreements across their own supply chains.

There are three models of supply chain complexity (Mentzer *et al.*, 2001). The direct supply chain comprises a purchasing organization, a supplier and a customer. An extended supply chain includes suppliers of the immediate supplier and customers of the immediate customer. An ultimate supply chain includes all the organizations from the ultimate supplier to the ultimate customer. This includes any number of intermediaries or 'middle men' that exist. See Fig. 3.1 for an illustration of the three types of supply chains.

The Melbourne Fashion Festival supply chain detailed above includes only immediate suppliers. These supply organizations will have their own supply networks, which are not reflected in Table 3.1.

Supply chain management refers to 'managing the suppliers and purchasers, covering all stages of processing from obtaining raw materials to distributing finished goods to final consumers' (Samson and Daft, 2009, p. 794). A supply chain should be robust, responsive and resilient (Klibi *et al.*, 2010). A robust supply chain is capable of providing sustainable value creation under all plausible future scenarios. A responsive supply chain provides an adequate response to short-term variations in supply, capacity and demand. Resilience is

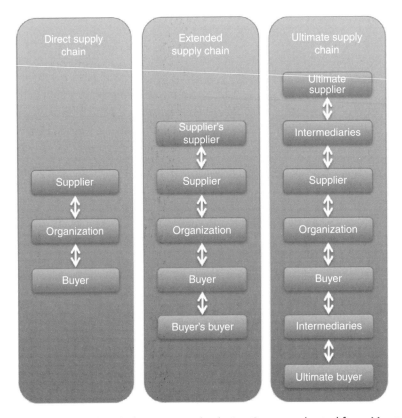

Fig. 3.1. Direct, extended and ultimate supply chains. Source: adapted from Mentzer *et al.* (2001).

Question

For an event manager, what issues emerge when the number of intermediaries in the network increases?

the ability of the supply to avoid disruptions (as much as possible), and to bounce back quickly when these inevitably occur.

MAKING, BUYING AND OUTSOURCING

In today's increasingly competitive business environment, the implementation of technological innovations (products or processes) can rarely be done in isolation. More and more, companies network with each other to combine resources and knowledge, allowing for the creation of competitive advantages. As organizations become increasingly specialized in what they produce, careful consideration is needed to determine what they should make and what they should buy. This is commonly referred to as the 'make or buy' decision. This is common practice within the organization of events. Table 3.1 provides insight into what the Melbourne Fashion Festival makes, and what it buys or 'contracts out' to other organizations. The organizing committee for the 2012 Olympics has contracted out the organization of the logistically challenging marathon event. London Marathon Ltd, owner and organizer of the annual London marathon, was contracted to produce the 2012 Olympic marathon.

A three-phase multi-attribute decision-making process increases the probability that the 'make or buy' decision is correct (Platts *et al.*, 2002). In the preparation phase, the relevant process or task is identified and specified. This is followed by data collection, the most significant phase. This requires specification, compilation and weighting of factors influencing the performance of in-house and external supply against each of these. In the third phase, analysis and results, the weightings and ratings are combined to provide a quantitative indicator of whether the merits of making are greater than the merits of buying.

Outsourcing refers to 'the transfer of activities to an external source' (Kotabea and Mo, 2009, p. 205). Organizations that produce something 'in house' and later decide to buy the resource of another organization are said to be outsourcing. The conventional argument in favour of outsourcing proposes that by doing so, companies should be able to 'improve their level of service, cut costs and free up time and capital to concentrate on what is most important – how they differentiate themselves and compete' (Bendor-Samuel, 1999). Outsourcing should not be used to refer to all purchasing decisions of an organization (Gilley and Rasheed, 2000). In their argument, outsourcing is premised upon 'the decision to reject the internalization of an activity' (p. 764) and that 'organizations having no choice but to acquire a particular good or service from an external source (because of a lack of capital or expertise, for example) are not outsourcing, because the internalization of the activity in question is not an option' (p. 765). For example, it would be inappropriate to say that an organization outsources the transportation of its international performers to an airline or that an event outsources the provision of space to a football stadium. However, an event may elect to outsource its sponsorship programme to a specialist sponsorship agency, and utilize a security organization to provide security staff, in preference for doing this internally. Facilities may also outsource the provision of food and beverage sales. In the USA, Centerplate runs the concession operations in at least seven major league ballparks including RFK, Yankee Stadium, AT&T Park, Safeco Field, Kaufmann Stadium, the Metrodome and Tropicana Field. Outsourceability is 'the degree to which it makes sense for a firm to outsource a given activity to improve performance' (Kotabea and Mo, 2009, p. 207). The factors that influence an organization to produce a resource internally or acquire the resource externally are summarized in Fig. 3.2.

The decisions to make or buy (and outsource) should not be driven by short-term cost reductions. These decisions are important strategic decisions for an event manager because

Internal production – make
- Cost considerations (less expensive to make the part)
- Need to exert direct control over production and/or quality
- Better quality control
- Secrecy is required to protect proprietary technology
- Unreliable suppliers
- No competent suppliers
- Quantity too small to interest a supplier
- Control of lead time, transportation, and warehousing costs
- Political, social or environmental reasons
- Emotion (e.g. pride)

External acquisition – buy or outsource
- Lack of expertise
- Suppliers' specialized know-how exceeds that of the buyer
- Cost considerations (less expensive to buy the item)
- Small-volume requirements
- Limited production facilities or insufficient capacity
- Indirect managerial control considerations
- Procurement and inventory considerations
- Brand preference
- Item not essential to the firm's strategy

Fig. 3.2. Factors influencing internal production or external acquisition. Sources: adapted from Burt *et al.* (2003) and Wisner *et al.* (2005).

they represent the potential to acquire or lose (or share) core competencies. The decisions reflect an organization's selection of the functions for which internal expertise is developed and nurtured, and those for which such expertise is purchased.

PROCUREMENT

Having made the decision to buy or outsource a service or product, attention must be given to the procurement process. Procurement refers to the acquisition of material, property or service. It includes such activities as purchasing, contracting and negotiating directly with the source of supply. Archer and Yuan (2000) detail a seven-phase procurement process. The phases include: (i) information gathering; (ii) supplier contact; (iii) background review; (iv) negotiation; (v) fulfilment; (vi) consumption, maintenance and disposal; and (vii) renewal.

A taxonomy of procurement options is detailed in Fig. 3.3. Movement from the left to right across the continuum is associated with an increase in the number of suppliers and an increase in transaction costs.

At the bottom of the continuum is in-house production, whereby the organization makes the good or produces the service internally. This is closely followed by subsidiary purchases, whereby the organization purchases from companies that it owns.

A joint venture occurs when the supplier and buyer create a third organization to manage their independent interests. Such cooperation reflects a very high level of cooperation between the organizations.

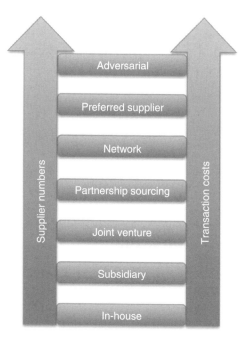

Fig. 3.3. Procurement taxonomy. Source: adapted from Parker and Hartley (1997).

Box 3.2. Events management software: an inside job.

Shane Hooks is a New Zealand sports event entrepreneur. His company, Brand New Day, organized a number of triathlon events and triathlon race series. To support these events, he developed events management software that would manage the registration for individual entrants, time athletes in the race, manage e-mail communications, provide online purchasing of event merchandise orders and an online post-event survey.

The success of this software prompted him to market the 'eventdirector' software to other events. For this purpose, he established a new company called Keep Left. Brand New Day owns 50% of Keep Left. The net result is that Brand New Day would contract Keep Left to provide the event director software for its events. In 2009, Hooks announced that Brand New Day would be moving out of the events business so that he could concentrate his efforts on his growing event software business.

Partnership sourcing (or collaborative sourcing) occurs when a purchasing organization relies upon a single source of supply or a small number of preferred suppliers. There are a number of advantages for partnership sourcing. These include avoiding unnecessary costs of excessive tendering and frequent competitions, fewer, dedicated suppliers, longer-term contracts, coordinated strategies between buyers and suppliers, a sharing of risks and rewards, more trusting relationships, and the pursuit of mutual benefit (i.e. 'win–win' outcomes). In the example of the Melbourne Fashion Festival, Arts Events Management Australasia (AEMA) is involved in producing many events. It is highly probable that AEMA utilizes many of the suppliers listed in Table 3.1 at its other events. For an event organizer that organizes multiple events, the key feature of partnership sourcing is that the organization may utilize many of the same suppliers for all of the events.

Network sourcing creates a virtual company but without moving to vertical integration. Building serial and multiple partnerships within the supply chain results in network sourcing. If the same organizations are involved in different supply chains, it is inevitable that conversations between employees of these organizations will lead to the organizations providing each other with opportunities beyond those facilitated by AEMA. Rather than a straight line, the supply chain would now resemble a spider's web where organizations are able to interact directly with each other.

A preferred supplier is an organization that has been approved by the purchasing organization and does not need to be subjected to further checks or an evaluation process in the future by the purchasing organization for subsequent transactions.

The adversarial model includes attributes such as tough negotiation, short-term contracts and playing off potential partners against each other. The limitations of the adversarial procurement approach are numerous. They include distant and/or superficial relationships; frequent tendering, which is both risky and expensive, heavy reliance on price as the key selection criterion; spot contracts or complex contingent claim contracting (i.e. bundling of goods), multi-sourcing, lack of trust and a reluctance to share information; and adversarial attitudes usually reflected in win–lose outcomes.

Event organizers are likely to consider a number of criteria when selecting supply chain partners. These include speed, time certainty, price, price certainty, flexibility, responsibility, quality, as well as the compatibility of the organization's values, cultures and brands. The latter features were evident in the decision of the Lincoln Agricultural Society to partner with EcoEvents. EPIC is an environmentally friendly, low carbon centre on the LAS showground. EcoEvents specialize in sustainable management solutions designed specifically for the events industry.

The creation of exchange relationships with suppliers and buyers creates a dependency on them. Focusing in on suppliers, the dependency of an event organization on any given supplier is in proportion to the importance of the resource controlled by the supplier and the availability of the resource from alternative suppliers. The bargaining power of suppliers, alongside the potential for new entrants, the bargaining power of buyers, the threat of substitute products, and the rivalry among competitors are the competitive forces that an event must contend with (see Chapter 10).

RELATIONSHIP MARKETING

Paraphrasing a definition of relationship marketing offered in the context of sport organizations (Buhler and Nufer, 2010, p. 25), relationship marketing in events refers to the establishment and maintenance of positive, enduring and mutually beneficial relationships between event organizers and their stakeholders. Adopting the relationship marketing philosophy is essential for organizations seeking to benefit from partnership sourcing (see above). The relationship management approach to managing supply chain relationships views relationship quality with suppliers as a key asset of the organization. This permits organizations to improve communications and better coordinate buyer–supplier relationships. These sorts of industrial buyer–supplier relationships are characterized by relatively long-term time horizons, non-market modes of governance and high levels of commitment and trust (Morris and Carter, 2005).

Relationship marketing within the supply chain seeks to create a long-term, conflict-free collaboration between the organization and its suppliers, in which all parties recognize each other's needs and exceed each other's expectations. As a high profile event, the London Olympics is under considerable pressure to act in a sustainable and responsible manner (see Chapter 9). The London 2012 ODA is the public body responsible for developing and building the new venues and infrastructure for the Games and their use after 2012. As noted previously, the ODA will establish relationships with over 2000 businesses. The ODA understands that in order for it to be regarded as socially responsible, it will need to ensure that these organizations are also responsible (see Table 3.2).

Relationship marketing also guards against opportunistic behaviour. Organizations in a buyer–supplier relationship can act opportunistically whereby they seek benefit at the expense of the other organization, thereby creating win–lose outcomes.

Table 3.2. Policies for suppliers to the London 2012 Olympics.

Anti-fraud Policy	LOCOG Sustainable Sourcing Code
Code of Practice on Gifts and Gratuities	LOCOG Packaging Guidelines
Code of Practice Regarding Conflicts of Interest	LOCOG Guidelines on Carbon Emissions of Products and Services
Brand Protection – Guidelines for Businesses	London 2012 Sustainability Guidelines on Corporate and Public Events
LOCOG Diversity and Inclusion Business Charter	Olympic Board Policy on the Use of PVC for the London 2012 Olympic and Paralympic Games
Information Security policy	Olympic Board Policy on the Use of HFCs for the London 2012 Olympic and Paralympic Games
Health, Safety and Environment Policy	LOCOG Child Protection policy
London 2012 Sustainability Policy	

Box 3.3. Making the boss look greedy.

Bruce 'The Boss' Springsteen is an American rock music icon with a strong working-class identity. In 2009, he performed in large venues throughout North America and Europe. The promoters that promote and the venues that present large-scale popular music concerts do not usually engage in the ticket sale and distribution process. Rather, they rely upon ticket agencies. It is estimated that Ticketmaster sells 90% of all tickets to large-scale popular music concerts in the USA. The organization has exclusive contracts with the largest and most popular arenas, meaning that if an event promoter hires a stadium they are obliged to use Ticketmaster as the ticketing agency. The ticket buyer pays Ticketmaster a sum that includes amounts separately designated as for the ticket itself and for any combination of service, convenience, processing and/or handling.

(Continued)

Box 3.3. Continued.

During Springsteen's 2009 US tour, fans seeking tickets for his Long Island and New Jersey shows were redirected from the Ticketmaster website to TicketsNow. TicketsNow is a secondary tickets site that is owned by Ticketmaster. This redirection to TicketsNow occurred even though 'face value' seats were still available through Ticketmaster. Springsteen and his management team were quick to condemn the practice. Springsteen's manager, Jon Landau, went public stating, 'We perceived this to have been a major abuse of our fans'. Springsteen also issued a statement via his website: 'Last Monday, we were informed that Ticketmaster was redirecting your log-in requests for tickets at face value, to their secondary site TicketsNow, which specializes in up-selling tickets at above face value. They did this even when other seats remained available at face value. We condemn this practice. We have asked this redirection from Ticketmaster to TicketsNow cease and desist immediately.'

In response, Ticketmaster issued an open letter of apology to Bruce Springsteen, Jon Landau and the entire Springsteen Tour Team. In the letter, Ticketmaster Entertainment CEO Irving Azoff wrote 'While we were genuinely trying to do the right thing for fans in providing more choices when the tickets they requested from the primary on-sale were not available, we clearly missed the mark'. By quickly condemning the practice and placing responsibility for it squarely at the feet of Ticketmaster, Springsteen was able to ensure that his reputation was not negatively affected. This study highlights the ability for an organization to be negatively affected by the actions of their supply chain partners.

Sources: www.rollingstone.com, www.billboard.com

NETWORKS AND CREATIVITY/INNOVATION

The creative process results in creative outputs – innovative ideas, products, services, procedures or processes. Creativity and innovation is a consequence of the interactions between people at the level of the individual, group, organization and inter-organizational network. Relevant individual characteristics include an individual's cognitive capacity, personality, motivational orientation and knowledge. Every innovation starts with a 'light bulb' or eureka moment within an individual's mind. There is not likely to be any shortage of new ideas for an event – the challenge is to ensure that these thoughts are expressed and captured by those with the capacity to implement them. The characteristics of the group and organization are instrumental in this process. Group characteristics include norms, cohesiveness of members, size, diversity and problem-solving approaches. For example, a group that does not encourage an individual to take risks, or challenge the existing way of doing things is not likely to help its members have and share innovative thoughts. Individuals with high creative potential coupled with a defective problem-solving approach will translate into ineffective group creativity. Effective groups require individuals who use and value different problem-solving approaches. Organizational characteristics include culture, resources, rewards, strategy, structure and technology. Network characteristics include size, diversity, distribution of power, and density. In terms of individual, organization and network size, there is likely to be an optimal number of people involved in the creative process. Too few and not enough diversity may be present. Too many people, and ideas get lost and people lose their confidence to speak publicly. Diversity, be it age, gender, ethnicity, familiarity with the problem, is generally regarded as assisting creativity. Network density increases the number of interactions between members of different organizations. The creative situation comprises all the social and environmental (i.e. contextual) influences on creative behaviour. These relationships are displayed in Fig. 3.4.

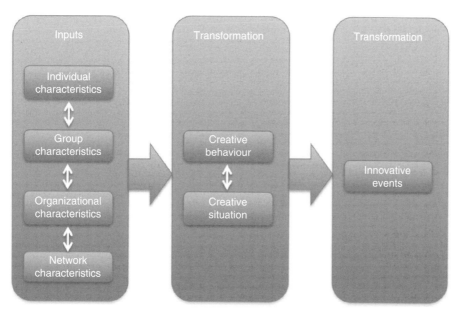

Fig. 3.4. Antecedent conditions for innovative events. Source: adapted from Woodman *et al.,* 1993).

In a study of a food festival, Mackellar (2006) identified a number of innovations that have occurred. These include social innovations, whereby community participation was increased and new applications of volunteer labour and their associated skill development were achieved. In terms of marketing innovations, businesses at the festival were approached by distributors willing to distribute their product for them in non-traditional outlets. An example of a service innovation is that a business developed a holistic health check for the festival that was also found to have a market beyond the festival. Businesses meet new suppliers of raw products and established process innovations. A new event committee structure was an indicator of organizational innovation. New lines of crops, new types of herb-based produce and new festival activities were examples of product innovation at the festival. Mackellar suggests that high levels of network density (i.e. the extent to which all members in the network are connected by direct ties) and social embeddedness (i.e. the extent to which economic action is dependent upon non-economic factors such as trust and goodwill) promote the capacity for innovation.

SUMMARY

Conceptualizing an event as an activity of a single organization fails to recognize the collaboration between organizations that is characteristic of all but the smallest of events. Just as there is specialization of tasks within an organization, there is specialization of organizational tasks and inter-organizational networks are generally essential to produce events. The development of an effective and efficient supply chain for an event is, therefore, a key consideration for event managers. Careful consideration should be given to what an organization produces internally and what external organizations are contracted to provide. Innovative events are a consequence of the people, the groups, the organizations and the networks that produce an event. For an event manager, thinking outside the box might involve thinking beyond the organization.

FURTHER RESEARCH

General reading:

Andersson, T.D. and Getz, D. (2008) Stakeholder management strategies of festivals. *Journal of Convention and Event Tourism* 9, 199–220.

Cousens, L., Barnes, M. and Dickson, G. (2008) Facilitating events management using a network perspective. In: Mallen, C. and Adams, L. (eds) *Sport, Recreation and Tourism Event Management: Theoretical and Practical Dimensions*. Butterworth-Heinemann/Elsevier, Burlington, Massachusetts, pp. 42–52.

Erickson, G.S. and Kushner, R.J. (1999) Public event networks: an application of marketing theory to sporting events. *European Journal of Marketing* 33, 348–364.

Useful websites:

Using sport effectively – www.sportworksuk.com

Supply Chain Professionals – www.supplymanagement.com

REVIEW QUESTIONS

1. For an event of your choosing, model their inter-organizational network. Ensure that your model categorizes organizations into similar groupings.

2. Competition today is not between individual organizations but between supply chains. Is this statement relevant to the events sector?

3. Apply Porter's Five Force model (1980) to the Melbourne Fashion Festival and an event of your choosing. Pay particular attention to the identification of competitors and substitute products and services. What similarities and differences are evident?

4. In the chapter, a spider's web analogy was used to help you understand a network sourcing within supply chains. In your mind, an event network is analogous to what? Map the features of an event to your analogue.

REFERENCES

Archer, N. and Yuan, Y. (2000) Managing business-to-business relationships throughout the e-commerce procurement life cycle. *Internet Research* 10, 385–395.

Babiak, K. and Thibault, L. (2008) Managing interorganisational relationships: the art of plate spinning. *International Journal of Sport Management and Marketing* 3, 281–302.

Bendor-Samuel, P. (1999) *Turning Lead into Gold: the Demystification of Outsourcing*. Executive Excellence Publishing, Provo, Utah.

Brinkerhoff, J.M. (2002) Assessing and improving partnership relationships and outcomes: a proposed framework. *Evaluation and Program Planning* 25, 215–231.

Buhler, A. and Nufer, G. (2010) *Relationship Marketing in Sports*. Butterworth Heinemann, Oxford.

Burt, D.N., Dobler, D.W. and Starling, S.L. (2003) *World Class Supply Management: the Key to Supply Chain Management*, 7th edn. McGraw-Hill/Irwin, Boston, Massachusetts.

Ebers, M. (1997) *The Formation of Inter-organizational Networks*. Oxford University Press, Oxford.

Gilley, K.M. and Rasheed, A. (2000) Making more by doing less: an analysis of outsourcing and its effects on firm performance. *Journal of Management* 26, 763–790.

Klibi, W., Martel, A. and Guitouni, A. (2010) The design of robust value-creating supply chain networks: a critical review. *European Journal of Operational Research* 203, 283–293.

Kotabea, M. and Mo, M.J. (2009) Outsourcing and financial performance: a negative curvilinear effect. *Journal of Purchasing and Supply Management* 15, 205–213.

Mackellar, J. (2006) An integrated view of innovation emerging from a regional festival. *International Journal of Event Management Research* 2, 37–48.

Mentzer, J.T., DeWitt, W.J., Keebler, J.S., Min, S., Nix, N.W., Smith, C.D. and Zacharia, Z.G. (2001) Defining supply chain management. *Journal of Business Logistics* 22, 1–26.

Morris, M. and Carter, C. (2005) Relationship marketing and supplier logistics performance: an extension of the key mediating variables model. *Journal of Supply Chain Management* 41, 32–43.

Parker, D. and Hartley, K. (1997) The economics of partnership sourcing versus adversarial competition: a critique. *European Journal of Purchasing and Supply Management* 3, 115–125.

Platts, K.W., Probert, D.R. and Canez, L. (2002) Make vs. buy decisions: a process incorporating multi-attribute decision-making. *International Journal of Production Economics* 77, 247–257.

Porter, M.E. (1980) *Competitive Strategy*. Free Press, New York.

Samson, D. and Daft, R. (2009) *Management*, 3rd Asia Pacific edn. Cengage Learning, Melbourne.

Toften, K. and Hammervoll, T. (2009) Niche firms and marketing strategy: an exploratory study of internationally oriented niche firms. *European Journal of Marketing* 43, 1378–1391.

Van De Ven, A.H. (1976) On the nature, formation and maintenance of relations among organizations. *Academy of Management Review* 1, 24–36.

Wisner, J.D., Keong Leong, G. and Tan, K.-C. (2005) *Principles of Supply Chain Management: a Balanced Approach*. Thomson South-Western, Mason, Ohio.

Woodman, R.W., Sawyer, J.E. and Griffin, R.W. (1993) Towards a theory of organisational creativity. *Academy of Management Review* 18, 293–321.

chapter 4

Funding, Sponsorship and Financial Management

Caroline Wiscombe

OBJECTIVES OF THE CHAPTER

Funding, sponsorship and financial management aims to provide potential events managers and those working in the industry with a comprehensive overview of the financial challenges of delivering and managing events. The chapter considers how events and events enterprises may be funded given the plethora of different organizational contexts in which they may be delivered. Sponsorship is discussed in its context as a major income stream for many voluntary, charitable and third-stream businesses, as well as a considerable revenue factor for private companies. Other sources of income are discussed including the growing impact of broadcasting rights on mega-events. 'Return on investment' is approached in a broad context, which again contextualizes information against a wide range of different events scenarios and draws on marketing approaches that are explored in greater depth in Chapter 7.

This chapter aims to:

- explain the role of funding and sponsorship in events' success;
- explain different forms of return on investment and how these can be calculated; and
- describe the process of financial management and identify why this should be monitored.

INTRODUCTION

On any given day, there is a huge number of events occurring worldwide. They can be large, global mega-events, such as the Olympic Games or the Football World Cup. Alternatively, they can be regional but world renowned, for instance the Edinburgh International Festival. Events can involve festivals and heritage, exemplified by the Mardi Gras celebrations in New Orleans held in February each year, or music and nightlife, which encompass Winter Restaurant Week in

New York City, New Year's Eve in Rome or Fisherman's Day in the Maldives. They can be very small, local events serving communities needs, or huge 'hallmark' events with a global following.

Sports and outdoor events are often focused on a particular activity such as the Day of the Virgin of Guadalupe Cliff Diving in Acapulco, Mexico, or the Wrangler National Finals Rodeo held in Las Vegas, USA. Arts or performance events may encompass music of all genres, which attract visitors on an annual basis, such as the Wagner Bayreuth Festival, or on a more infrequent basis, such as the Oberammergau Passion Play held every 10 years. Alternatively, they may be one-off events hoping to develop a following that may drive a more regular occurrence, such as the Restfest touring digital film festival in Seoul.

Children and families are not forgotten by events organizers, particularly around the holiday periods. Flambarts Festival is held annually in Dreux, France, while Christmas Through The Ages is an annual event in Kensington Gardens, London. Events sometimes verge on the weird and wonderful; such events include the annual Esclade in Geneva, Switzerland, and the Skin Two Rubber Ball weekend in London.

In the planning and organization of any event, whether large or small, driven by public, private or third-stream organization, the most important underpinning guarantee of success is the management of finance. This includes ensuring enough income of all types, including ticket sales, advertising, media coverage, donations, grants, funding or sponsorship, is sufficient to cover all costs and expenses. It also includes building in controls for expenditure that ensure accountability. Successful financial management may mean making a profit, if the event is for a privately run organization, or a surplus for third-stream, charitable or voluntary fundraising activity. It also requires the development of processes that prepare budgets or forecasts, and report on and evaluate the performance of the event.

Funding and sponsorship is a vital ingredient in the success of events as it forms a major part of the income streams for organizers. Corporate sponsorship in particular provides vital revenue and its withdrawal can cause severe financial difficulties. The economic recession of 2007–2009 caused many corporate sponsors to reassess their commitments; The Masters golf tournament at Augusta National Country Club, Georgia, USA, is a major annual sporting event. The tournament brings in over US$100 million to the economy of the city but in 2009 it was seriously affected by four major corporations alone cancelling sponsorship to the caterers, Kwoka, causing a loss of revenue of more than US$70,000 and a direct relationship to the employment of temporary workers, many of whom use the event to earn college fees and tuition. Similarly, the Renault Formula One (F1) team lost its sponsorship partway through the 2009 season, which was a severe blow for both the crew and drivers, but also for the wider sport.

The financial challenge of managing and delivering events is therefore multifaceted. The delivery of income streams, which include funding and sponsorship, as well as the handling of costs and expenses, through sound financial management, are vital. The investment into events must be justified, particularly where organizers are seeking to provide longevity of purpose, perhaps by developing annual or biennial events. Where events management fails to consider all elements of finance and financial planning, success may be less than judicious.

Box 4.1. The Edinburgh International Festival (Income).

The Edinburgh International Festival runs for almost a month in mid-August to early September annually. It brings an estimated £200 million to the Scottish economy each year and attracts hundreds of thousands of visitors. It is a registered charity and the organizers aim to 'break even'. Break even is a term that describes a situation where income equals

(Continued)

Box 4.1. Continued.

expenditure and the organizers make neither a loss nor a profit. If the organization made year on year profits, it could no longer remain a charity with the associated tax benefits that this status brings.

Its income streams, which reached £9.6 million in 2009, are multifaceted; 23% of income comes from ticket sales. In 2009, box office sales reached £2.58 million and accounted for 398,760 attendances at festival events.

However, despite the perceived success of ticket sales, this is not enough to cover the costs and expenses of putting on the festival, which covers a wide variety of entertainment genres from comedy to drama, huge orchestra pieces to individual artists and commissions; in total 180 performances with more than 2200 performers taking part. Grants from the City of Edinburgh Council and the Scottish Arts Council provide a further 50% of income with 27%, or £2.59 million, from sponsorship, donations and other earned income (e.g. retail sales of festival merchandise).

Sponsorship and donations come from a wide geographical area as well as from diverse groups. Principal supporters become Proscenium Club members, and include BP, Caledonian Hilton, City Inns, Standard Life and Scottish & Newcastle UK. Foreign government support comes from countries including Australia, Germany, Switzerland, the USA, Romania and Singapore. Many trusts and foundations provide funding; these may be in charitable, education or arts foundations. Not all funding provided is 'cash'; many 'in kind' supporters provide income by offering services. These include Capital Solutions, Dimensions (Scotland) Ltd and Malmaison. In each of these groups fall a number of hotels that measure success of their donations through the recorded occupancy rates. In 2008, occupancy rates during the festival were 88.9% and this rose to 91.3% in 2009.

Business sponsorship is vital to the festival's income stream therefore identifying the ways in which the festival can support corporate brands is crucial to the 'selling' of sponsorship; this may be through brand alignment with festival, such as Homecoming Scotland, or through the corporate social responsibility initiatives felt by sponsors to be vital. Outreach programmes in the local community, employee reward programmes and hospitality opportunities all play an important role in attracting sponsorship. However, media coverage also plays a growing role. In 2009 television broadcasts appeared on many international, national and regional programmes including the recording of festival performances for a Japanese documentary. Radio coverage was even more extensive with over 13 countries receiving direct radio commentary. Further media coverage saw journalists and bloggers covering 380 titles and websites. This provides huge incentives for sponsorship alignment.

Sources: Various

Activity

Think about an event you know. List all the things that are needed to run the event and try to estimate the costs and expenses that are involved in running it. What does your list look like? How much did you estimate the costs to be? Use all the sources available to you to see if you were right!

FUNDING

Funding is a diverse term. It is used by all kinds of organizations to describe the money needed to develop an event. Funds or funding may be used for capital expenditure (the term used to describe expenditure for items that will be there long after the event has been and gone, such as transport infrastructure or a stadium) or for recurrent expenses used in day-to-day operations. The way funding is organized may be dependent upon the type of organization planning the event; these can be described as private organizations, public organizations, third-stream or voluntary bodies or can combine private and public partnerships.

Funding of private events organizations

Private organizations are usually sole traders, perhaps a wedding event coordinator, limited companies with the addendum 'Ltd' added to their trade name, or public limited companies (PLC) that trade their shares on the stock market. A private organization exists to make a profit, whether for the benefit of its sole owner, or a group of owners or partners. Profit is the term used to describe money left over when all the income of a private organization is larger than all the costs and expenses, and is declared on a periodic basis – sometimes annually but also more often an interim profit and loss account may be produced. The type of organization is determined by the ownership of the business, and this dictates how taxes and liability for losses are accounted for.

For a private organization funding is usually determined by loans and borrowings, which could be short term, up to 1 year, or long term, up to 20 years. This type of borrowing is termed 'debt finance' and is usually available to provide cash for investment in facilities or equipment (termed assets). If the asset will remain for longer than 1 year, such as buildings, this is termed fixed assets. Where the asset will be used up more quickly, such as stocks of food or beverages, these are called current assets.

When the economic climate is in a downturn it is a lot harder for small and medium-size organizations to borrow money because banks and other financial institutions worry that the business will not be able to pay back the interest on the loans. A business plan is used to help the financial institution decide if the organization really understands its market, potential and its ability to support such loans. The capital borrowed will always, in accounting terms, equal the assets of the organization.

A PLC has another opportunity to raise funding by issuing more shares in its business. This is known as 'equity finance'. Like a loan or borrowing it provides access to cash, but instead of paying interest to a financial institution the organization will have to pay a share of the profits to the shareholders. In some large share issues this may also mean handing over some aspects of management or ownership control.

Once an events organization generates profits, these can be used to develop the business. This is called retained earnings. When a financial institution is deciding whether to lend funds for debt finance they will consider how much retained earnings are also being introduced. The more the retained earnings the more positive the lending situation becomes, as owners are showing they are not just taking out all the profits to pay themselves a dividend but using the generated cash to buy more assets for the business. The business becomes more valuable the more assets it owns.

Publicly funded organizations

Publicly funded organizations include the police, schools, universities, health services, museums and art galleries, among others. Many of these organizations arrange or attend events to raise awareness for their product or service. Alternatively, public-funded organizations may support events organizations or provide events for public entertainment, leisure or tourism purposes.

In the UK public funds provide a wide range of leisure and recreational services that may include events. Events, both large and small, may be held in local authority facilities where no direct payment is made for access, such as urban parks, beaches and country parks, or could be held in theatres, arts centres or sports centres where a charge is levied. In addition, many towns still have 'civic halls', which are used to house events and festivals.

Funding for recreation should be part of a sound regional strategic plan; for more on strategic planning see Chapter 10. Event organizers seeking funding through local government agencies should satisfy themselves of the mission and strategy being developed and provide evidence that their event will contribute to the authorities' aims.

Event organizers may be working on behalf of local and regional governments to provide entertainment as a part of the recreational life of the area. While funding is usually guaranteed for such work, there is always an accountability of the expenditure on such activity, particularly where losses are continually made and the public support for such events falls away. Government offices are answerable to the taxpayer and may have difficult questions to answer if funds are not used appropriately. A question of probity in difficult economic climates makes the expenditure of public funds on entertainment, raised as it is through taxation, difficult to justify. Box 4.2 looks at this in more detail.

Box 4.2. Walsall Illuminations: losing public appeal.

The Walsall Illuminations are a council-funded project running for 5–6 weeks each September to November. The Illuminations are held to provide an attraction for both locals and visitors, and tourism numbers, retailers and traders all provide positive feedback on their worth. However, since 2003 attendance figures have steadily deteriorated and in the 2008 season the Walsall Metropolitan Borough Council, which runs and organizes the event, made a deficit of £167,000, despite its costs and expenses coming in under the approved operational expenditure budget. This was the third year the event had run at a loss.

The income target for 2008 was £670,000, which included a budgeted surplus of £50,000. The only income allocated from external funding was £40,000 and this was affected by a shortfall of anticipated funding from Black Country Tourism; instead of £30,000 the Council received only £6000. Therefore, the impact of ticket sales and attendance is much larger than for some other events and any downturn immediately affects the 'bottom line' (the term used for the final figure when all income less all costs and expenses are calculated).

Date	Attendance figures	Operational outturn (£)	Result
2003	193,000	£35,000	Surplus
2004	163,000	–£51,000	Loss
2005	188,500	£40,000	Surplus
2006	157,000	–£49,000	Loss
2007	120,000	–£184,000	Loss
2008	111,000	–£167,000	Loss

(Continued)

Box 4.2. Continued.

In order to rejuvenate the event the council would need to invest in a radical change to the current offering, which includes dated attractions, less than exciting food and beverage offerings and vintage storylines. While the event was due to take place in 2009, eventually the Council succumbed to public pressure to strategically reposition the illuminations in line with refurbishment of the venue, itself subject to a lottery funding bid; thus the event may not now run until 2012 at the earliest.

The financial challenge is in the use of public funding for this event. In restaging it the council must have a sustainable income strategy and understand fully the effect of the event on the local economy. In addition it must explore the use of sponsorship opportunities as it seeks to increase its income stream, thereby assuring the public taxpayer that it is using every opportunity to cover costs and expenses.

Sources: Various

Third-stream organizations

Third-stream organizations are those with charitable or non-charitable status who work to provide support and funds to those 'in need'. They do not seek to make a profit but to provide goods and services to those less fortunate than themselves.

Sometimes the 'event' is the charity, as in the case of the Glastonbury Festival, which supports a number of third world and environmental projects. In other cases charities or voluntary groups use an event to contribute income to their core work. In either situation, either core funding from the parent organization is contributed thus providing start-up funds, which are paid back after a successful event, or other forms of funding are sought. These can include special fundraising at a number of levels (some ideas include dinner dances, auction nights, trivia evenings and so on), selling merchandising (pens, scarves, T-shirts and ties are just some examples) or using lotteries and gaming (such as bingo, raffles, gaming machines).

Third-stream organizations are more likely to apply for grants and funds from government sources and from other charities set up to sponsor particular activities; The Edinburgh International Festival, for instance, applied to the Leverhulme Trust for funds to set up a director's workshop.

Box 4.3. Edinburgh Military Tattoo: the search for funding.

The Edinburgh Military Tattoo has been one of Scotland's most iconic events for 35 years. It has attracted a sell-out audience of 217,000 people for the last 10 years and is thought to be worth around £50 million to the city's economy. Major concerts organized at the same venue are worth a further £5 million per annum.

The grandstands used for spectators had been used for 75 years and a replacement arena would cost in the region of £16 million. Replacing the current arena required a better design to enable the speedier erection of the stands in front of the famous castle. In order to achieve this, groundwork to move the network of utilities pipes and cables buried under the esplanade has to be undertaken, the removal of the existing stands to be organized and development work to the foundations of the castle has to be carried out – an enormous logistical task in itself.

(Continued)

Box 4.3. Continued.

Three public bodies, the Scottish Government, Scottish Enterprise and Edinburgh City Council, agreed, after a great deal of consultation and lobbying, to each provide £3 million toward the project. The remainder of the funds, some £7 million, will be funded by the Tattoo from a combination of its own funds and corporate sponsorship. By 2009 it had taken years to reach this agreement and the organizers still face 2 more years of implementation of the project before the new seating can be used.

Sources: Various

SPONSORSHIP

Sponsorship is an agreement between a company or organization and an event organizer where the company gives either money or the equivalent value 'in kind' for instance goods or services, in exchange for the right to be associated with the event. This can include the company name on team shirts, on advertising banners, in press advertisements or whatever is agreed in order to improve the awareness or image of the company. The more high profile the event usually the greater the ability for events organizers to attract sponsorship; however, this does not stop very small events attempting to attract sponsorship in order to increase their income streams, perhaps by the donation of a cup or prize from a retail outlet. The reward for the sponsor is usually not philanthropic; they will be seeking exploitable benefits usually in the form of promotion or publicity. Events managers need clear targets for the achievement of sponsorship and to make back-up plans in case these cannot be achieved; therefore, monitoring of budgets will have the added complexity of being based on the timing of income from sponsorship.

Sponsorship has developed rapidly over the past 30–40 years, but the global economic climate of the 2007–2010 period caused many companies to ensure that a measurable return on investment is being achieved. This makes sponsorship harder to attract. In 2002 over £6.3 million was provided to festivals in the UK alone, around 14% of the total sponsorship market. Fifty one per cent of sponsorship is usually directed at sports, which rose by 65% in 2005 to reach a mammoth worldwide total of US$43.1 billion (Masterson, 2007).

In order for events managers to attract sponsorship they need to understand clearly what sponsors might expect and is realistically achievable. Sponsorship falls under the category of 'marketing expenditure' for corporate or business sponsors and the marketing solutions provided by this means of communication need to be more effective and efficient than other forms, such as direct advertising. Other marketing options are discussed in Chapter 7 but usually sponsorship objectives are divided into four broad categories: direct sales, brand awareness and external and internal corporate awareness. Competitive advantage provides a fifth category linking all objectives together (Masterson, 2007). It is not easy to link these objectives to a direct return on investment. If sales only occurred because of sponsorship, and this can be objectively and accurately measured, then it is usually easier to attract as a form of income; thus direct sales at events might be those where food and beverages are offered on an exclusive basis, which provides measured income for the supplier, and may convert consumers to their products in the future.

Brand awareness is less tangible but can help in brand recognition. How events managers offer this brand awareness varies. Media Trust offers sponsor names and logos on three training diaries produced during the year, priority to speak at events, logos on their events calendars, links to sponsor websites through their weekly e-mail updates as well as logos and profiles on all marketing and printed materials. The National Union of Students (NUS) offers sponsorship, which supports face-to-face dialogue with students and their officers and attendance at two major events per year. Sponsorship entitles high-profile brand awareness. However, not all events offer this type of branded activity. Corporate advertising at The Masters golf tournament is very subdued. The grounds are untouched, with the three main sponsors using secluded private chalets for their hospitality guests. Brand awareness is limited to television advertising, which is kept to 4 minutes per hour of commercial spots versus the normal 15–18 minutes per hour afforded to sponsors during other Professional Golf Association (PGA) tournaments. Events managers attempting to access sponsorship therefore need to be clear about what they can offer in terms of brand awareness and how this is more efficient and effective than other forms of marketing solution.

Corporate image is often a key driver in sponsorship. Corporate social responsibility (CSR), which you can read more about in Chapter 9, often impacts on corporate image. The use of sponsorship to promote particular events and partnerships is often key to corporate image and knowing the image changes, or CSR initiatives being used by potential sponsors can provide lucrative revenue. Linking the event to cultural, educational or minority groups can provide good sales techniques for this aspect of sponsorship.

Box 4.4. The Carmel Bach Festival.

Sponsors of the Carmel Bach Festival contribute to a series of free musical opportunities, which opens the performance of baroque music to a growing educational strategy accessed by a wider audience. The Bach Festival is a world class, 16-day celebration of music and ideas inspired by the historical and ongoing influence of J.S. Bach and is hosted in Carmel, California. Founded in 1935, it began as a 3-day festival of open rehearsals and musical performances, and for more than 70 years the series of musical events has continued to bring the sounds of the Baroque and beyond to communities of the Monterey Peninsula. Comprising nationally and internationally renowned performing artists, the Festival orchestra and chorale, along with a strong local chorus, contribute to a summer schedule featuring full orchestral and choral works, individual vocal and chamber ensemble concerts, recitals, master classes, lectures and informal talks, in addition to interactive social and family events, which is visited by those from local communities, the wider USA and overseas.

There are four main educational strands provided, which allow access to a wide range of community groups:

1. Community concerts, which started in 2003, and were developed to bring the magic of music to the entire family and to demonstrate the high standard of performance young people are capable of achieving. The free community concerts are informal and incorporate interactive hour-long performances presented by members of the festival orchestra, festival youth chorus and/or young artist performers.
2. Free open rehearsals allowing music students to study the development of the different performances with festival Music Director Bruno Weil leading the ensemble in a series of onstage working sessions, in preparation for the main concert series.
3. Free pre-concert talks, which inspire learning about classical music and the concerts through an informal talk and discussion series. David Gordon, the festival's Education

(Continued)

Box 4.4. Continued.

Director, introduces the day's main musical performance by describing the origins of the music in the context of history and the composers' lives.

4. Free community ticket availability: the programme allows for free access to musical events for organizations such as the Boys and Girls Club, community college music students, elder care facilities, church groups and summer school programmes in the counties of Monterey, San Benito and Santa Cruz.

These would not be possible without the sponsorship of a large number of patrons and the contribution of over 300 volunteers who undertake a wide number of tasks from helping out in the festival office, to acting as ushers or providing hospitality for the musical artists.

Source: Carmel Bach Festival (2010)

Activity

You are the newly appointed director of the Carmel Bach Festival and one of your first new strategies is to extend the educational and outreach programmes associated with the event. Make a list of ideas to support this strategic direction as well as engage new sponsorship.

Competitive advantage is an overwhelming driver for potential sponsors. In November 2009 the Virgin Blue Airline Group agreed to the sponsorship of the Sydney Mardi Gras for 4 years. The group contains three airlines, V Australia, Virgin Blue and Pacific Blue. The three airlines will serve as the official airlines for the Sydney event and will promote Mardi Gras via their communication network, which encompasses 28 Australian cities and towns alongside 13 international destinations. The combination of long-haul aircraft, domestic Australian flights and short-haul to the Pacific Rim countries makes Virgin an ideal sponsor. The competitive advantage to Virgin is in it being the official and 'sole' airline involved. Therefore if one sponsor can get competitive advantage by being a sole, or major, sponsor, this again can provide a good sales technique.

Damage to lucrative sponsorship deals can come in a number of forms, not least is the inability for events managers to ensure that posters, hoardings and other visible sponsorship sites are theirs to publicize. In 2004, the Sydney Mardi Gras was hit by a non-sponsors campaign to attract the 400,000 revellers to their brand by putting marketing advertising along the 170 bus shelters lining the parade's route. Already struggling to find sponsors, the organizers then failed to attract the corporate sponsorship it was seeking.

Attracting sponsorship

Any events organization needs clear plans to attract sponsorship and they need to understand clearly the economic and marketing drivers involved. Different categories of sponsor will require conceptually different returns on their investment, whether in profitability or net worth, or a more altruistic component. Those who seek to attract sponsorship to particular community events would emphasize that 84% of people think better of brands who seek to support the local community directly (SBI, 2009).

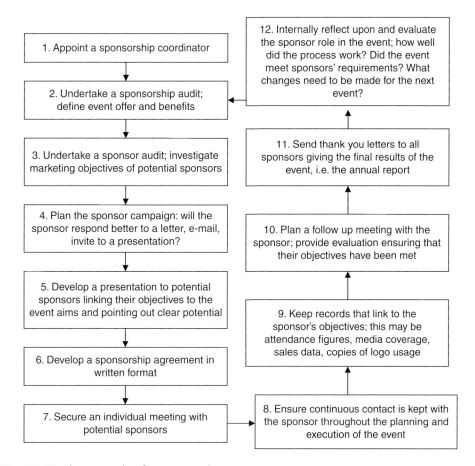

Fig. 4.1. Twelve-step plan for sponsorship.

When meeting any sponsor the secret to a successful outcome is preparation. Being clear about the aims and outcomes of the event, and how they link to the sponsor's marketing plans, is crucial. The sponsorship agreement should be in writing and clearly state what will be provided to the sponsor as part of the package; for example, this may include free tickets to the event or hospitality packages. Providing clearly evaluated outcomes, reflection on the results of the event and thanks will add to the potential of getting the sponsor to assist in any future events you organize. Making this the role of one person within the planning team will ensure clear lines of communication and responsibility for the process (Fig. 4.1).

Other income

Funding and sponsorship form two very important income streams for events organizations. Other income streams may be derived from ticket sales, merchandise, broadcasting fees, advert sales and concessions.

Ticket pricing strategies: for many events organizers the price of the ticket is not the sole source of income and therefore will not be priced according to the costs and expenses of the organization, unlike, say, a restaurant business. Pricing strategies will be crucial to the success of the event, however, and might produce discussions on ensuring value for money or maximum impact to a particular target group. Often events organizers will consider discounts for larger groups, early-bird discounts or the creation of special categories of attendees, particularly for patrons or sponsors of the event. The addition of extra hospitality to a ticket price might attract a premium. It is usual for events organizers to build into their ticket pricing strategy the opportunity of a number of free tickets. These may be used for bartering of in-kind services or to alleviate potential problems – for instance the Glastonbury Festival gives the local community free tickets to the event to 'apologize' for the congestion caused by the increased traffic during concerts. Ultimately ticket pricing may be more 'art than science' but the size of the event or similar events can provide a good benchmark to which events organizers can relate. However to get the best price, scientific methods, techniques and investigations, as well as consideration of the distribution mechanism, need to take place (Preuss, 2001).

Merchandising: events organizers may find the notion of merchandising hard to understand. However, the purchase of a scarf or pen, T-shirt or mug with the event logo attached to it seems, for many participants and spectators, to be both essential and necessary. The merchandise provides an opportunity to revisit the notion of the event long after it has ceased to be. In addition, merchandise may add to the value of sponsorship by giving sponsors the opportunity to see their 'logoed' items on stalls. Events organizers can seek ways to take orders for goods to be supplied post-event, thus ensuring money is not lost in pre-ordering too many items. Pricing merchandise is again difficult but as a minimum should cover all costs of retailing the item.

Broadcasting fees: for mega- or hallmark events broadcasting fees provide an increasingly large percentage of their overall income; broadcast fees for the summer Olympics in 2008 were worth US$1715 million, up from US$100 million in 1980 (Gratton and Solberg, 2007). Winning broadcasting rights is a competitive market and events organizers will ensure the best value for money they can achieve.

While this has provided events organizers with valuable income or sponsorship, it can often come at a price. Broadcasting rights to events covers television, radio, Internet and mobile phone streaming and sometimes its impact has changed event control with many mega-events now work toward maximizing the broadcast audience, rather than the live event.

While many small events organizers may feel that this is only relevant to large mega-events, there is a strong bond to be found between many radio stations and events provided by small clubs and local or regional organizations. The possibilities created should not be ignored, as the public increasingly look to events to provide broadcasted entertainment.

Advert sales: an event is surrounded by fences, flags, poles, lorries and so on. In addition, the event will have a programme, with pages and space on those pages that can be used as advertising. Any space that is both moveable and static can be 'sold' as advertising space. The events organizer must consider the logistics in having many advertisers or fewer advertisers with more hoardings. Events organizers need to plan this income carefully and, as with sponsorship, appeal for advertisers who may be able to find a distinct advantage in advertising at, or with, the event.

Concessions: within the confines of any event are numerous sales opportunities. For families, there must always be balloons and light batons at any night-time event. Food and drink stalls also provide opportunities to 'let' space for a fee. The provision of concessions can earn events organizers more revenue than trying to organize the facilities themselves as often specialist concessionaires will be able to foresee the needs of the market in terms of volume and type. Once an event is established the organizer may provide more and more rules to its concessionaires; for instance Glastonbury Festival insists that all stalls use recyclable materials and dispose of their waste using environmentally friendly means.

Box 4.5. Tall oaks from little acorns grow …

Lyme Regis in Dorset, England, a seaside resort with a permanent population of around 3500, hosts a number of cultural and heritage events each year. In 2009, there were 21 main events and festivals according to the town council events diary. The events range from a Jazz Festival, Artsfest and 'Candles on the Cobb' to carnival and regatta and fundraising for the Lifeboat Guild.

In 2009 it was estimated that sponsorship from the 117 retail outlets of the town provided income of £398,970 to the events' organizers. Not all sponsorship is given in cash, but raffle prizes, advertising in programmes and on posters, food costs and sustenance to participants, utility provision, fabrics and decorations all contribute. Some businesses will also provide man-hours to support particular events by selling programmes, tickets, preparing food and so on. The events generate tourism both from local visitors, day trips and those taking longer breaks. It has been shown that this sponsorship directly links to the income of retail outlets by £1.9 million and generates the equivalent of 43 full-time posts.

In consideration of the withdrawal of sponsorship as a cost-cutting exercise in a difficult economic climate, retailers need to think long and hard about the effect, not just on event's organizers, but on the town's overall economy before decisions are made.

Source: Wiscombe (2009a)

Return on investment

A return on investment (ROI) is important for all events and their organizations; however, there are a number of different systems through which their economic, social and environmental impact can be justified. While this chapter focuses on a financial or economic return for investment, as a particular financial challenge, there is increasing pressure from government, underpinned by the public, for any organization to move beyond just bottom-line profits and provide a more value added conceptual basis that revolves around social and environmental as well as economic parameters.

All funding and sponsorship need to be accountable. This accountability may differ according to the funding and sponsorship parameters; for many government departments and authorities sponsorships of events is undertaken to provide clear social, economic and technological drivers; for sports events this funding may be related to the number of medals achieved or the notion of more participants in particular activities *but not all targets are set in advance.*

For all corporate business, however, decisions on investment targets need to be set that are specific, measurable, achievable, relevant and time specific – in other words, they are SMART. These SMART objectives may be linked to market share, profitability, performance, productivity, social responsibility or innovation, but must clearly be understood by the events manager. Wherever funding and sponsorship come from, events managers need to be clear as to how the return on investment is to be measured.

Financial profits

The measurement of financial returns is usually based on a calculation of return on capital employed (ROCE); however, care is needed in defining 'capital' as well as in the notion of 'return' (Wilson and Joyce, 2008). For an individual event the notion of capital may be harder to quantify if equipment and facilities are used on an ongoing basis and a contribution only is needed to account for its use. In other events all equipment and facilities may be built and used for one event only and be written off in terms of future activity; the famous Bird's Nest Stadium used at the Beijing Olympics might be an example of this type of capital. The organizing committee for that event built a fit-for-purpose stadium whose investment was only counted for that one event, if it is used afterwards that would be a bonus, not an essential requirement.

That said, the return is counted as profit (all income less all costs and expenses) as a percentage of capital. Profit is subject also to some debate. Some writers do not include deductions for interest on any debt finance, whereas others insist all costs and expenses, except tax liabilities, in the period should be used (Wiscombe, 2009b).

Consistency is the key to analysis of ROCE and a full explanation should be given to stakeholders to explain how the calculation has been derived. The formula in its simplest format is:

$$\text{ROCE} = \frac{\text{Profit}}{\text{Capital employed}} \times 100$$

Of course the measurement of ROCE in this format can only be used as an economic calculation in profit or surplus making organizations – those in the private or charity sector. Government investment or third-stream funding would look at the economic impact of the event in a much broader context.

Economic impacts

The economic impact of events is clearly a rational argument for investment and funding decisions (Wiscombe, 2009a). The wider multiplier effect of events is well documented but not all economists agree that the initial investment is worth the huge costs associated with them. The idea behind economic impact of mega-events for instance is based on three key factors:

1. Direct effect of investment through the building of stadia, development of transport infrastructure, housing, increasing accommodation for competitors and spectators and so on.
2. Consumer spend during the event, not just on tickets but on food, accommodation, flights, or travel and transport.
3. Indirect effects, which are caused by the stimulus of the direct effects; this is described as the 'multiplier effect' (Tribe, 2005). This concept is extremely powerful and can be used to predict any number of effects from the initial injection of capital (see Chapters 10 and 11).

Box 4.6. FIFA World Cup 2018 or 2022 – economic impacts for funding and sponsorship.

Milton Keynes Council agreed to submit a compliant application to enable the successful completion of the bid for Milton Keynes 2018 World Cup host city status. The agreement was reached on the basis that the project committee had used extensive media coverage to promote the bid in the local region to encourage public support for the expenditure; an independent review of the economic impact of hosting the 2018 FIFA World Cup had estimated a minimum economic benefit of £130 million for each host city, as well as benefits beyond this in terms of the profit and branding of the city. Inward investment would follow, which was not yet quantifiable, international and national prestige of the city would be raised, and the plan would limit the council to not more than £65,000 in any one financial year. The total funding plan to be approved is £250,000. If it worked in accordance with the criteria, the economic payback would increase the investment by 520 times its original value.

Pricewaterhouse Coopers (PwC) is backing the 2018 World Cup bid, and was named as its first sponsor, by acting as business advisor to the campaign. They will provide a full economic impact assessment, guidance on tax, and guarantees and advice on budget to the bid team. The company regard the sponsorship as providing access to a number of networks who will be applicant host cities, allowing them to introduce themselves and their services.

Sources: Various

The arguments for and against the economic benefits of mega-events are important, as persuading governments to invest in the bidding process will not last forever. Events managers will be increasingly asked to develop *ex ante* and *ex post* evaluations. If one were to discredit the other, the current vogue for mega-event sponsorship, particularly sports events, may change (Szymanski, 2002). Financial management of mega-events is therefore even more crucial to their success – poor financial planning will impact on results but also affect future funding.

Box 4.7. The financial management of Mardi Gras.

Mardi Gras in New Orleans, Louisiana, USA, is one of the largest, most famous and most spectacular parties in the world, drawing hundreds of thousands of revellers. The event had its roots in the region's earliest settlers and has become quite unique, beginning its celebrations on 'Twelfth Night', the feast of the Epiphany. The success of the New Orleans Mardi Gras, sponsored by such corporate underwriters as Pepsi Cola© has led to a number of spin-off events using the same 'Mardi Gras' name both in the USA and overseas.

Sydney, Australia, holds one such event, staging a 'Mardi Gras' annually for around 24 years before the event reached financial collapse in 2002. In seeking sponsorship from the Council in 2005, which amounts to free use of the city's parks and streets, parks clearing for the events, waiver of hire fees for the use of banner poles, a listing as a 'Hero Event' on the city website, and reimbursements of costs for barricades for the parade, New Mardi Gras had to ensure prudent financial management and evidence of risk management processes, as well as ensuring the events were clean and green, committed to environmental sustainability. The event has a turnover of AU$3m (£1.18m) and is now managed by a more commercially aware team that needs government funding as well as commercial sponsorship to ensure its survival.

Sources: Various

> **Questions**
> - What suggestions could you propose for the Sydney Mardi Gras organizational team to help ensure future financial success?
> - What are the key financial elements that they must consider?

The Olympics

No discussion about the economic impact of mega-events would be complete without at least a few words on the Olympic Games. Governments have supported bidding processes for the Summer Olympics with a list of objectives that range from increases in tourism numbers to the regeneration of urban areas. The Olympics is not only an exemplar of the financial complexity that underpins the planning and management of events but now involves the spending of billions of dollars with funding sources needed for everything from the construction of facilities and stadia to the operation of the events themselves. The event is awarded to a city that, through an organizing committee, needs to raise sufficient funds to ensure a quality event.

A wide range of funding arrangements have been used to finance the Olympics. In 1980 Moscow provided a Games entirely supported by public funding, whereas the 1984 Los Angles Games were 98% supported by private funding (Preuss, 2004). Over time the financial sources have become global, with an impact from consumers all over the world; wherever the Games are staged, the USA plays a key role as 70% of the top sponsors and 55% of TV broadcasting rights are funded by that country (Preuss, 2002).

By the time London bid for the 2012 Games there was an understanding among governments that the Olympic Games had changed its financial constructs. Since the 1980s the organizing committee was confident that the event would provide a surplus, and that part of the legacy would be increased sports facilities and adequate infrastructure capable of housing the athletes, tourists and media representatives (Preuss, 2002).

The financial premise of a 'surplus' no longer holds true, and maintaining budgetary control is essential to maintaining viability. Added to this is the experience of Athens, which, after building completely new fit-for-purpose stadia, has failed to capitalize on the infrastructural legacy. There are other benefits, however; the Sydney Olympics were heralded as a great success. This event in 2000 overcame some of the very loud objections to the use of the public purse to sponsor the Games. It managed to sustain enthusiasm through the perceived rewards arising from place-specific attributes (perceived evaluation of the host nation's role, city and people in the world economy), countered outdated Australian stereotypes, stimulated future overseas tourism and investment, as well as providing new urban infrastructure (Waitt, 2003).

Organizers of future Olympics need to heed the lessons learned by other mega-events and Games both by considered budgetary constraint but also in ensuring the infrastructure legacy is assured. Benefits can be uncertain, but with investments of public money it would be expected that a post-Games income from land and accrued property, such as the athletes' village, would provide additional proceeds (House of Commons Committee of Public Accounts, 2008).

Sponsorship evaluation

All sponsorship should be evaluated, if not by the events manager then certainly by the income provider. Continuous evaluation of all monies used in sponsorship is even more important in uncertain economic times, and has led sponsors to withdraw from future events projects, even though they may contribute substantially to the CSR initiatives of the organization. While a continuous and iterative process will occur, the post-event evaluation will be measured against the original SMART objectives set.

There are three key areas of sponsorship evaluation. The first is in direct sales, the second in brand image and the third, more tenuous again, will be in overall financial gain or company worth. Much of the evaluation needs to be measured and for large, hallmark and mega-events, companies will spend considerable time assessing the impact by survey and questionnaire, usually from independent consultants, as well as assessing the impact on sales and company value.

Sales effectiveness is one aspect of sponsorship evaluation; nevertheless, it may not be easy to assess as the link between purchases and the sponsor is so nebulous. British Telecom (BT) is a major sponsor of the 2012 Olympics but the notion that customers are flocking to purchase telephone or Internet services from them because of this sponsorship cannot instantly be measured. More easily measured would be the sales generated by a sponsor who has provided a function or service at an event and received direct sales as a result.

One way of measuring the results of an event would be the media exposure it receives. Events managers should measure the amount of 'air time' that is received through public relations exercises. In addition, they should measure the column inches in newspapers, magazines or other journals. Managers are also making inroads into measuring the amount of Internet exposure the event receives, whether via YouTube, Facebook or other networking sites. Advertising on TV and via Internet or radio is expensive. Through mega-events, much smaller amounts of money will provide airtime for sponsors, which can be consistently accessed. However, while airtime or column inches can be measured, the actual effect of the accrued media coverage must then be ascertained. This is termed 'communications effects' and again this will be covered further in Chapter 7. Suffice to say that the sponsor will measure brand awareness and recognition, brand attitude or image, brand recall and brand performance as a result of their investment.

Large corporations that use sponsorship of events as a large part of their marketing campaigns believe that greater dividends for shareholders, or increase in worth of shares on the stock market, can be directly attributed to sponsorship campaigns. There is no doubt that if a corporation makes significant expensive sponsorship investments, usually over periods of time, the organization would expect the bottom line to increase; this would allow other knock-on measurements of company worth, share value or market share to be attributable to the marketing investment.

However large or small the sponsors' investment, it is always worth the events organizers understanding the volume exposure they can offer, the image they can present and finally the type of consumers who will be targeted by the sponsors' presence.

Activity

Consider Box 4.2 – Walsall Illuminations – and write a report providing Walsall Metropolitan Borough Council with an operational plan to attract income and investment to their Illuminations event. Describe the steps they might take to increase funding, attract sponsorship and also develop other income streams.

FINANCIAL MANAGEMENT

Financial management requires an attention to detail that may not be easy to achieve among an events organization team. A few extra pounds or dollars to hire the marquee, a fall in sponsorship income and a few tickets remaining unsold will not seem important to some members of the planning board. Financial management requires careful planning and to those interested in events management as a career, this can appear off-putting, as it insists that teams work with clarity and precision; this does not always work well with those who are more creative in their approach and simply think that income will follow their fantastic ideas. Those taking the financial management role must be authoritative and insist on compliance with the set financial parameters of the project. These are recorded in a set of accounts, sometimes via a spreadsheet, other times by using dedicated software. The understanding of the set of accounts, or financial records, is important and those in charge of financial management should take time to explain how the account is set up, as well as the parameters. Setting those parameters can be a major challenge and are driven by the budget account.

Budget

Any event manager must realize that in staging an event there will be an anticipated level of funding in order to put on the event, and a set of costs and expenses to be paid. It is important to first forecast what all the expected expenses will be and also build in a contingency fund for things that may not be expected. A realistic income should be anticipated and can include funding, sponsorship, ticket sales, merchandising and advertising income, and so on. None of this is easy to ascertain and may take some level of experience.

It is important to keep a check on this income and expense; this is termed a budget. A budget can be developed in a simple spreadsheet format, see Fig. 4.2, or could use sophisticated software, such as 'eventpro'©. Budgets are not, however, a one-off statement of account; they will develop and improve in sophistication as the planning of the event moves through its various stages. The budget may well have been set up to monitor milestones over the planning period. Therefore an expense called 'advertising' at the start of the project might later be divided into a number of different headings, for instance newspapers, local radio and magazines. This helps the marketing manager to see where performance is on track or where additional efforts need to be made.

Question

Look at the budget in Fig. 4.2. Note the layout of figures. Can you find out, using a calculator or spreadsheet, how the figures actually make sense?
- Income – Direct Costs = Gross profit
- Gross profit – Expenses = Net profit or net surplus
- Where would you seek to make savings in costs and expenses in order to improve the surplus?

Some aspects of the expenses budget may have to be cut if income is not being generated as quickly as had been thought. This is monitored through the cash flow account.

	£	£	£
Income			
Bars	76125		
Venue Hire	14428		
Project Funding	51600		
Car Park Charges	48048		
Events Tickets	25393		
Cloakroom	933		
Café	520		
Donations and Interest	100		
Interest on the Savings			
Account	31		
Total Income		217178	
Direct Costs			
Bar Stock	28371		
Bar Staff	6645		
Security	20576		
Duty Management	14438		
Sub Contractors	9580		
Advertising and Promotion	7316		
Equipment	1261		
Equipment Hire	2760		
Licences	1677		
Cloakroom	1428		
Cleaning	5753		
Café	807		
		100612	
Gross Profit			£116,566
Expenditure			
Salaries and Wages	34602		
Duty Management	3396		
Tutors	5390		
Fees	10775		
Staff Training	1000		
Project Expenses	7258		
Volunteer Expenses	574		
Utilities	7325		
Repairs and Renewals	5104		
Cleaning and Waste	3904		
Security	611		
Computer Software	2438		
Equipment	793		
Depreciation	4150		
Insurance	9801		
Advertising and Promotion	921		
Telephone and Internet	2126		
Travel	960		
PPS Licence	781		
Subsistence	311		
Bank Charges	286		
Bad Debts	1881		
Other	856		
		105243	
Net Surplus or Loss			£11,323

Fig. 4.2. A budget for a small voluntary run events venue that has an educational remit.

Box 4.8. London 2012 budget nightmares.

The House of Commons Committee of Public Accounts Fourteenth Report was commissioned to investigate the budget for the London 2012 Olympic and Paralympic Games. Its summary highlights the problems and pitfalls for mega- and hallmark events in setting and complying with budgets.

'At the time of London's bid to host the Olympic and Paralympic Games in 2012 the cost of the Games was estimated to be just over £4 billion. The costs were to be met by public sector funding of £3.4 billion, with a further £738 million from the private sector.

'After London was awarded the Games, the Department for Culture, Media and Sport and the Olympic Delivery Authority reviewed the cost estimates and in March 2007 announced a budget of £9.325 billion. The Department has stated that public sector funding will not exceed this figure. The March 2007 budget included contingency provision of £2.747 billion. This sum was not included at the time of the bid despite Treasury guidance that budgets for major projects should allow for the tendency to underestimate costs.

'Since March 2007, £500 million of the programme contingency has been allocated to the Olympic Delivery Authority to cope with early financial pressures. Clarification over the delivery structures for the Games means that the Olympic Delivery Authority incurs tax liabilities in the normal way, and this has added a further £836 million to the earlier cost estimates. The March 2007 budget also included a preliminary estimate of £600 million for policing and wider security, over and above the cost of site security during construction. No estimate for the cost of policing and wider security was included at the time of the bid. In addition, the Olympic Delivery Authority's programme delivery budget has risen to £570 million, compared with an original estimate of just £16 million.

'While the cost estimates have increased by £5.3 billion, the public funding required to meet these costs has increased by £5.9 billion due to significantly lower expectations for private sector funding. Some £4.9 billion of this increase is to be met by the Exchequer and £675 million by the National Lottery, bringing the total Lottery contribution to £2.175 billion. The final cost to the public sector will depend on proceeds arising from the disposal of assets after the Games, in particular, the sale of land on the Olympic Park, as well as the share of profits expected once the Village is converted into housing and sold. The estimate of £738 million private sector funding towards the cost of venues and infrastructure at the time of the bid was revised to £165 million (less than 2% of the total funding) in the March budget.

'In addition, while the Olympic Village had been expected to be fully funded by the private sector, the March budget included a £175 million public sector contribution to the Village. Private sector construction firms have a vital role in delivering the Olympic programme, but the Olympic Delivery Authority has had difficulty in achieving competition between bidders for contracts to deliver the main venues, with only one bidder emerging for the Main Stadium.

'The prospect of longer term benefits from hosting the Games was central to London's bid. The Government has set out five high level legacy promises but more detailed plans have not yet been finalized. It intended to publish a "Legacy Action Plan" early in 2008, and the Olympic Delivery Authority will be working with the London Development Agency during 2008 to set out arrangements for use of the Olympic Park after the Games.'

Source: House of Commons Committee of Public Accounts (2008)

Questions

- Imagine you are a financial director of the London 2012 organizing committee. How would you advise them to proceed in their financial management following the House of Commons review in March 2008?
- You may find it interesting to note that the organizing committee advertised the financial director post a number of times. Could you provide some ideas as to why this might have been?

Cash flow monitoring

Once income and expenses have been thought through, it is important for the entire event project that the timing of the income and expenses be carefully controlled. If expenses are due for payment before income has been generated, then the event may become 'bankrupt' before it can get off the ground. Sometimes income generation is so poor that decisions on whether the event should go ahead may have to be taken that limit the organizer to less loss. Devil's Dyke, a music event in East Sussex, was cancelled in the summer of 2009 because of poor ticket sales. The organizers decided that it was better to cancel than to lose even more money in the development of the event. This is why the cash flow account is so important (Fig. 4.3).

It is worth noting that while depreciation and bad debts are part of the budget account, they do not appear in the cash flow statement, as they are not part of the money flow in and out of the organization. If at the end of a month the cash is not in the business to pay the next month's bills, action will need to be taken to increase income, or to defer payment. This can sometimes be negotiated with suppliers but needs careful handling.

It is important to note that some events, especially hallmark or mega-events, need to monitor cash flow for years, not just months, in advance of the event date.

Management or project accounts

A management account will run for the length of the project. It uses the budget as its basis and as each line of income, cost and expense is spent, this is logged and compared with the budget figures. Changes and discrepancies are noted, with those in charge of particular departments or costs centres explaining the differences (Fig. 4.4). If costs and expenses for an event are growing out of control it is at a management or project meeting that this will be noted and actions taken to either reduce the cost or increase income to accommodate the changes. Where public money is part of the funding this monitoring will be vital in providing detailed understanding of where the money has been spent. Some public funding can only be used for certain costs and expenses. This may mean that sub-accounts are kept for the funding body concerned showing exactly where and how their money has been allocated.

Income and expenditure accont (sometimes termed a 'profit and loss' account)

The income and expenditure account for a private company will record the results in terms of profit or loss. For third-stream or public companies the results should at least 'break even'. An event may be part of a larger organization but it is usual for each individual event to have its own income and expenditure account, which follows the format similar to a budget, and will

	Jan	Feb	March	April	Etc
	£	£	£	£	£
Receipts					
Bars					
Venue Hire					
Project Funding					
Car Park Charges					
Events Tickets					
Cloakroom					
Café					
Donations and Interest					
Interest on the Savings Account					
Total Receipts					
Less Payments					
Bar Stock					
Bar Staff					
Security					
Duty Management					
Sub Contractors					
Advertising					
Promotions					
Equipment					
Equipment Hire					
Licences					
Cloakroom					
Cleaning					
Café					
Salaries and Wages					
Tutors					
Fees					
Staff Training					
Project Expenses					
Volunteer Expenses					
Utilities					
Repairs					
Renewals					
Cleaning					
Waste					
Security					
Computer Software					
Equipment					
Insurance					
Telephone					
Internet					
Travel					
PPS Licence					
Subsistence					
Bank Charges					
Other					
Business Rates					
Wages/National Insurance					
Professional Fees					
VAT					
Drawings					
Total Payments					
Net Cash Flow	Receipts - Payments				
Opening Balance	From December Closing Balance				
Closing Balance	Opening Balance + Net cash Flow				

Fig. 4.3. Cash flow account for a small, voluntary run events venue that has an educational remit.

Costs and Provisions	March 2007 Budget (£ Million)		Estimates at November 2004 Bid (£ million)		Difference (£ million)
Olympic Delivery Authority Budget					
Core Olympic Costs	3081		1966		1115
Infrastructure and regeneration	1673		1684		−11
Contingency	500		0		500
Sub-total		5254		3650	1604
Other (non ODA) Olympic		388		386	2
Other Provisions					
Policing and wider security	600		0		600
Tax	836		0		836
Programme Contingency	2247		0		2247
Sub-total		3683		0	3683
Change to Budget schedule on costs and provisions		9325		4036	5289

Fig. 4.4. Project account for the London 2012 committee showing expenses only.

Questions

- Where has the London 2012 committee strayed from its original budget? What might be the consequences of this overspend?
- Do you think that the original budget was not thought through enough? Where might obvious changes have been included?

---

often be viewed alongside the budgeted figures, for ongoing or final comparisons to be made. Income and expenditure accounts follow accepted accounting protocols or generally accepted accounting principles (GAAP).

Balance sheet account

The final account will provide the overall organization, or its individual projects, with a balance based on the total funding provided. The capital invested will always equal the assets (both fixed and capital, which together make up the net assets). The balance sheet captures the situation of the 'worth' of the event or organization on a fixed date so if cash is spent on equipment the day after a balance sheet is developed then the account no longer remains accurate (Fig. 4.5).

	£	£	£
Assets			
Fixed Assets			
Premises			
Equipment			
Current Assets			
Cash in Hand			
Cash at Bank			
Stock			
Debtors			
Less current liabilities			
Creditors			
Net Assets			Balance
Financed By:			
Long Term Liabilities			
Capital Invested by Owner			
Profit Account			
Total Capital Employed			Balance

Fig. 4.5. A draft balance sheet layout for a sole trader.

Annual reports

Finally, for any events organization or department, it is good practice to generate an annual report. This may list one event or a multiplicity of events that make up the portfolio. The detail within the report will be limited to reporting the success or losses of the event to the appropriate audience. An annual report will contain more information than the financial statements required from businesses for tax reporting purposes; as a minimum businesses need to provide an annual 'profit and loss account' and a 'balance sheet' to the appropriate government department so that taxes can be determined (in the UK returns are made to HM Customs and Revenue by sole traders and limited companies).

In their annual reports PLCs will detail the financial information of the organization, including its aspirations for the future, to its shareholders with the purpose of explaining the profits the organization has made, and how it proposes to allocate them. If the PLC needs to retain some of the profits to reinvest then this will lower the cash payout, called the dividend, payable to shareholders. For tax purposes a PLC registered in the UK makes its financial returns to Companies House.

Charities, while providing financial information, might focus much more heavily on the purpose or mission of the organization and how it has fulfilled its obligations. If an organization registered as a charity for tax purposes, the Charities Commission will want to receive enough information to know that all costs and expenses are accurate and able to be counted against income; for instance trustees (those who sit on the board of charities) can claim for hotel accommodation and sustenance for any meetings, but not for alcohol. Charitable organizations can claim tax-free fees for a meeting room but not for restaurant meals. The rules for registered charities are complex and professional advice should be sought both before registering with the Charities Commission and before the submission of final accounts, otherwise trustees can be held liable to prosecution.

Public-funded organizations often report on wider issues than finance. The economic generation the event has provided or social capacity will often be of more importance than the final accounts per se. The environmental changes provided by the event or the media presence may also provide evidence of success, over and above financial records.

Sole traders tend not to provide formal annual reports but simply submit their 'income and expenditure account' and 'balance sheet' to the taxation authorities. However, this information does help to provide information for future funding or sponsorship bids and therefore a summary of activity for the year, and the way the organization has provided its services, could help entrepreneurial events organizations take stock and help to move forward; collation of such data can help to provide a reflective and holistic review.

SUMMARY

Organizers face a major challenge in providing enough income to ensure a sustainable future for many, even hallmark, events. Recent economic warnings to many regular event organizers, including those whose cases have been discussed in this chapter, mean facing severe financial challenges in the future.

Mega-events are more and more expensive to stage and need increasing amounts of funding and sponsorship, from all sources of potential income, to sustain their quality thus the agreement of major sponsorship, such as that provided by Milton Keynes Council to support the World Cup 2018 or 2022 bid by committing £250,000 in support to become a host city in June 2009 was a major boost to the organizers. Core funding of major events, such as the Edinburgh International Festival, is under threat with organizers being warned to expect budget cuts of up to 4% from the City Council for 2010 and the Scottish Government's 3-year £6 million backing coming to an end in 2011, with no guarantee of renewal.

Providing sponsors and funders with clear returns on investment is key to the income challenge, which for many events cannot depend on ticket sales alone. Those returns can be economic but will also include providing strong messages on the events' image that can link with a products' branding message and clear opportunities that access target markets. Measurement of results is vital and events managers should move much more positively to measure these results for smaller sponsors, showing how they have been enhanced by the investment.

Some government funding, or removal of funding, is being used to change events and their structure to provide images that sit better with the philosophy of the city, rather than the organizers, and lack of strong financial management provides clear opportunities for this to happen; the Houston city goal to change their Mardi Gras from a 'bacchanalian revelry' into family entertainment led the Park Board to use budget deficits as an excuse to slash US$800,000 expenditure from a US$1 million budget, thus doing away with live bands, previously a cornerstone of the event (Rice, 2007).

In summary, the most creative of events managers cannot develop their ideas without income; income in all its forms is vital to events success. The financial management to ensure that income covers all costs and expenses is important and the monitoring of this, and returns on the investment made, should follow accepted principles.

FURTHER RESEARCH

An excellent review of sponsorship return on investment is given by:
Masterson, G. (2007) *Sponsorship for a Return on Investment*. Butterworth-Heineman, Oxford.

Other articles providing a good background to sponsorship are:
Lamont, M. and Dowell, R. (2008) A process model of small and medium size enterprise sponsorship of regional sport tourism events. *Journal of Vacation Marketing* 14, 253–256.
Crompton, J.L. (1993) Understanding a business organization's approach to entering a sponsorship partnership. *Festival Management and Events Tourism* 1, 98–109.
O'Hagan, J. and Harvey, D. (2000) Why do companies sponsor arts events? Some evidence and a proposed classification. *Journal of Cultural Economics* 24, 205–224.
Mishra, D.P., Bobinski, G.S. and Bhabra, H.S. (1997) Assessing the economic worth of corporate event sponsorship: a stock market perspective. *Journal of Market Focused Management* 2, 149–169.

For more information on the impact of the Olympics read anything by Holger Preuss, who has written a plethora of articles, books and conference papers on the topic, and:
Adranovich, G., Burbank, M. and Heying, C.H. (2001) Olympic cities: lessons learned from mega-event politics. *Journal of Urban Affairs* 23, 113–131.
Kasimati, E. (2003) Economic aspects and the summer Olympics: a review of related research. *International Journal of Tourism Research* 5, 433–444.
Veraros, N., Kasimati, E. and Dawson, P. (2004) The 2004 Olympic Games announcement and its effect on the Athens and Milan Stock Exchanges. *Applied Economics Letters* 11, 749–753.

REVIEW QUESTIONS

1. Choose an event and write a sponsorship audit clearly explaining the benefits of funding the event.
2. Pick one major brand and clearly link the marketing objectives to the sponsorship audit.
3. Explain how you would evaluate the performance of the sponsorship provided by the brand to the event you have suggested.

REFERENCES

Carmel Bach Festival (2010) Carmel Bach Festival. www.bachfestival.org (accessed 10 January 2010).
Edinburgh International Festival (2009) Annual Report. Edinburgh International Festival, Edinburgh.
Gratton, C. and Solberg, H.A. (2007) *The Economics of Sports Broadcasting*. Routledge, Abingdon, UK.
House of Commons Committee of Public Accounts (2008) The budget for the London 2012 Olympic and Paraplympic Games. *HC 85* (22 April 2008). Her Majesty's Stationery Office, London.
Masterson, G. (2007) *Sponsorship for a Return on Investment*. Butterworth-Heineman, Oxford.
Preuss, H. (2001) Olympic ticket pricing. *European Journal for Sport Management* 8 (Special Issue 2001), 37–62.
Preuss, H. (2002) Economic dimension of the Olympic Games. Centre d'Estudis Olimpics (UAB) International Chair in Olympism (IOC-UAB).
Preuss, H. (2004) *The Economics of Staging the Olympics*. Edward Elgar, Northampton, Massachusetts.
Rice, H. (2007) Isle tosses Mardi Gras Bands: city says axing live acts, forced by deficits, will support effort to attract families. *Houston Chronicle*, 22 September 2007.

SBI (2009) Brands and corporates. www.sbi.co.uk (accessed 3 November 2009).

Szymanski, S. (2002) The economic impact of the World Cup. *World Economics* 3, 169–177.

Tribe, J. (2005) *The Economics of Recreation, Leisure and Tourism*, 3rd edn. Elsevier, Oxford.

Waitt, G. (2003) Social impacts of the Sydney Olympics. *Annals of Tourism Research* 30, 194–215.

Wilson, R. and Joyce, J. (2008) *Finance for Sport and Leisure Managers*. Routledge, Abingdon, UK.

Wiscombe, C.A. (2009a) Coastal communities and events: the case of Lyme Regis. Paper presented at *Coastal and Resort Destination Management: Cultures and Histories of Tourism*, 19–20 October 2009, University of Girona, Spain.

Wiscombe, C.A. (2009b) Financial awareness for travel operations management. In: Robinson, P. (ed.) *Operations Management in the Travel Industry*. CAB International, Wallingford, UK.

chapter 5

Delivering Live Events

Ade Oriade, Peter Robinson and Steve Gelder

OBJECTIVES OF THE CHAPTER

Efficient management of event operations is pivotal to the success of an event irrespective of its scale and category. However, the complexity of the operations will vary from one event to another depending on the type of event and, perhaps most importantly, the size of the event. This chapter explains that successful events are a consequence of effectively managing resources to support the needs of event attendees. Based on this, the chapter explains event planning and management from operational perspectives utilizing operations management principles, theory and models.

The objectives of this chapter are to:

- explain the key stages of designing and delivering an event;
- contextualize events management within the broader operations management context;
- provide a guide to successful events management; and
- highlight the myriad processes and requirements of delivering live events.

To achieve these objectives, this chapter is divided into four distinct sections to identify the process for designing, setting-up, delivering and closing down an event. Emphasis is placed on day-to-day operational elements and activities including venue choices, site and facility design, quality and capacity management, event production and risk and safety management. The four sections are:

- Part A – The Event Idea
- Part B – Pre-event Planning
- Part C – The Big Day!
- Part D – The Big Tidy-up

INTRODUCTION: OPERATIONS MANAGEMENT

According to Naylor (2002, p. 5), 'Operations management is concerned with creating, operating and controlling a transformation system that takes inputs from a variety of resources and produces outputs of goods and services needed by customers'. Singh (2008) refers to operations management as the productive heart of an organization, the purpose of which is to deliver timely, reliable and accurate service to the end-users. While different authors have defined operations management differently, central to most definitions is the notion that operations management is the management of those processes and systems that transform resources acquired by the organization from its macro-environment, into services and products that meet the needs of customers. This is illustrated in Fig. 5.1.

Operations management has its theoretical roots in manufacturing as 'production management' but is now also applied to the service sector. As the service industry expands, the applicability of operations management to the sector increasingly become evident. There are two main perspectives that scholars have identified in the field of management: strategic and operational perspectives. The main focus of this chapter is the operational perspective; this is not underplaying the importance of strategic management. Strategic management is discussed in Chapter 10; however, references will be made to strategic perspectives in this chapter given their interdependent nature.

Operations management is sometimes viewed as a department within an event organization. This stand-alone approach isolates operations as a distinct functional department in parallel with other key areas such as marketing, human resources and finance. An alternative approach is to conceptualize operations management as a function that permeates every department of an organization. Operations, therefore, are not the responsibility of a single department within an event organization. A third, more holistic conceptualization views operations as a process that not only permeates across departments, but also incorporates relevant external organizations. Adopting operational perspectives and incorporating the three views is very useful in event planning and management. This multi-dimensional approach facilitates understanding of individual activities and tasks to be performed in the 'production' system, the relationship that exists between departments, and the operations and role of the external suppliers.

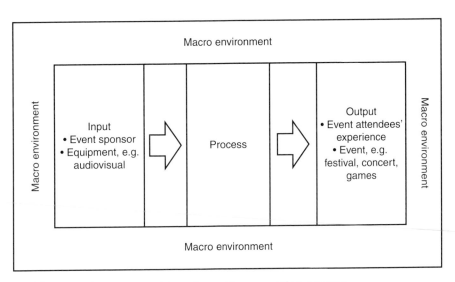

Fig. 5.1. The event input–output transformation operation process.

PART A – THE EVENTS IDEA

The planning of any event should always start with the overall vision or aim: what is the desired outcome of the event? What is the event intending to achieve? Is it to educate, to entertain, to sell a product, to make money, to celebrate an historic event? Masterman (2004) highlights the importance of 'event benefits', be they economic, political, social, cultural or environmental (see Chapters 1, 2 and 12).

The needs assessment model (Goldblatt, 1997) asks the questions Why, Who, When, Where and What, in relation to the proposed event (see Chapter 2). Bowdin *et al.* (2001, p. 70) asks:

- Who is the customer?
- Which specific needs are being satisfied?
- What are the organizers attempting to accomplish?

This is a good starting point and helps to clarify the rationale for staging the event. Shone and Parry (2001) see this initial action as the 'brainstorming phase', where ideas for an event are discussed among the organizing team.

The importance of this stage of event planning cannot be understated, as the cost of staging events and the increasing levels of accountability across the whole spectrum of events requires clarification, and more importantly, a justification for the resources utilized. This is imperative, whether it is for reasons of strategic importance to the organization, for financial gain or to satisfy environmental need.

The final idea for the event is likely to be encapsulated in a mission or vision statement. This may be 'an event to raise awareness of …' or 'an event to launch a new product', for example.

PUBLIC, PRIVATE AND THIRD SECTOR EVENTS

The rationale for an event is also affected by the scope of the event organizers, as events will, inevitably, fall into three categories:

Public sector: where the reason for the event is most likely to be determined by its legacy, its benefits for the local community, or its role in tourism development or a celebration. In this instance, the event is usually funded through taxes (which means that organizers have to justify the need for the event) or it is publicly funded, but recovers the costs of the event through income generation.

Private sector: This covers a multitude of activities that are designed to generate income, and may be delivered by tourist attractions, commercial companies and event organizers such as wedding planners. In addition to generating profit directly, events in this category also include product launches and trade fairs where the initial investment is repaid through increased projected long-term sales. There are also a number of fundraising events developed in the private sector as part of a corporate social responsibility agenda (see Chapter 9).

Third/voluntary sector: This includes events run by charities, communities and individuals as fundraising, commemorative or celebratory events, and may or may not be designed to cover costs. Very often events are funded by sponsorship and donations.

Examples of these events are presented in the following pages.

Box 5.1. Public sector event – The Black Country Olympics.

The Black Country Olympics began in the early 1970s as an event organized between the four boroughs that make up the Black Country: Walsall, Dudley, Wolverhampton and Sandwell. As well as sporting events such as swimming, trampolining, judo, netball and golf, the games also included a range of what could be regarded as 'recreational activities', traditional pub games: bar billiards, dominoes, crib, etc.

In 1994, a proposal document was presented to the Black Country Executive Committee effectively rebranding the games as the 'Youth Games of the Black Country'. This refocus towards youth sport was designed to encourage participation in sport, assist in sport development strategies and promote community identity. Thus the annual event would contribute towards local government policy for sport, healthy lifestyles and community cohesion.

Over the years the structure and format of the event have evolved; the venue for the games has alternated between the four boroughs but in recent years has settled in one borough. The event has moved from a 2-day weekend format to completion over 1 day.

Other regional and national local authorities have adopted the ideals of the original games, and to celebrate the millennium, a national event was staged in Southampton. Each borough has its own strategy for selecting participants that often accords with local policy on sport provision. A common method has been to utilize the school sport leagues to select entrants. In keeping with original Black Country Olympic ideals around equity, the modern games have categories of sport for people with disabilities.

Key stakeholders for the games have included interested parties from across the three leisure sectors:

- Black Country Local Authorities
- Black Country Sports Partnership
- Schools/colleges
- Sports clubs
- Coaches
- Volunteers
- Sport governing bodies

The annual event is funded through contributions from the four Black Country boroughs, the county sports partnerships (BCASP) and over the years has been supported by private businesses such as Beachwood Audi and Sonex printers. The games have utilized local sporting celebrities over the years with a number of high-profile athletes attending to provide PR and add status to each event.

Box 5.2. Private sector event – ADAC International Truck Grand Prix.

This is a major event in the truck racing calendar, held each year at the Nürburgring Circuit in Germany. The event is presented here as a case study that explains the planning behind most motorsport events. Although truck racing, and indeed Formula One (F1), World Touring Cars and other international motorsport series have a popular following, the reality is that alone these events would be unfeasible. They have huge set-up costs and rely upon the event providing excellent entertainment, ideally to encourage people to visit for the

(Continued)

Box 5.2. Continued.

whole race weekend. The ADAC event lasts for 3 days and attracts 150,000 people. Truck races are relatively short; indeed even an F1 Race is only 2 hours, so to ensure a profitable event numerous other activities are developed alongside.

At the ADAC GP, the circuit is a shortened version of the one used for F1, and the extra space is used to host an evening rock concert. This encourages spectators to stay for the full event, and it becomes like a festival. There will be supporting races, other attractions and parades and opportunities to see areas such as the Paddock. At the ADAC event, these include the Sports Car Challenge, historic vehicles, and Go & Stop races. All these events will have their own race series and will work together with the ADAC organizers to develop a major event that will attract a broad audience, whose reasons for going may not relate in any way to the core purpose of the event.

Major events such as these are usually organized within the private sector and have numerous complex relationships to manage. These include the Circuit owners and managers, the FIA (Fédération Internationale d'Automobile as the world sport governing body), the Race Series promoters, concert organizers, trade and exhibition displays, and catering providers. There will also be commercial rights holders involved and they, together with each team taking part, will need to ensure profitability or promotional coverage as an outcome of a race weekend, the only exception being the governing bodies.

FEASIBILITY PLANNING

Once the ideas have been discussed and an agreement has been reached on the broad nature of the event, it should then be subjected to a detailed feasibility study. Feasibility is viewed by Bowdin *et al.* (2006) and Tassiopoulos and Damster (2004) as turning the vision into measurable aims and objectives. This should incorporate a stringent evaluation of the resources required to conduct the event and an understanding of the limitations for the event. The limitations alone can be very challenging: consider the logistics involved in organizing the funeral of Michael Jackson within a very short timescale. Compare this to the 6-year lead-in to the London Olympics.

The feasibility study can be regarded as crucial for a number of reasons:

- to minimize the risk of failure (business failure or health and safety risk management failure);
- to assess the financial requirements (potential income – expected expenditure);
- to identify appropriate management structures;
- to identify appropriate marketing strategies; and
- to identify other 'primary' resources needed – manpower, equipment, expertise.

Areas covered in feasibility studies vary according to the aims and focus of the event. For example, an event that is purely commercially driven will need to undertake a thorough financial analysis to ensure the primary objective is achieved. Events in the public sector need to measure their likely impact and benefit compared with the investment of public funds, while those in the third sector often start small and grow over a period of time.

Once the principle for holding the event is agreed, it then requires a more developed focus to ensure that it achieves the original aspirations (mission or vision) for holding it. This requires aims and objectives to act as a framework for delivery.

DEVELOPING AN 'OPERATIONAL' STRATEGY

To achieve the mission, or vision, of an event, a set of objectives is essential. These should be based upon the accepted SMART principle that the objectives are:

- **S**pecific: clear and concise targets, which are
- **M**easurable through targets, that are
- **A**chievable and
- **R**ealistic to ensure that targets can be met, and these need to be
- **T**ime-limited so that there are systems to monitor the progress towards completion.

For each aim there should be a number of objectives (between three and five) that together achieve the aim. An objective therefore should be seen as a specific/measurable target that is designed to be a crucial tool in assessing the intended outcomes of the event. The success or failure of any event is naturally aligned to the initial objectives set.

The concept of aims, objectives and actions can be applied where each event objective can be broken down into a series of contributory actions. These can then be achieved by gathering information, understanding internal and external influences and identifying what will need to be done to achieve the organizational objectives.

Much of this information can be collated through environmental scanning tools, such as SWOT and PEST, which will be discussed in Chapters 7 and 10.

Activity

For an event that is designed to launch a new product (regional level), formulate a set of aims and objectives.

Once the strategy has been developed, a method to achieve the actions is required. This is, in effect, project management tailored to the delivery of events.

PROJECT MANAGEMENT

Project management has been used by business organizations for decades to achieve their organizational objectives. There are ways in which the 'tools' of project management and operations strategy can be applied to the delivery of events. There are three approaches that are discussed here, and the final choice will be determined by the scale and scope of the event:

- Gantt charts;
- critical path analysis; and
- work responsibility matrix.

Gantt charts

Developed in 1917 by Charles Gantt, this chart, in its simplest form, is a bar chart that shows the sequence of tasks that are required to complete a task or an event (Fig. 5.2). The fundamental requirements are to 'break down' the whole event into smaller units, using the technique of

Fig. 5.2. Simple Gantt chart for an event.

work breakdown schedules (Tassiopoulos and Damster, 2004). The 'unpacking of the whole event' into singular work elements that are the responsibility of the event team or outside agencies, allows for incremental planning and facilitates clear lines of accountability (Burke, 2006).

In order to identify tasks and present them in a chart that visually displays the event from the initial planning stages through to closedown and evaluation tasks requires event planners to ask questions:

- What is needed?
- What is needed now?
- What do you need before that?
- What tasks can run concurrently?
- What are the milestones?
- What is the priority?

Critical path method

Within the scheduling of activities undertaken to deliver an event, the concept of the critical path method (CPM) must be applied. The idea was originally developed to consider the 'time–cost trade-off' (Burke, 2006); this suggests that if certain 'critical' tasks are not completed on time, it will have a detrimental impact upon other actions. The 'linking' of all of the event tasks/actions and the estimated duration should produce a timeline that identifies how long the event preparation should take (Tum *et al.*, 2006).

Some of the reasons why these estimates can be little more than a best guess include the reliance on legal sanctioning such as licences, which dictate legal compliance based on issues such as stadium safety, alcohol sales or other licensing activities that are time constrained by their application processes and the initial delays that occur when trying to confirm artists and equipment.

In order to assess the critical path, there must be a clear understanding of the types of actions that can be undertaken in 'series' and the actions that can be undertaken in 'parallel' (Burke, 2006). An example would be the need to confirm a venue or location for an event in order to:

1. Establish the capacity of the event and thus the maximum number of potential attendees (imperative for income projections).

2. Identify the specialist equipment needed.

3. Include the venue details on the initial promotional launch.

Work responsibility matrix

A work responsibility matrix lays out the major activities in the project and identifies the responsibilities of each stakeholder/group member involved in the event. It is an important project communication tool because all stakeholders can see clearly who to contact for each activity that may impact upon their area of work.

The work responsibility matrix will vary between events, not only as a function of the scale and scope of the event but will also be dependent on the specific focus of the event and the resultant priority areas. For example, there are some people who will be more 'critical' to the successful outcome of any event, such as a Health and Safety Officer, the local police, landowners or artists' agents. People who are responsible for these primary areas should report directly to the event manager.

PART B – PRE-EVENT PLANNING

The organizing committee

All events need to be planned by a 'committee', with tasks assigned to different team members. If an event is being organized by an existing organization then it may be the responsibility of the heads of department to form an organizing committee. When the event is being organized by a voluntary group, it is often more difficult to assign tasks and decide who is 'in charge'. In some cases, the 'committee' may comprise different suppliers and stakeholders from different businesses. There is likely to be conflict involved here!

Annual events, especially those that are in the private sector, often have a paid committee, where staff are assigned specific tasks and may work on a full-time, part-time or seasonal basis. This is common practice for seasonal events such as agricultural shows. It is entirely possible for one person alone to organize medium-sized events, but there is no substitute for having someone else to check that all the details are complete and to help with administrative tasks such as making name badges or delegate packs.

Setting out terms of reference (an operational guide to the way the committee operates) helps to manage decision making, conflict and commitment. The structure for the organizing committee is often seen as an organizational chart with leadership and roles and responsibilities clearly defined. Figure 5.3 shows the difference between a simple structure and a more complex structure for a larger event.

Not all events require a committee and professional event organizers may work independently, overseeing all aspects of delivering an event. This is also true of specialist event jobs such as

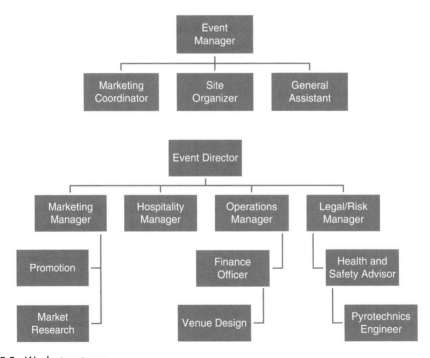

Fig. 5.3. Work structures.

wedding coordinators. In some businesses, the event manager relies upon other departments to support them. In a hotel, the event manager will rely upon the restaurant manager and the housekeeping teams for event support.

CHOOSING A VENUE

Having developed an event idea, the choice of venue is essential for success. There are many factors to consider and different events will have very different requirements. Some of the factors to consider in choosing an event venue are:

- Target market: location decisions will significantly impact upon different user groups, with distance and accessibility being key considerations.
- Accessibility and public transportation: sufficient parking at a site is crucial and, where this is not possible (such as inner city venues), sufficient alternatives need to be available, close to the venue, and anyone attending the event should be aware of any parking charges. Attendees at events may be reliant upon public transportation. A location close to major transport hubs is essential for a conference where delegates are likely to arrive by train or plane.
- Venue theme and ambience: the co-branding potential between a venue and the event should be considered. For example, a historic venue will complement an event with a medieval festival more effectively than a modern conference centre would. Similarly, a motor museum would be an ideal site for a conference for automotive parts manufacturers.
- Venue capacity: in simple terms, the venue should not be too big and it should not be too small. No one wants to spend their day crammed into a small room becoming hot and uncomfortable. However, over-capacity can create a perception that the organizers have not been as successful as they hoped in filling the space.
- Venue reputation: potential consumers may not differentiate an event from the venue. If people perceive the venue negatively, this will almost certainly spill over to their perception of the proposed event. This is called reputation interdependence.
- Venue availability: the venue must be available to stage the event. It may not always be possible to have the ideal date at a venue.
- Venue catering: a venue may insist on providing catering or using its own external suppliers. It should never be assumed that hiring a venue provides full independence for catering decisions.

There are many different types of venue offering a wide range of service and facilities to maximize their market appeal. Some examples of typical venues and the events they host are identified below:

- Football stadiums: music concerts, meetings, conferences, parties, weddings, celebrations.
- Racecourses: car shows, conferences, weddings, other equestrian sports.
- Stately homes and estates: conferences, exhibitions, concerts, outdoor sports, weddings, garden themes.
- Conference centres: conferences, meetings, weddings, celebrations.
- Tourist attractions: specific events at the attraction, weddings, conferences, meetings.
- Exhibition centres: trade fairs, product launches, public exhibitions, conferences.

Box 5.3. Festivals.

Festivals are made up of a range of different types of events with a common theme and are often marketed as an entity separate from any single event. It has become quite accepted that festivals themselves might 'piggyback' on other festivals where the themes can be associated. An example of this would be The New Orleans Jazz and Heritage Festival, which features performances, exhibitions and activities that link the music and the history of New Orleans.

Heritage festivals and events tend to look at unique aspects of a particular place and may feature architecture, theatre, music, heritage walks and exhibitions of art and culture. Dublin, for example, has a Franco-Irish Book Festival, a St Patrick's Festival, a Bloom Festival and a Dublin Irish Writers Festival. Add to this the activities that associate with Trinity College, such as Bloomsday, which is advertised as 'the day in 1904 on which all the action of James Joyce's novel *Ulysses* takes place'. This unique event is celebrated every year on 16 June by Joyceans all over the world and involves a walk through old Dublin.

Piggybacking on these activities are alternative activities, often staged by minority cultures or groups, who benefit from the association with the mainstream activities. In Dublin, these include the Dublin Pride Festival, the Festival of World Cultures, the Dublin Viking Festival, Hallowfest and the Temple Bar Chocolate Festival.

Study provided by Lexie Mathieso

Events can be staged in purpose-built venues or in venues that are adapted from their original or primary purpose. Wherever an event is held, choosing the right venue is usually the first step.

Question

Consider an event you have recently attended. What were the main requirements for the event venue and do you think the organizers got it right? What improvements would you suggest?

STAGING AN EVENT

The equipment required at events will vary according to the type of event and its venue. There is a multitude of equipment available and some examples are provided here in the context of requirements. Further details of specialist equipment are identified in other sections of this chapter.

- **Getting to the event**
  - Is the venue signposted?
  - Is additional signage required either inside or outside the venue and surrounding areas?
  - Are different car parks being used for different groups (e.g. members, VIPs, premium ticket holders, stall holders, performers)?

- **Vehicular access**
  - Are additional traffic control systems required before and or after the event? While arrival times are generally staggered, most people leave a venue immediately after the event has finished. This is where congestion will be at its greatest.
  - If the event finishes at night, do car-parking areas need additional lighting (e.g. temporary 'tower lights')?
  - Are pedestrian walkways clearly differentiated from vehicular pathways?
- **Stage, lighting and sound**
  - Stage hire is only the start of the real cost of having a stage on site. Staging also requires delivery, erection (usually requiring specialist plant equipment) and electrical fittings.
  - Lighting needs can be considered in terms of both core activity and for the attendees, especially as they enter and leave a venue.
  - The sound from the core activity (i.e. conference address, music concert) needs to be projected to the audience. Additionally, the event organizers may wish to have their own public address system to communicate with attendees.
- **Communication**: Given the spatial footprint of the event and need for timely communication, event staff will not always be able to rely on face-to-face communication. Mobile phones, two-way radios, panic buttons and pagers all have uses at events. Alongside this communications hardware, consideration needs to be given to the protocols for its use. For example, will the communication be 'open', whereby all people can send and receive messages to everybody, or will communication be 'restricted'?
- **Power/energy**: All of the above may place heavy demands on energy. This may not be problematic for purpose-built and/or indoor venues, but can be for outdoor events. In these circumstances, the event may need generators to provide sufficient power.
- **Stages**: Building an outdoor event site is not without its problems and heavy plant equipment required for building stages may churn up event fields if the weather has been even slightly wet. This makes it difficult for other vehicles to get deliveries on to the site and can be very unpleasant for those attending the event. Metal roadways can be built to minimize damage but may need to be acquired at short notice and these actually create slip and trip hazards for the public so they need to be removed before the public arrive and put back before the site is cleared.
- **Themed events**: Events can be themed in many ways. There are businesses that specialize in fancy dress and props to decorate events. Fireworks may be needed and specific colours of linen, chair fabrics and even 'comedy actors' may be part of the experience.
- **Sanitation**: In temporary venues, the supply of toilets and waste removal is particularly pertinent. There may be a need to provide additional toilets, or provide all of the toilets. Waste removal – litter and other forms of rubbish – may need to occur while the event is operation. Overflowing bins are unsightly, for example, and they may need to be emptied throughout the day.
- **Catering** is usually provided by other companies with the capacity to provide not only food and drink, but also seating and marquees to provide a comfortable environment. The event organizer may levy a site fee for these businesses in exchange for providing a ready-made market of potential clients.

All of the above can be provided and managed in-house by the event organization. Alternatively, the event may elect to outsource the provision of these resources to specialist companies. For some event companies, it makes sense to buy equipment. An exhibition venue that regularly hosts trade shows may as well invest in the equipment needed to host the show rather than renting it in. There is a fairly simple cost calculation for this shown in Box 5.4.

Box 5.4. Hire or buy?

This example uses a training company as an example. A training company will regularly need a data projector. This will cost around £900 to purchase. If the company uses venues where this equipment is provided free of charge then there is no need to invest.

However, if the company delivers 90 training sessions each year and the hire cost (at the venue or from an independent distributor) is £20 per session, then the total hire cost is £1800 over a year.

This equates to the purchasing cost of two data projectors, and with a 1-year guarantee, there is a saving of £900.

If the number of courses each year was 50, representing a hire cost of £1000, then it may be a safer option to use the equipment provided at a venue as there is little scope for contingency if the equipment fails, whereas this is the venue's responsibility if they own it.

Box 5.5. Lighting up the Singapore Grand Prix.

The Singapore Grand Prix is most notable as the F1 Circuit's first night race. Staging this event, however, requires considerable planning and development.

The circuit is over 5 km long – specialists Valerio Maioli S.p.a were chosen by F1 racing's governing body, the FIA, to deliver the lighting package.

Because of the nature of the event and the risk of accidents that could be caused by too much glare, or reflection from the road surface, or blinding mist from car tyres in wet conditions, no ordinary lighting would do.

The final solution was achieved through strategically positioned lighting projectors around the track. Once the hardware was chosen, the delivery infrastructure was the next challenge. In total, this required:

- 108,423 m of power cables.
- 240 steel pylons.
- 1600 light projectors.
- A total power requirement of 3,180,000 W.
- 12 twin-power generators, sound deadening and a control room to monitor power and fuel.
- Each projector consists of a 2000-W white metal halide lamp installed at 4-m intervals on the aluminium truss.
- This gave an illumination measurement of around 3000 lux, which is four times brighter than the average sports stadium.

Contingency planning includes a back-up power system through the generators to cover one for failure, power-loc connectors to replace cables quickly and safely while alternative power sources and phases would allow neighbouring projectors to continue working. To avoid impacting on broadcast quality, the lights and camera equipment were fitted to the same side of the track.

The only challenge that remains then is for the F1 teams to find visors and visor strips that work under the lights and for the FIA to continue to find new and exciting ways of presenting the F1 event.

Sources: Various

LICENCES AND PERMITS

Ensuring that the event has the correct licences and permits in place is essential. The event must also have specific licences for playing music or video in public places, for serving alcohol (unless this is subcontracted) and for holding an event. In many countries, event sites are licensed for maximum numbers of attendees and for certain times to limit disturbance late at night. Venue owners and event organizers must have relevant insurance in place.

CREATING THE THEMED EXPERIENCE

Authenticity, 'ambience' or 'atmosphere' is created through the service experience, linked to the theme of the event. For example, a medieval-themed dining event would be greatly enhanced by costumed servers, medieval music and the use of old-fashioned language, but the perfect themed setting would be ruined by staff dressed in T-shirt and jeans, making little effort to deliver good service (see Fig. 5.4).

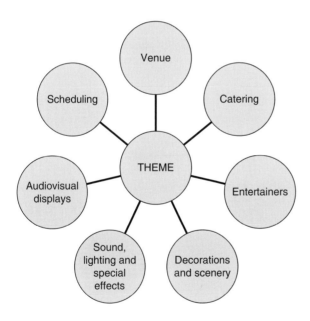

Fig. 5.4. Creating a theme.

TICKETING

Ticketing requirements vary depending on the type of event. From an operations perspective, there are two primary decisions: ticket levels and ticket distribution.

Many events offer a variety of ticketing levels – the more expensive tickets come with a range of privileges including priority seating, priority parking, refreshments and behind-the-scenes tours. For example, a horse racing event may have three ticketing levels: Centre

Course only (low price); Centre Course plus one grandstand and bar access (medium price); and Centre Course, premium bars, grandstand by the start/finish and restaurant access (highest price).

The development of these ticket packages is a marketing decision, not an operational one. However, ensuring that the access is provided to ticketholders and that non-ticket holders do not receive access is clearly an operational one. When these packages are being developed, consideration must be given to the policies and procedures that will need to be implemented to ensure that it functions smoothly.

Ticket distribution can be managed in a number of ways. The event may choose to utilize a ticketing agency (e.g. Ticketmaster) or it may elect to sell and distribute the tickets 'in house'. Tickets may be sold before the event by offering:

- advance booking through the event website;
- ticket sales through an agency;
- tickets can be bought in advance and:
  - collected on the day;
  - sent in the post;
  - printed out after booking.

Many attendees will prefer to purchase and physically receive their ticket before the event, as it reduces the likelihood of queuing before the event. Selling tickets on the day provides additional implications from an operations perspective – additional staff needs to be employed, cash handling and or EFTPOS/credit card systems need to be introduced. It is common practice for events to charge more for tickets purchased on the day of the event to offset these additional costs. Advance ticket sales should allow quicker access, discounted prices and predictability of numbers for event organizers; although for first-time events, visitors may underestimate the popularity of the activity.

An additional ticketing issue for events where demand exceeds supply is the secondary ticket market, or what is popularly referred to as ticket scalping. Ticket touts are difficult to stop and solutions are not always practical. Most events do not offer a refund or resale service, a practice that can minimize touting. However it is often very clear when an event will be popular and will sell out, making touting a valuable activity to those involved who buy the tickets at the retail value and sell them on at a vastly inflated price after all other tickets are sold. Many believe this is morally and ethically wrong and many major events now require photo ID as part of the ticketing system. On the other hand, it may be quite reasonable for someone who cannot attend for genuine reasons to sell their ticket on if the venue does not offer a buy-back/resale system.

VENUE DESIGN

Venue design is crucial to many events. Dedicated conference and exhibition centres are designed as multi-use facilities and have the capacity to change the use of space. They have demountable arenas, large open spaces and large access areas to allow vehicular access to the building. The only design consideration is the layout of the room to meet the needs of different users. Often large exhibition venues do little more than hire out space, car parking and equipment to an organizer, and then employ their own staff to manage the impacts on the venue. This may include car park staff and security staff. The venue may also provide toilets, restaurants, ticketing facilities and an online box office in advance of the event.

Figures 5.5, 5.6 and 5.7 demonstrate different ways of managing exhibition and conferencing space to facilitate different types of events. Figure 5.5 shows the ways in which rooms can be designed for different activities. A theatre-style layout is ideal for product launches, while boardroom formats work well for meetings and training courses, and the banqueting set-up is ideal for celebration events. Of particular note with the latter is that it is advisable to leave a chair out of each table to ensure no one has their back directly facing the stage, maximizing the view for everyone at the table.

For trade fairs, most established exhibition centres use exhibition cells or pods, which are versatile partitioned structures that allow exhibitors to have different sized spaces. This is advantageous because it means that different prices can be offered for cells of different sizes, in different positions. A large cell by the entrance to the exhibition will be more valuable than a small cell at the back where there is less visitor footfall (Fig. 5.6).

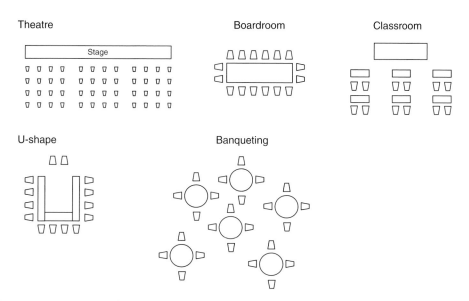

Fig. 5.5. Common conference room layouts.

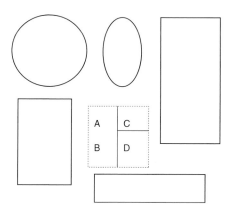

Fig. 5.6. Trade fair layouts.

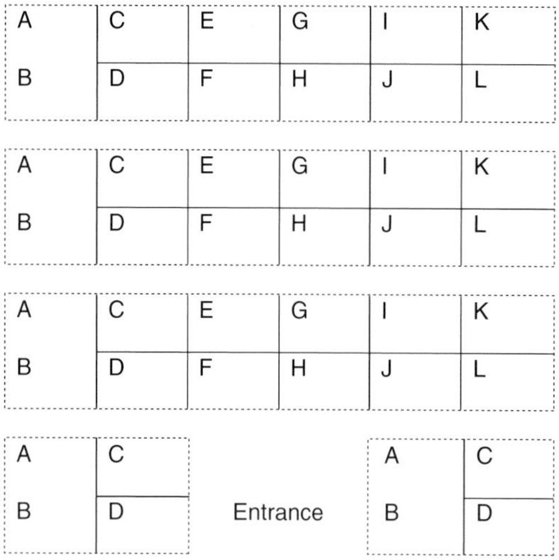

A	C	E	G	I	K
B	D	F	H	J	L

A	C	E	G	I	K
B	D	F	H	J	L

A	C	E	G	I	K
B	D	F	H	J	L

A	C			A	C
B	D	Entrance		B	D

Fig. 5.7. Show layouts (e.g. car show).

From an exhibitor's perspective, it is important to consider how the space will be used and furnished. It is advisable for the display to feel open and inviting, as anything that feels deep and narrow will be off-putting to visitors keen to avoid the risk of any 'hard-selling' from companies once inside the display area.

For some exhibitions, such as motor shows and other public exhibitions, exhibitors may design their own stands and displays to maximize brand impact and glamour. Car shows are an excellent example of this approach to exhibition design where cars are displayed on ramps, erected on top of displays and in public viewing areas, and the stands include sales and meeting rooms and corporate hospitality facilities such as bars and cafes. In this instance, the floor area is designed to allow a mix of these display areas together with traditional exhibition cells, and the cost of the space is based upon both footfall and total square or even cubic footage.

For many other events, especially outdoor concerts and festivals, where the site is simply 'a field or two' much more planning is required to ensure that there are distinct areas and that access and egress to the site and to the event area is clear and provides sufficient space. A country fair for example may need separate catering areas, trade areas, display areas and then arenas where competitions can take place. Care should be taken when designing an event's layout so that complementary facilities and amenities are located together. For example, first aid, lost property and lost children would happily co-exist but, because of their noise, generators should not be placed alongside camping areas as they would keep people awake.

Activity

Using an event of your choice, or an idea for an event, choose a venue you know and design a layout for the space.

SITE PLANNING

Site plans are essential for everybody involved in designing an event. There are numerous components that need to be included and for major events, different information is required. While people attending an event need to see where everything is, the site plan for contractors may require more specific information, measurements and GPS data.

This means that two different site maps are required. An example of a basic public map is given in the case study for a country fair, but there will certainly need to be a different map for event organizers to ensure that the event set-up is correct. The list below illustrates common inclusions on site maps, although these will not all be needed at all types of events:

- Scale
- Entrance and exits
- Roads and parking
- Information/administration
- First aid
- Emergency access
- Lost children
- Water
- Electricity/generators
- Camping areas

- Lost property
- Toilets
- Food and catering areas
- Marquees
- Displays/exhibitions
- Direction pointer (North)
- Rings and demonstrations
- Storage area
- No-access areas
- Lighting and cabling

- Rubbish bins
- Pathways
- Phones
- Cash machine
- Media centre
- Performers' area (Green Room)
- VIP access
- Different ticketable areas
- Fire marshal points

Box 5.6. The site plan (Fig. 5.8).

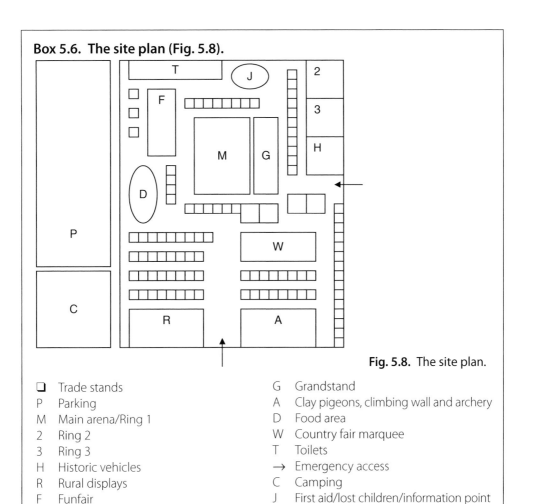

Fig. 5.8. The site plan.

❏	Trade stands	
P	Parking	
M	Main arena/Ring 1	
2	Ring 2	
3	Ring 3	
H	Historic vehicles	
R	Rural displays	
F	Funfair	

G	Grandstand
A	Clay pigeons, climbing wall and archery
D	Food area
W	Country fair marquee
T	Toilets
→	Emergency access
C	Camping
J	First aid/lost children/information point

(Continued)

Box 5.6. Continued.

The advantage of a site plan such as this example for a country fair is twofold. First, it is an essential tool for event managers who need to plan out the site – often a more detailed plan with measurements will be used – this is important to ensure that there is sufficient space for emergency vehicles, visitors and site vehicles.

There will be strict rules in place to minimize vehicles on the site once the gates open, although depending on the location of facilities such as toilets for example, some access may be essential in order that these can be cleaned and maintained during the event.

In the days before the event, the event team will be kept busy managing arrivals on the site and ensuring that everything is laid out as expected in the event plan. This is also important, as many trade stands will have paid for a certain space and for parity, traders need to keep to their designated area.

The event team should have already given out a contract that defines the amount of space that can be used and the distance into the thoroughfare in front of their stand within which they can place display boards and advertising.

Other requirements of a site plan may include the power routes for heating and lighting, locations of speakers, generators and water points, plus acceptable cable routes to avoid anybody tripping over cables or other site equipment.

RISK MANAGEMENT

Risk management provides a system with which to identify hazards, evaluate the likely risk and the severity of anything going wrong, and as a result being able to put in place measures to make the event as safe as possible.

There is always a risk of something going wrong at events, and the larger the event generally the higher the risk. In order to minimize risk, event managers can carry out a risk assessment. A risk assessment involves identifying potential hazards, and then measuring the risk factors and seeking solutions to minimize the level of that risk. If, in risk assessing an event, hazards are identified that cannot be managed to make the event safe, the activity should be removed (e.g. bungee jumping) or the event cancelled. Risk management is an ongoing event process.

Box 5.7. Health and Safety policy in the UK.

Health and Safety (H&S) legislation in the UK only applies to organizations with five or more employees. This means many organizers are not required to develop an explicit H&S policy although they do need to conform to H&S legislation. Regardless of size, it is worthwhile having an H&S policy for any size organization because it demonstrates:

- commitment to health and safety;
- responsibilities for all tasks for all people; and
- procedural health and safety and compliance with guidance and rules.

(Continued)

Box 5.7. Continued.

A Health and Safety policy should include:

- A current certificate from an insurance company showing that the organization has employers' liability insurance, public liability insurance and third party insurance.
- A Health and Safety Law poster for employees. Organizations should also be encouraged to provide information leaflets about Health and Safety issues.
- Action to be taken in the case of fire, how to raise the alarm, what to do when the alarm is sounded, how to call the fire brigade, fire escape route, muster points, emergency exits, fire extinguisher points, fire doors (as designated on the fire certificate).
- Location of first aid point/box, name and location of trained first aid persons or the appointed person.
- Copy of any specific information or posters regarding regulations that apply to individual premises where it is a requirement of those regulations to display information.
- Up-to-date risk assessments.
- An organizational Health and Safety plan with responsibilities outlined.

There is also a legal requirement to give people access to copies of the health and safety policy.

Study provided by Debra Wale

In order to assess these risks fully, it is necessary to categorize them. Firstly, risks can be categorized as low, medium or high and then the severity of the possible outcome is also considered. To do this, it is necessary to look first at the areas of an event where problems can occur. These include:

- Crowd management
- Alcohol
- Contingencies: fire, first aid, emergencies
- Installation of equipment and services
- Safety of equipment
- Food safety
- Water quality
- Lighting
- Breakdown
- Cash handling
- Noise levels
- Chemicals
- Weather
- Bites and stings
- Parking
- Electrical storms and lighting
- Electrical and gas safety

These risks apply to everybody involved in organizing an event, as is demonstrated in this example of a risk assessment (Fig. 5.9).

Risk Assessment Form

Event/Work covered by this assessment	Charity bike ride at a Forestry Commission Site

Activity or task and the persons involved	Approximately 150 cycling participants, volunteer marshalls and event organizers, plus some contact and space shared with the public.

Assessor (PLEASE PRINT)		Date of assessment		Date of reassessment

Existing safety measures and people at risk	Guidance on the use of cycle routes is provided by the Forestry Commission. Participants hiring bikes will be given helmets by the hire company

Hazard No.	Nature of Hazard Posing Significant Risk	Risk Rating (from below)	P*	S*	Proposed Action
1	Cars, bikes and pedestrians together	6	3	2	Existing signage designated parking
2	Risk of injuries on bikes	9	3	3	All participants must wear helmets Additional safety wear advised for Red Route
3	Participants becoming lost	4	2	2	Maps for all participants Marshalls available
4	Participants unable to complete the circuit	4	2	2	Maps for all participants Marshalls available 1 vehicle available to collect stuck participants from nearest access points (shown on maps)
5	Head injuries	6	2	3	All participants must wear helmets Additional safety wear advised for Red Route 1st aiders available Marshalls to have emergency numbers

Fig. 5.9. Risk assessment for a charity mountain bike event.

6	Minor injuries	9	3	3	All participants must wear helmets Additional safety wear advised for Red Route 1st aiders available Marshalls to have emergency numbers
7	Major injuries	2	1	2	All participants must wear helmets Additional safety wear advised for Red Route 1st aiders available Marshalls to have emergency numbers
8	Injuries/accidents with non-participants	1	1	1	Signage warning other people about the event
9	Security of money	4	2	2	Money to be kept in safe
10	Falling branches	2	2	1	Forestry Commission close site when winds above 43mph
11	Slips, trips, falls	4	2	2	Appropriate clothing and footwear advised for marshalls and staff
12	Lone working (Marshalls)	3	1	3	All Marshalls to have mobile phones Marshalls will be rotated to ensure all present Most will work in pairs and be close to public areas such as car parks

*P = physical risk control; S = safe system of work, i.e. procedural risk control.

Scoring System

Hazard severity	Likelihood of occurrence
5 = Very high (multiple deaths)	5 = Very high (100% certain to occur)
4 = High (death or serious injury)	4 = Likely (small change = accident)
3 = Moderate (injury or disease)	3 = Quite possible (may happen)
2 = Slight (minor injury)	2 = Possible (low or minimal risk)
1 = Nil (no risk)	1 = Not likely (no risk present)
0 = Not applicable	0 = Not applicable

Risk rating = Severity x Likelihood
Greater than 10 = critical risk

Fig. 5.9. Continued.

Activity

Conduct a risk assessment for an event of your choice.

First aid

First aid is an extremely important consideration, as this allows the event organizer to provide care to anyone who is injured at their event. Although actual legislation and/or rules differ around the world, 'best practice' for the numbers of first aiders required at events is the ratio of two first aiders to every 1000 people, and a minimum of two at any event.

WHEN IT GOES WRONG

There have been a number of notable accidents at events with high numbers of injuries and fatalities. Whatever the cause of the accidents at the time, once the initial aftermath has passed, public policy is often reviewed to enhance event safety. The two examples in Box 5.8 provide UK-based illustrations. It is imperative that event managers and venue managers do all they can to ensure a safe environment for event employees and event audiences who have a right to expect a safe and well managed event environment.

Box 5.8. Football disasters.

The Hillsborough disaster occurred in 1989 at Hillsborough football stadium in Sheffield. Ninety-six Liverpool football fans were killed as a result of being crushed against each other after being trapped inside fencing used to separate areas on the terrace (at this time football terraces were standing room only).

Prior to the Hillsborough disaster, football stadia already had to comply with the Safety at Sports Grounds Act (1975) that concentrates on stadiums that hold 10,000 spectators or more. The stadium has to provide a 'reasonable safety' level in order to gain the certificate. These factors include:

- a maximum number of spectators;
- grouping of spectators;
- number of entrances and exits;
- records of attendance and maintenance;
- existing provision of barriers; and
- seating arrangements

Two years before the Hillsborough disaster, 56 people were killed in a terrace fire at Bradford City Football Club. This led to the Fire Safety & Safety of Places of Sport Act (1987), an amendment of the 1975 Act, which required stadia to ensure that there were:

(Continued)

Box 5.8. Continued.

- Means of escape in the case of a fire: emergency exits and routes should be kept clear at all times and should open in the direction of escape.
- The means for fighting a fire: considerations should also be given to the layout, dimensions, the number of emergency routes and exits, and the provision of doors within these routes.
- Risk assessment: the responsible person must carry out a fire safety risk assessment, and implement and maintain a fire management plan.

The Taylor report (commissioned after the Hillsborough disaster) required the compulsory refurbishment of all the grounds in the country, turning them into all-seater stadiums (the Football Spectators Act 1989). The following list illustrates the new responsibilities of football stadia:

- better stewarding;
- easy to get to fire escapes;
- an anti-crush design of stadium;
- fire evacuation procedure;
- fire prevention systems (sprinklers);
- clear signage for escape; and
- all-seater design stadia.

Study provided by Debra Wale

Question
What other event disasters have led to improvements in legislation?

CRISIS MANAGEMENT PLAN

> … [T]he greatest damage … can be caused not by an event or the disaster itself but by the manner in which a crisis is managed, particularly in the context of communication and information provision.
>
> (Pender and Sharpley, 2005, p. 286)

It is essential that crisis management plans be in place before the crisis occurs. Page (2003) proposes the management challenge of a crisis thus:

- Crises are often short term but impacts are longer term.
- 'Stable' businesses transformed into chaos.
- Concept of crisis and chaos highlights need for flexibility and adaptability.

Van Walbeek (2004) suggests that the following components are required for crisis situations:

- leadership (crisis coordination);
- adequate emergency response;

- victim identification;
- media relations;
- family assistance;
- information dissemination; and
- internal and external communications.

Pender and Sharpley (2005) identify four principles underpinning crisis management in tourism:

- coordination (complex array of public and private sector organizations);
- collaboration;
- communication; and
- commitment (all parties should accept that a crisis will occur and all involved in the development of the crisis management plan must be committed to it).

Effective crisis management relies on a plan to manage incidents that have taken place. This is usually planned in advance and included in a contingency plan.

THE CONTINGENCY PLAN

Despite the best endeavours of event planners, things can and do go wrong at events. The contingency plan is designed to outline the responses required from event organizers if something unexpected happens. In order to deliver this effectively, event managers need to anticipate the full range of disasters and plan accordingly.

In advance of any event, the events team should be familiar with the contingency plan so they are prepared for action. This will increase the speed with which 'Plan B' can be implemented. In certain situations, event managers will need to make a 'go or no-go' decision.

Question

For an event of your choice, what might lead to a decision to delay, postpone or cancel an event only 1 hour before going live?

While most event managers' first instinct is that 'the show must go on', there will be situations in which the correct decision is postponement or cancellation. The plan should contain site maps, access routes and scenario planning, and for major events, this needs to be developed in partnership with the emergency services.

THE CONTROL CENTRE

It is entirely possible to write checklists for every aspect of an event, but there are so many different events, with so many different requirements that it would be impossible to produce a single list that would apply to any event. As the event looms, some degree of overall control

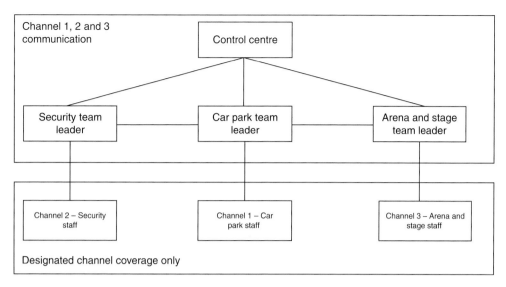

Fig. 5.10. Communication design.

is essential and checklists may include specification sheets for specific aspects of an event, run sheets, which are explained later, and programming schedules to coordinate music, different acts, synchronized fireworks and other elements of the event display.

On the day, these and the contingency plan need to be located in the event control centre. This should be a central point where key staff members are based. It should be reasonably secure, possibly providing facilities for keeping money safe, and having broadcast and communication facilities.

A control centre may be a shared resource with other event staff, such as commentators and first-aiders, although at major events it is best to ensure that the control centre is accessed by a restricted number of staff or even designated key holders. At major venues, the control centre may have large numbers of staff involved to coordinate public activities, media and broadcast coverage, VIP guests and facilities management.

The key function of the control centre is to manage communications during the event. For simple events, communication may be based upon mobile phones, although this is risky in areas of low mobile signal, and for events that take place in a large area it is necessary to check for coverage first. It is better to use two-way radio systems, some of which require a licence, especially when the site is close to other radio users such as airports. Once the technology is chosen, there needs to be an agreed system for communication, which can be achieved through the use of different radio channels. An outline of a communication system is shown in Fig. 5.10, based upon a three-channel two-way radio system at an outdoor music concert.

REHEARSAL AND PRODUCTION MANAGEMENT

'Shows' are often hosted as part of a tour programme and are, therefore, self-sufficient in a venue such as a theatre or concert hall. However, when the event is being hosted at a special venue, perhaps one where the staging and sound system are brought in specifically (such as an open-air concert), then there should be one member of the events team responsible for liaising with the show's production manager.

For some events, there may be several different acts and the production may be managed in-house within the event team. This will require a detailed production schedule, with 'run sheets' for specific staff detailing tasks that are required at different times. This may include details of fireworks performances, certain musical sequences, carrying equipment, changing stage sets or, where celebrities are involved, meeting the requirements of the performer's riders. The rider is an addition to the event contract that has been much publicized by 'celebrities' in recent years, making very specific requests such as certain drinks or specific equipment provided in changing rooms and requiring facilities for their 'entourage' – the group of staff who provide a range of services including make-up artists, security staff, hairdressers, personal assistants, catering staff and more.

Even for small events, it is important to run through the plans and check not only that everything is in place, but also that the plans will work in reality – it is very easy to forget about the fact that what may appear to work on paper may not go to plan when there are several hundred people on site. One example of this may be a 'walkabout' open-air theatre performance in an outdoor location, where different acts are staged in different locations within a garden or parkland setting. It will be necessary for the performers to know where each act will be staged and it is equally important for the organizers to be able to ensure that the public know when and where to go, and that any areas or walkways that the performers require are kept clear of the audience.

It is essential to check that all the equipment works, especially lights, speakers and software, and this should be done well in advance of the event starting to allow time to source replacement equipment.

Question

What are the most important aspects of planning and preparing for an event?

Box 5.9. The National Trust events programme.

This is a UK-wide events programme that covers events at every National Trust property open to the public. The National Trust (NT) is a UK-based charity that cares for historic buildings and the natural environment. The Trust delivers a number of events at each of its 400-plus properties, and these are designed to achieve several goals.

1. Income generation.
2. Raising awareness of the charity and the work it does.
3. Developing new audiences, including younger audiences and those that are hard to reach.
4. Fundraising for new developments, restoration work and general funds.
5. Partnership development with other organizations.

At a national level, the Trust produces guides to organizing events that each property should try to host. These include Easter Egg Hunts and Family Fun Days. The latter are often designed as treasure hunts and trails based on popular children's books.

(Continued)

Box 5.9. Continued.

Some NT properties regularly host conferences and private events such as weddings as part of their longer-term property plans. Some properties, such as Stowe Landscape Gardens, even employ a wedding planner, as this is a valuable and important market for the property. The larger NT properties play host to a number of major music concerts each year, from classical proms to modern artists. These are major events that attract new and existing customers to the Trust. Likewise, fireworks displays are also popular at some properties. Most properties host smaller events such as outdoor plays performed by theatre companies, and some hold exhibitions of costumes from films recorded at the properties.

As well as delivering events designed at national and regional office levels properties are also encouraged to develop events that relate to the site, such as costumed interpretation and special tours. Over recent years, the Trust has broadened its retail and catering offers through the traditional winter 'closed season' and has supported these with special indoor events.

PART C – THE BIG DAY!

On the day, or for the entire duration of an event (if it continues for several days), the event organizers have a number of functions to perform, the majority of which are based on the planning and preparation that have taken place prior to the event. Part C presents and explains the operational functions that take place during the event. It must be noted that these activities are not discussed in any particular order as these activities run concurrently.

UNDERSTANDING DEMAND FOR EVENTS

In general economic terms, *demand* is the quantity of a product/service that people are willing and able to pay for. This is not necessarily the same as the amount that is actually purchased, as levels of supply may not be sufficient to satisfy demand. For instance, the Take That Reunion concert sold out in just a few days after the box office opened and many more people were willing and able to buy tickets but could not because no more tickets were available. In this light, we can classify demand as follows:

- Effective/actual demand: the number of people actually participating in/attending an event.
- Suppressed demand: the population that cannot participate in/attend an event due to circumstances such as:
  - Potential demand: lack of purchasing power, but would like to participate/attend. If circumstances change this form of demand can be converted to actual demand.
  - Deferred demand: constraints such as shortages of supply (e.g. seats) can be converted to actual demand if the venue can accommodate the demand.
- No demand: the part of the population with no desire to participate in/attend an event.

Greasley (2006) identifies three strategies for reconciling capacity and demand: level capacity, chase demand and demand management. In adopting level capacity strategy, the processing capacity is set at a consistent level throughout the planning period irrespective of changes in demand. This strategy is usually put in place to meet 'average' demand where inventory is used to absorb variations. The application of this strategy in event operations is very common for differentiation and ease of control. However, this does not allow tapping of the full potential of the market in peak periods. On the other hand, the adoption of chase demand strategy enables the planner to match output to demand levels over time. Capacity may be adjusted by manpower planning. Smart managers always keep a list of casual staff that can be called at short notice in case of insufficient capacity (staff shortage). Often these staff are trained by and have worked for the organization in the recent past. On this basis, they are conversant with the organization's culture and mode of operation. The demand management approach attempts to change demand to fit capacity by altering and/or transferring demand from one point of service to another, from peak periods to quiet periods or by altering the marketing mix. Redirection of visitors from a busy attraction or sub-event to a less well attended one is an example of the adoption of this type of strategy.

It must be noted that capacity planning is part of the pre-event functions that managers and organizers of events undertake. It is a precursor for the management of capacity on the day of the event or during the entire period of the event; hence this and associated concepts are discussed here to provide better understanding of capacity management process.

CAPACITY MANAGEMENT

Hill (2005) explains that capacity encompasses the resources an organization possesses to meet the needs of customers, process information and provide service and is an amalgam of the systems, equipment, labour and facilities required to create the event. Capacity in events will include the number of workers available to serve during an event; the number of seats available in a concert hall; the number of attendees that can be physically accommodated in a given space or the number of people a site can accommodate before the quality of the attendees' experience is adversely affected. It becomes very important that when planning an event organizers must consider appropriate levels of capacity to meet the projected number of attendees, as this ensures the effective management of visitors' experiences.

In event operations, capacity management is an integral function, which aims to harmonize the level of operations with demand in order to obtain a good balance between costs and service provision. Hill (2005) describes capacity management as an essential responsibility of the operations function that seeks to match the level of capacity to the level of demand in terms of both quantity and the skills mix to meet the service specification. Many venues have a maximum capacity stated within their licence.

The success of event operations depends largely on the ability to vary demand to fit capacity; hence, prediction of demand becomes inevitable. The ease of aligning demand to capacity varies from event to event. Generally, in the service industries, predicting demand can be a tricky task; however, event organizers try to make demand as predictable as possible. The ability to predict demand is the basis for formulating suitable operational plans to manage attendees' experiences. There are two main options open to planners in forecasting demand: they can either adopt qualitative or quantitative techniques.

It should be noted that while these approaches to capacity management are exceptionally useful, the alternative simple solution for some events, such as concerts, is to sell tickets in advance of the event (see Chapter 5, Part B) or to use a 'pre-booked tickets only' policy, but this may pre-emptively limit audience attendance.

Qualitative techniques, also sometimes referred to as strategic forecasting techniques, are usually used for long-term estimates. These incorporate decision maker's intuition, emotions, personal values and experiences (Heizer and Render, 2006). They are mostly descriptive; however, quite a number of qualitative forecasts will need interpretations, and statistical and numerical explanations and representations to make them meaningful. The qualitative class consists of:

- the Delphi technique;
- strategic issues analysis; and
- scenario analysis.

The *Delphi technique* is perhaps the most popular of the qualitative techniques used in eliciting and consolidating judgements of experts about a subject's future. This technique is particularly useful where prior data of the subject matter is scarce or not in existence. It involves the selection of a panel of experts from relevant areas of expertise. Their ideas and/or opinions of the subject form the basis of future estimates. These opinions are circulated to all the members for reactions, opinion polling, sharing and revision. This process forms a continuous loop to achieve a desired or acceptable consensus.

Strategic issue analysis is useful in assessing emerging strategic issues. For instance, it is used in monitoring the effects of changes – socio-economic changes (habits, tastes and income level), political changes (perception on war, policies on terrorism) and regulatory changes (EU regulations, domestic regulations on immigration matters, etc.). This involves systematic observation of these variables and their resultant effects on events. Examples that are currently very relevant to the events industry include diseases such as swine flu (events can propagate the spread of disease because there are lots of people in a small area), natural events such as the volcanic ash cloud, and economic (in)stability.

Scenario analysis involves the estimation of complex events especially where financial implication variables play a central role. This method allows the integration of variables in explaining future occurrences. It also allows the description of events and their implications. Scenario analysis provides an organization with models of outcomes corresponding to various external and internal stimuli.

The second form of forecasting technique, the *quantitative approach* is the most often used technique at the operational level. Mostly, it employs one or more mathematical models that rely on historic data and can employ causal variables to estimate future outcomes. The quantitative category encompasses the following:

- judgement techniques;
- counting techniques;
- time-series techniques;
- causal techniques; and
- system simulation.

Judgement techniques rely on human judgement and experience and are composed of three main methods: naive extrapolation, staff opinions and expert opinions (the judgement technique is sometimes categorized under the qualitative approach).

- Naive extrapolation is the most commonly used (Sanchez *et al.*, 1995) and it involves the use of current demand as forecast taking into account any known influence.
- Staff opinions, also known as sales force estimates, take into consideration staff knowledge and proximity to information concerning demand when estimating future sales.
- Expert opinions involve recognition of knowledge and experiences of superior officers and specialists as invaluable in making future estimates.

Counting techniques consist of two main methods: market testing and market research.

- Market testing is used mainly for products where a consumer panel is provided with a specimen or samples of a new product to be introduced to the market. The panellists' reactions, comments and opinions form the basis for product development and demand forecast.
- Market research is method that involves the typical survey of a representative sample of a targeted population with the view of gauging and assessing likely courses of action. This is achieved through a variety of ways, including direct or telephone interview, self-filled or assisted questionnaires, observation, and interactive or information technology-assisted means. For reliability and validity, the sample size and selection are very important factors to note.

Time-series techniques are the most common and simple-to-use forecasting techniques. Historical data in time series have four major components; they are trend, seasonal, cyclical and random components. Time series consist of simple averages, moving averages, weighted moving averages and exponential smoothing. Time-series forecasting necessarily follows a sequential process, which involves the following steps:

- collection of data;
- assessment of data and intended technique;
- application of forecasting technique;
- interpreting and extrapolating the data;
- deciding on future course of action; and
- balancing supply and demand.

Time-series forecasting

1. Simple averages consider the sum of the data from the previous period divided by number of occurrences. Simple averages assume that demand is constant and therefore consider all data in forecasting. They are less reliable if the data pattern changes.

2. Moving averages are similar to the simple averages except that they consider the variations in demand over time and disregard some old data that is not relevant to future forecasts.

> Moving average = total demand in previous n period/n, where n is the number of previous period (which is usually a fixed number chosen according to the needs of a given operation)

Moving averages are very sensitive to changes, adjustable by altering the value of n. A low value of n produces a more responsive forecast, whereas a value that is too low will produce a too-sensitive forecast (Waters, 1996). Care must be taken in determining the value of n.

3. Weighted moving averages, unlike the simple or moving averages, work by assigning weight to each period. The most recent data is assigned greater weight than the old one and this highlights the recent information. The difficulty with this method lies in assigning weight and determining order of importance of various periods.

4. Exponential smoothing is a widely used method; like the weighted moving average, it treats data as less relevant as they get older and makes use of weighting factor in forecasting demand. This method employs both previously forecasted and actual sales figure.

> Mathematically expressed as $NF = \alpha D + (1 - \alpha)F$, where NF is new forecast, α is the smoothing constant, D is actual sales of previous period and F is previous period forecast.

In order for the aforementioned time-series techniques to deal with patterns other than constant time series, a model for seasonality and trend is required. Data in event operations could be seasonal and, therefore, the need for calculating the Seasonal Index (SI) arises. SI is the actual demand for a season/average demand for a season. The seasonal index assists in forecasting complex time series by splitting observations into separate components. These components are individually estimated and afterwards put together to obtain the whole forecast (Waters, 1996).

Causal techniques like the time series use historical data to forecast demand but normally build their models around variables with the bid to forecast cause or relationship. They become very useful when forecasting interrelated variables. For instance, an event organizer may want to know the effect of food quality on attendance. These techniques consider the negative and positive correlation of various variables. They could be quite complicated and involve complex mathematical modelling but they are very effective methods of monitoring changing interactions between environmental factors. It should be noted that the majority of these techniques are available on commercial software, so an operator only needs the basic rudiments of computer usage and sets of reliable data. The techniques under this umbrella include linear regression analysis, multiple regression analysis and econometric modelling.

- Linear regression analysis or simple correlation involves finding the relationship between two variables x (independent variable) and y (dependent variable). The linear equation is expressed as $y = a + bx$. For example, our hypothetical effect of food quality on attendance can be examined in which case event attendance will be the dependent variable (x) and food quality is the independent variable (y).
- Multiple regression analysis like its simple counterpart also looks at cause–effect of variables, but in excess of two. It is mathematically expressed as $y = a + b_1x_1 + b_2x_2 + b_3x_3 + \ldots$ In this method rather than looking at the effect of food quality only on attendance, other variables like advertisement, repeat attendees and so on can be added and form the basis for the forecast.
- Econometric modelling uses combination of linear and multiple regressions simultaneously in forecasting demand. This method is capable of incorporating a number of independent variables simultaneously. It is well suited for forecasting long-term demand and is an effective method of monitoring changing interactions between environmental events.

The *system simulation* method examines the structural properties of industries and economic sectors and is a useful method of forecasting trends. This also involves intensive mathematical modelling and calculations, which are made simple using software.

CROWD CONTROL

Again, this is one of the areas where the effectiveness of the planning process can be ascertained. Controlling crowds at a regular horse racing event is a very different proposition to crowd control at events such as Notting Hill Carnival or the Glastonbury Festival where there may be up to 150,000 people in attendance. Having a large crowd at an event is not a bad thing in itself and can be used as a yardstick to measure success, but having a magnitude of people moving in different directions all at one time can constitute health and safety issues. It is the responsibility of the event organizers and all parties involved, such as the police and independent security companies hired by the organizers to ensure that people are moved in a safe manner.

A variety number of methods can be employed to control crowd, these include:

- zoning;
- route mapping;
- colour coding; and
- redistribution/channelling.

Accreditation (ticket checking) is important to ensure that the right types of people are admitted; however, if the accreditation process is not efficient it can be counterproductive and bottlenecks can build up if the checking system at the entrance if it is not fast enough. Experience will inform planners about the type of layout to employ (see channelling in the section below) to ensure all areas where visitors move about *en masse* are managed safely. This could include car parks, admission points and around main stages and arenas at times when headline acts or show finales are taking place.

The three keys to success in crowd control are cooperation among stakeholders, efficient communication between operatives and the crowd and regular communication between operatives and the control centre. Effective communication between gate and security staff and the crowd is essential: people don't want to be ordered around, they want to see reason. Security personnel should take their time to explain, in a friendly and helpful manner, why the crowd is being redirected rather than just ushering them away from an activity or attraction. Crowd control is about ensuring and assuring safety. Provision of guidelines and warnings is part of the responsibility of the event team and crowd controlling staff to ensure safety.

QUEUE MANAGEMENT

As stated in a preceding section, one of the major operational issues is the tricky nature of prediction of demand, particularly where event attendees' arrival is variable. This will result in uneven human traffic and is likely to lead to congestion at peak periods. Experienced event managers managing recurring events are able to determine when human traffic will build up and put in place measures to prevent unnecessary queues. Planners and managers of a one-off event that requires the buying and checking of tickets at the gate may not enjoy the same privilege. One of the key concepts in managing queues is queuing theory. Slack *et al.* (2007, p. 346) define queuing theory as 'a mathematical approach that models random arrival and processing activities in order to predict the behaviour of queuing systems'.

If there is excess demand for an event and tickets sell out in advance, then some of this demand will go elsewhere. If there is excess capacity at the gate for ticket sales then people will queue to purchase tickets. At times, the excess demand may not have any other alternative than to wait, for instance where there is turnaround of capacity such as at events where people come and go or where tickets have to be purchased at the entrance. In this instance, capacity planning and control is best managed by giving consideration to the attendees' experience. Yeoman *et al.* (2004a) suggest that the role of organizers in managing queues is concerned with the trade-off of the cost of providing quality service and the cost of event attendees waiting in line. This view suggests that queues should be as short as possible, to ensure, for example, prospective attendees standing in queues do not leave without buying a ticket and likewise their wait in the line should not detract from their enjoyment of the event, although the negative aspects of queuing can be mitigated through the use of performers to entertain the people. Some organizations try to engage customers while waiting in line. They do this by creating focal points or activities to diffuse their sense of 'waiting' for too long; in this case, queuing itself will become part of the event experience.

A queuing system in this sense consists of *channels* and *phases*. The channels represent the ticket sale points and phases relate to the number of service points where the visitors in line will stop. It would be justifiable to design this element of an event so that the visitors and the activities they take part in during the queue form part of the system. Haksever *et al.* (2000, cited in Yeoman *et al.*, 2004b) submit that a product layout could be single-line channel or multi-line channel. A single-line channel queuing system refers to one ticket selling point and a single queue while on the other hand a multi-channel queuing system will comprise of more than one ticket selling point with one single line. Whichever queuing system an event organizer chooses will be determined by the event size and nature. It is not uncommon that attendees to some events may not need to queue. It is also possible to arrange admissions to offer ticket collection, credit-card-only payment and advance ticket queues for those who purchased tickets in advance.

One area of key importance is the management of traffic away from the event site where tailbacks can easily lead back several miles, and for several hours, impacting especially heavily on rural communities when events take place in rural areas, and many rural events use fields as car parks, which are especially susceptible to the weather, and rain can quickly lead to churned up ground and the use of tractors to get people on and off the site.

THE CORPORATE MARKET

This is especially important because it is one of the most lucrative aspects of events, whether at a specific conference or corporate facilities at a sports event. This is 'a goose that lays golden eggs', as organizations all over the world, particularly in boom periods, entertain and pamper their productive employees, valuable clients and hard working executives with the intention of enhancing teamwork, leadership and communication skills.

Since this market is an economically significant one, it is advisable that event organizers pay particular attention here. Capable staff must be recruited and assigned to undertake the operation of corporate events and activities. Likewise, it is important to have a dedicated member of the organizing team assigned here to ensure that things run smoothly even if the main operation is contracted out. A wide range of amenities and facilities are often made available to guests in this category of high-level events. Such facilities may include, but are not necessarily limited to cloakrooms, welcome signage and high levels of comfort.

Whatever the type of event, the location of corporate services and hospitality must be such that the guests enjoy a premium view of the main activity or event. Corporate guests should be located in such a way that they will experience minimal difficulty in terms of access.

TRANSPORT

Almost all facets of events are transport-driven. This includes the transport of equipment to sites and the subsequent transport of attendees. For many events, arrangement for transporting attendees and equipment is a major part of the planning and operation process. This arrangement may span a range of areas and activities such as corporate transfer, study tours and other travel-related events. It becomes essential that managers of events are conversant with transport systems in the area where any given event is being held. For instance, suitability and interconnectivity of different modes of transport should be considerations. As there are various activities and status of individuals involved, managers need to consider a wide range of options available to them including the standards and availability of transport. Celebrities attending events are likely to need secure parking. Musical groups will all require parking for coaches. People visiting an event using public transport also need to be considered.

The transportation system comprises the carriage, motive power, terminal and way. Although an event manager has little or no influence on the quality of the road and terminal, the choice of carrying unit must be such that put the safety and comfort of the passengers at the top of the priority list. Consideration of the 'way' component of the transportation system is also important, particularly in terms of sustainability and corporate social responsibility. There are three main modes of transport: water, land and air. Ideally, the venue of an event will be accessible by at least one of the modes of transport identified. It is possible for a venue to be served by two or all of the three modes. Where this is the case, it is better for attendees to reach the event through many means and the likelihood of reduced strain on one mode. A good example of a multi-modal venue is the National Exhibition Centre (NEC) in Birmingham, UK, which is served by a railway station, excellent parking facilities and an airport.

There are numerous organizations that provide transport services. Such organizations include coaches, taxis and public companies to mention just a few, and most offer 'luxury' options to include executive cars, limousines, executive coaches and tour buses. While event managers may not be directly in charge of the operational running of transportation, the coordination of the transport of both people and equipment remains their responsibility.

International events with multiple venues require enormous efforts in coordinating attendees' transfer. This is not to say that small to medium sized events do not require effort in term of coordination of transportation. As a matter of fact, managers of small and medium-sized events have the opportunity of being creative with the way they go about transporting people. For instance the organizers of the European Union of Tourist Officers Conference in Nottingham in 2008 transferred the delegates from their hotel to the venues of the conference in buses running on biofuel. A guide on the bus provided a brief explanation on how the bus runs and its impact on the environment. This to some extent provided a discussion forum for some of the delegates and a lively environment generally for the duration of the trip.

In some other types of events, there may be a need to transport important personalities like politicians, celebrities and royals; in this case, a more appropriate means may be through an individual's private vehicle or through limousine transfer where the event organizers are responsible for getting the VIP to the venue. Whichever means they use in getting to the venue, it is advisable that the organizers provide a dedicated entrance that is fully manned to ensure their safety. Where the provision of a dedicated entrance is not feasible, organizers must ensure that the main entrance is kept clear at the time of their arrival and a secured space is provided for their vehicles. Parking for other attendees that might have travelled in their cars or group-hired vehicles is also important. More importantly, service routes and access for wheelchair users and other people with disabilities must be well managed. There are also an increasing number of events investigating public-transport-only options to get to venues, this will include the London 2012 Olympics and has been successfully implemented at the British Motorshow at the Excel venue in London.

In terms of movement of equipment, depending on the type of event, transport may range from simple one-van trips to the complex coordination of a fleet of trucks moving stages, sound equipment, electricity generators, bill boards, seats and other equipment. In some instances, the movement of specialist equipment, for example computer servers, scientific equipment, circus materials and animals (animals are not equipment in the real sense but they may be regarded as 'specialist equipment' here as most will have to be transported in a special way), may be involved. This 'equipment' needs to have arrived well before the start of the event. A special entrance and parking facility, fully manned by professionals, must be dedicated to them. The entrance must be kept clear to avoid delay in case some delivery or participants coming with their equipment run late. The Chelsea Flower Show in London has so many vans visiting during the run up to the show that a stacking system is coordinated 3 miles from the venue for contractors setting up show gardens.

General points to consider in terms of transport include:

- general access to the event location/site;
- emergency access to the event location/site;
- disabled access;
- pedestrian access;
- loading and staff access;
- traffic flow;
- drop-off/pick-up point;
- vehicle routing;
- public transport service;
- other transport infrastructure like parking, signage and lights; and
- other facilities – breakdown/towing service.

ACCOMMODATION

Part of the planning activity is to determine whether the event will involve participants' and attendees' accommodation and whose responsibility it is to organize, book and pay for this. In most cases, attendees are responsible for their own accommodation. Even then, it is important to ensure that attendees to overnight events are well accommodated, whether they are responsible for paying for their accommodation or not. The planners in their initial determination of location for an event, particularly one that requires an overnight stay, should consider the availability of appropriate accommodation if they want to optimize attendance and goodwill, and should investigate opportunities to offer accommodation and/or dining packages for event attendees in partnership with local businesses.

Often accommodation for special guests and some categories of participants is organized and paid for by the event organizer. Where hotel accommodation is involved, the guests would be informed, through their joining instructions, the name of the hotel, location and contact details including a website address for the guests to request any information not supplied. In some instances, delegates are given a list of hotels to choose from, often with negotiated discounts. Whatever the case, there is a need to detail a person who will oversee the coordination of accommodation as part of their responsibility, depending on the nature and size of the event. Special guests may value a special welcome. This is advisable, as it is a sign of courtesy and enhances goodwill between the guest and the event organizer. One of the major issues some big events have to address is accommodation. Where this is not considered, it may generate disaffection from some stakeholders such as residents of the area where the event is held and event attendees. Some events, particularly major festivals, provide motor homes for temporary accommodation, and many participants invest in their own motor homes. While this may avoid the need for the organizer to consider accommodation, they do need to think about parking!

PART D – THE BIG TIDY-UP

The saying 'it's not over until it's over' holds water in case of planning, staging and managing events. The event is not yet concluded until after the clean-up and event review. This final part of this chapter centres mainly on cleaning up and review and evaluation, the two parts that constitute event closedown.

THE BIG CLEAN-UP

The big clean-up is not limited to clearing rubbish and rearranging the event venue in readiness for the next event. If the meaning of cleaning up is restricted to this, some event organizers would not have to bother about cleaning. If an event took place in a hotel's function suite or conference hall, the hotel will be responsible for the physical cleaning. However, there are other things that need tidying up, such as returning hired equipment, paying outstanding bills, debriefing event staff, disposing of one-off equipment and so on.

From the above, it can be concluded that the big clean-up includes two main components: physical and administrative cleaning up. The scale of the event will determine the magnitude of cleaning up to do. For big events, it is advisable to have a schedule for clean-up. The first point of call would be a staff debrief. Event staff will have to understand that the event is not yet over until every cleaning up task is completed and should also understand that this stage is equally as important as all the others and affects the reputation of the organization. Tasks that have not been assigned because of oversight or because of new developments would have to be assigned to appropriate member of staff. Failure to clean up effectively may mean that the owners of the site will not allow the event to return in the future.

The next step is for everybody involved with the clean-up to get to work. Dismantling and removal would be necessary where temporary structures such as offices and stages are involved. Organizers need to bear this stage in mind when entering into agreement with contractors. A lack of detail and foresight can result in incurring unnecessary costs, which will affect the event budget eventually. A major musical event is an example where construction of temporary structures is inevitable. Obviously hired equipment has to be returned. It is important to know whose responsibility it is to return them, if there is any extra cost involved and/or if there is a refund of deposit due. At times, one-off equipment has to be disposed of or ownership may have to be transferred as part of the event legacy; in this case, a proper handing-over needs to be arranged.

Clearing up should be approached methodologically with health and safety in mind, as people are likely to be in a hurry to go after 'a hard day's work'. Stackable items should be properly stored and instructions for manual handling correctly observed when carrying and lifting. Managers and team leaders need to be on hand to supervise and assist where necessary. One thing that can give an event, particularly those held in public spaces, a bad image with the local people and government is the issue of rubbish. Removal of rubbish needs adequate supervision; a manager should be assigned to inspect the site after this has been completed. Ideally not only does rubbish need to be removed, but recycling should be encouraged.

REVIEW AND EVALUATION

Event evaluation is concerned with observing, measuring and monitoring the implementation of an event so that its outcome and implementation process can be accurately assessed.

'It matters not where you begin the process. It is essential that every phase be considered, visited and understood' (Goldblatt, 2002, p. 56). The event review and evaluation process is intrinsically linked to the event planning process. It is a strategic necessity for the achievement of organizational goals and event success. Evaluation may involve components/parts of event processes or a comprehensive review of all phases. In this case, the primary concern is with a comprehensive post event evaluation in alignment with the event objectives.

The determinants of effective event evaluation include:

- the event objectives;
- time frame;
- performance indicators; and
- the design of evaluation process.

Often event evaluation is constrained by cost, a lack of sufficient time, knowledge of importance/usefulness of evaluation and the requirements of stakeholders. Efficient design of event evaluation provides organizers the opportunities to ascertain the effectiveness of the event and learn how to improve on their performance. Collecting and processing the right type of data in this sense cannot be overemphasized. Managers can use either of the two main approaches: quantitative or qualitative, for gathering and analysing data. Both can also be used together in the evaluation of an event. Specific methods that can be used include:

- observation;
- surveys;
- interviews;
- focus group; and
- impact assessment.

Data analysis is an important aspect of this process and requires knowledge and dedication. Quantitative methods will require the knowledge of statistical techniques. On the other hand, analysing qualitative data will require such data to be broken down into themes; these could be based solely on the established performance indicators or other criteria that may be determined by the situation or by key stakeholders. In some cases, the evaluation may be required to be reported in written form. It is advisable that organizers keep record of reports, as they are sources of rich information to guide future events.

Factors to consider in reporting evaluation include the following:

- user specificity;
- reader friendliness;
- timing;
- ethical considerations;
- accuracy; and
- coverage of key aspects of the event.

A full discussion of event evaluation is included in Chapters 10 and 11.

SUMMARY

As identified at the start of this chapter, operations management cannot stand alone as a management tool and it is closely integrated with every function of the event. What this chapter has demonstrated clearly is the scale and scope of operations management. Everything that has been discussed here relates to any size of event. Events provide an exciting operational challenge and it is in the delivery of operations management that success or failure will be delivered. Events managers must have a keen eye for detail and an ability to lead and manage teams to be successful in this role.

FURTHER READING

To read more about operations management:
Slack, N., Chamber, S. and Johnston, R. (2007) *Operations Management*, 5th edn. Prentice Hall, Harlow, UK.

For current events:
The Event Magazine available at: http://www.theeventmagazine.com/

For event planning:
Special Events Magazine available at: http://specialevents.com/

REVIEW QUESTIONS

1. Given everything you have read in this chapter, what are the biggest challenges for the events industry?
2. Considering your answer to question 1, what events do you feel are the lowest risk to manage?
3. Design an events management plan for an event of your choice.
4. Write a contingency plan for a major music festival.

ACKNOWLEDGEMENT

The authors are grateful to Lexie Mathieson from Auckland University of Technology for providing case study material for this chapter.

REFERENCES

Bowdin, G.A.J., McDonnell, I., Allen, J. and O'Toole, W. (2001) *Events Management*. Butterworth Heinemann, Oxford.

Bowdin, G.A.J., Allen, J., O'Toole, W., Harris, R. and McDonnell, I. (2006) *Events Management*, 2nd edn. Elsevier Butterworth-Heinemann, Oxford.

Burke, R. (2006) *Project Management: Planning and Control Techniques*. John Wiley & Sons, Chichester, UK.

Goldblatt, J. (1997) *Special Events: Best Practices in Modern Event Management*. CAB International, Wallingford, UK.

Goldblatt, J. (2002) *Special Events: Twenty-First Century Events Management*, 3rd edn. John Wiley & Sons, New York.

Greasley, A. (2006) *Operations Management*. John Wiley & Sons, Chichester, UK.

Heizer, J. and Render, B. (2006) *Principles of Operations Management*, 6th edn. Prentice Hall, Englewood Cliffs, New Jersey.

Hill, T. (2005) *Operations Management*, 2nd edn. Palgrave Macmillan, Basingstoke, UK.

Masterman, G. (2004) *Strategic Sports Event Management: an International Approach*. Elsevier Butterworth-Heinemann, London.

Naylor, J. (2002) *Introduction to Operations Management*, 2nd edn. Pearson Education, Harlow, UK.

Page, S.J. (2003) *Tourism Management: Managing for Change*. Butterworth Heinemann, Oxford.

Pender, L. and Sharpley, R. (eds) (2005) *The Management of Tourism*. Sage Publications, London.

Sanchez, N., Miller, J., Sanchez, A. and Brooks, B. (1995) Applying expert system technology to implementation of a forecasting model in food service. *Hospitality Research Journal* 18/19, 25–37.

Shone, A. and Parry, B. (2004) *Successful Events Management: a Practical Handbook*, 2nd edn. Thomson Learning, London.

Singh, P.J. (2008) What is operations management and why is it important? In: Samson, D. and Singh, P.J. (eds) *Operations Management: an Integrated Approach*. Cambridge University Press, Port Melbourne, pp. 3–36.

Slack, N., Chamber, S. and Johnston, R. (2007) *Operations Management*, 5th edn. Prentice Hall, Harlow, UK.

Tassiopoulos, D. and Damster, G. (eds) (2004) *Event Management: a Professional and Developmental Approach*, 2nd edn. Juta Academic, Landsdowne, South Africa.

Tum, J., Norton, P. and Wright, J. (2006) *Management of Event Operations*. Butterworth Heinemann, Oxford.

Van Weelbek, B. (2004) Crisis management: could you cope if the unthinkable happened? Available at: http://www.hospitalitynet.org/news/4016241 (accessed May 2004).

Waters, D. (1996) *Operations Management*. Addison-Wesley, Harlow, UK.

Yeoman, I., Robertson, M. and McMahon-Beattie, U. (2004a) Visitor management for festivals and events. In: Yeoman, I., Robertson, M., Ali-Knight, J., Drummond, S. and McMahon-Beattie, U. (eds) *Festival and Event Management: an International Arts and Culture Perspective*. Elsevier Butterworth-Heinemann, Oxford.

Yeoman, I., Robertson, M., Ali-Knight, J., Drummond, S. and McMahon-Beattie, U. (eds) (2004b) *Festival and Event Management: an International Arts and Culture Perspective*. Elsevier Butterworth-Heinemann, Oxford.

chapter 6

Successful Staffing of Events

Sine Heitmann and Christine Roberts

OBJECTIVES OF THE CHAPTER

This chapter provides an overview of the management of people at events by introducing the various elements involved in human resource management (HRM). First, human resource planning (HRP) is outlined, alongside the need for strategic alignment between the human 'resource' and the event itself. Secondly, the chapter introduces volunteers as a unique and crucial group of employees within the events industry. Constituents of effective staff management are then reviewed, namely recruitment and selection practices, performance management, employee motivation and welfare policies.

The objectives of the chapter are to:

- discuss the importance of effective HRM;
- explain how recruitment, selection and training policies improve performance management; and
- explain how employee motivation can reduce labour turnover.

INTRODUCTION

Working within the events industry is significantly different from that of other industries, in that motivations for work, job roles and length of service are all largely heterogeneous. Given the large scale of event typologies and the way in which the industry has evolved, it is fair to suggest that the variety of events and subsequent job roles within events are limitless; however, typified careers within this domain exist for conference and banqueting, wedding planners, festivals organizers, sales, security, venue managers, theatre and arts and event managers. This diversity of jobs results in a range of different needs when it comes to managing the employees and coordinating the various event areas and their staff. Additionally, a hefty proportion of events industry workers participate on a voluntary basis. Reasons for work, therefore, cannot be primarily justified through the desire for economic returns but rather the desire for acquisition of experience, achievement, involvement in an area of interest or good cause all contribute towards reasons for work of this nature.

This chapter will introduce general ideas on the management of human resources (HR) within an event and look at the challenges that are presented to an event manager, be that as part of the banqueting department of a hotel, a conference centre, a local community-run charity event or a mega sports event. First, the chapter looks at the strategic importance of HRM and planning of staff within the events industry. Secondly, key HRM practices are introduced, such as recruitment, selection and performance management. Finally, this chapter provides an overview of key welfare policies that are relevant to the event manager.

HUMAN RESOURCE MANAGEMENT FOR EVENTS

As highlighted by the HRM cycle (Fig. 6.1), HRM is concerned with attracting, developing and retaining suitable employees for an event. This process applies to any industry, and in order to effectively manage HR, organizations need to establish recruitment and selection procedures, performance management policies and employee motivation strategies. When considering events, however, there are two specific requirements that differentiate HRM from other industries.

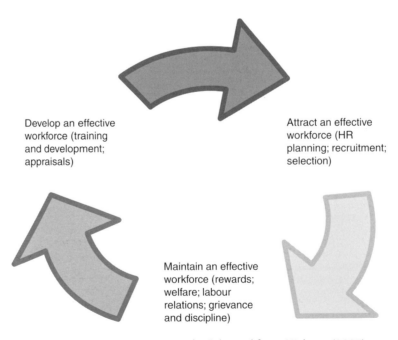

Develop an effective workforce (training and development; appraisals)

Attract an effective workforce (HR planning; recruitment; selection)

Maintain an effective workforce (rewards; welfare; labour relations; grievance and discipline)

Fig. 6.1. Human resource management cycle. Adapted from Nickson (2007).

First, events have a 'pulsating' organizational structure, which means that as the event approaches the volume of staff required vastly increases, and then decreases ever more speedily once the event is drawn to a close (Hanlon and Jago, 2004). This means that most employment offered at events is short-term in nature and staff are required to work to tight deadlines.

Secondly, the majority of events rely heavily on volunteer employment to the extent that without these individuals, many events would cease to exist. This type of workforce has to be managed differently from paid employees without compromising on fair treatment (Van Der Wagen, 2007).

These two challenges will be discussed throughout the chapter to highlight the unique nature of HRM at events. Before detailing the various elements of HRM, preparatory stages (i.e. HRP) have to be considered.

PLANNING FOR STAFF

HRP plays a significant role in the success of any event and poses a key question to event managers: do we have the right amount of people with the right skills at the right time and at the right price? Within the events industry, the role of an employee stems wider than merely providing manpower for the delivery of an event; careful selection of staff members also contributes to conveying a message and legacy of the event itself. The strategic perspective of HRM and HRP therefore requires that staff requirements be aligned with the overall objectives and the legal necessities of the event.

If costs need to be contained, effective staff management can contribute by improving staff/volunteer productivity, reducing absenteeism or decreasing staff numbers. If the quality of an event needs to be improved, managers may consider adopting improved recruitment and selection processes, expanding training opportunities, increasing number of staff, and providing more attractive benefits and rewards. If organizational effectiveness needs improving, better job design, changes to organizational structure or improved team working could be possible solutions (Bowdin *et al.*, 2006). This may all be achieved through careful staffing methods, and HRP can provide essential information at the beginning of an event. The following provides an overview on what is involved in HRP.

Just as any planning requires forecasting, prediction and estimates, planning for events is no different. Information has to be gathered at the very beginning of the planning process (see Chapters 2 and 5). The first stage requires the HR manager to analyse the labour markets (both internal and external to the organization). The internal labour market includes existing staff and volunteers and helps the event organizers to establish whether there is already a pool of staff available at their disposal, thus determining the HR supply.

Having the right number of staff is a crucial factor as too many staff can reduce profit, but too few staff can result in a below average outcome, and legal issues such as licences, fire regulations and security may also determine both required numbers of staff, and also the right number of staff with the correct qualifications. Generally, the right estimate is based on managerial judgement from past experience, but simple calculations can help in this process.

An event manager should not only look out for the right amount of staff, but also needs to look at the quality of staff and assess whether s/he has the right type of staff with the right skills. The catering for an event requires staff to have a background in hospitality, whereas stewards need to be good in conflict management and the marketing staff needs to have good sales skills.

These discussions can go into further detail depending on the event in question. If there are any shortages in staff (quantitative or qualitative), the external labour market is assessed in order to cater for these demands. At this point, considerations for recruitment and selection as well as training and development policies become important, which will be discussed later. While a small-scale local event can draw on volunteering staff from the local community, a wedding requires more professionally trained staff. A large-scale mega-event needs much longer planning for the numbers of volunteers that are needed. The London 2012 Olympics started recruiting for volunteers in 2009, whereas the core committee and permanent staff had been recruited much earlier.

Professional, well-established events like the Olympics or event departments within a hotel have the background and experience to establish a suitable organization structure. Should an event be organized and operated by a local community, it is most likely that virtually all staff will be volunteers, with any financial payment to selected individuals being quite negligible. In these situations, the organizational structure of the workforce is largely self-enforced and self-managed; role selection, authority and commitment are at liberty of the individual and general socialization into the committee group. For example, the Peter-and-Paul-Festival (see Chapter 9) is a community run festival in which a local committee organizes and coordinates the various aspects of the festival and more than 3000 locals are volunteering their time to make the festival a success. While there is the equivalent of an organizational structure, it is less formalized.

Questions

- Use an event that you are familiar with and look at the objectives – what kind of employees would you look for to employ? What skills and qualities do these employees need?
- Use the Internet to identify a hotel with a conference department or a well known mega-event like Glastonbury or the Olympics – what kind of organizational structure have they got in place? How are duties and responsibilities allocated?

As the internal and external labour market analysis has to take paid and unpaid workers into account, the question of outsourcing has to be considered. As events have a particular demand cycle for staff ('pulsating effect'), many event organization employ agencies to conduct the recruitment of additional staff, particularly in the case of volunteers. Shortages in skilled areas such as catering or security can be remedied through the use of outsourcing or contracting agencies that have a pool of staff available for specific events. Other large-scale events such as Glastonbury work together with the charity organization Oxfam, which recruits volunteers for the festival (see Box 6.2).

Based on the labour market analysis, an organization is able to draw up an HR operational plan or personnel management action programme, which includes a more comprehensive strategy to contribute towards further questions, such as:

1. 'How do we attract new employees?' – Recruitment and selection plans can be implemented, which includes job analysis, job descriptions, person specifications, recruitment policies and selection practices.

2. 'Once we have attracted new employees, how do we make sure that they are doing the required job?' – Training policies and schedules can be drawn up to induct, train and develop new and existing staff, ensuring that they deliver the goals and objectives of the event.

3. 'How do we make sure that staff are at the right place and the right time?' – Logistics have to be taken into account and this is where events differ from other organizations because of a more complex rota.

4. 'How do we make sure that performance is managed and adequately recognized?' – Performance management and recognition policies are needed which detail motivational techniques, rewards and pay.

The most important role of HRM within events planning is the integration of multiple projects with different timelines, which all require HR aspects such as staffing, development of policies and procedures, training and performance management, alongside rewards and recognition. While in most cases these projects have similar requirements, some have more specific demands. For example, training has to be provided to any project groups, but the team that prepares the event site has to start earlier than the catering or security team. Similarly, the training of staff, particularly volunteers, often adheres to differentiated timescales; dependent on the nature of the job role, volunteers may be required to attend training well in advance of an event, or merely turn up on the day of the event and be present in briefing sessions. Strategic integration of HRM should highlight these requirements alongside directing the most effective way in which to manage such multiple tasks. Integrating the efforts of all personnel is essential in order to achieve a cohesive workforce.

Questions

- Consider the Gantt chart in Chapter 5 on event planning and identify the different project groups. At what points would you include HR planning, recruitment and training for staff?
- Consider the forecasting techniques in Chapter 5 (under capacity management) – which ones can you apply for HR forecasting and planning? Which one do you think is the most suitable one?
- Using an event that you are familiar with, go through the event planning process and identify how many staff you need at each point and for each project group.

VOLUNTEERISM

The events industry relies on volunteers and volunteers are important in terms of continuity and success. Volunteering is unpaid and individuals may participate in a large array of job roles, including fundraising, promotion, administration duties such as registering participants and updating records, organizing events, committee work, first aid and warden duties. A sports event, for example, may require scorers, referees and registrars, where a festival may require ushers, merchandise sales, backstage runners and hospitality. Unlike the relationship with paid employees, the reliance on volunteerism has resulted in unusual power relationships observed between volunteers and management.

Consideration must be paid to the event typology and the kind of volunteers it may attract. Volunteers in general are more likely to be female, aged between 16 and 19 years, holding no formal qualifications; however, the characteristics of event volunteers are slightly more complex. On a global scale, it is often observed that volunteers reflect the characteristics of the people the event aims to attract. Sports events, for example, tend to attract high numbers of young, male volunteers. For example, almost 200,000 of the 320,000 volunteers that applied for the Beijing 2008 Olympics were students. Additionally, the job typology has shown to attract patterns of volunteer characteristics, for example, older populations tend to volunteer more for administrative, secretarial and committee job roles (Ralston *et al.*, 2005). Volunteers are generally local residents to the area of which the event is held, often sporting a genuine interest in the cause. The aims, therefore, are to recruit a regular supply of volunteers, training and develop their abilities and sustain their involvement to ensure the continuation of the event. These patterns of participation can be considered for effective marketing and recruitment of volunteers.

Volunteer mobility is relatively high, whereby entering and exiting employment occurs far more rapidly. Managers therefore, cannot expect the same level of commitment from volunteers as paid staff. A successful relationship between managers and volunteers hinges on agreed levels of satisfaction, preferably built into events management objectives. It is essential, therefore, that organizations understand and accentuate motivations as experienced by the volunteer, as discussed in Box 6.1.

Box 6.1. XVII Commonwealth Games, Manchester.

In May 2001, HR recruiters initiated a large-scale publicity initiative aiming to employ 10,000 volunteers to assist in the operation of the Manchester Commonwealth Games. This highly challenging task was achieved through tactical target marketing within catchment areas that: (i) share the characteristics of typical volunteers; and (ii) were most likely to benefit from the volunteer scheme. The initiative was largely aimed at areas suffering deprivation and/or social exclusion, ensuring an allocation of at least 1000 volunteer opportunities filled by these community groups. Volunteers were encouraged to participate by the training opportunities that would further their own prospects within employment. They were able to work towards and achieve accredited qualifications (such as health and safety, teamwork, first aid, customer care and host nation training), alongside gaining valuable work-based experience within a variety of events industry pursuits, such as stewarding, security, catering, medical assistance, tourist assistance and even operational job roles. Additionally, volunteers were given the opportunity to work alongside those with similar sporting interests in support of the internationally acclaimed event.

Volunteer feedback demonstrated positivity, with comments suggesting that the experience was worthwhile and unforgettable; their involvement was fun and rewarding. It was evident that the friendly, enthusiastic nature of the volunteers was gratefully received and noted by a number of athletes and spectators. Moreover, the passion and hard work of the volunteers were acknowledged by the media, resulting in an improved, positive image of the residents of Manchester. In addition, the profound attention led to high levels of interest from local government and a number of key funding bodies.

Financial support was later offered to the city to encourage the continuation of volunteers' initiatives. This resulted in the formation of the Manchester Event Volunteers (MEV) group, which has continued to run successfully. The purpose and aims of the MEV are: to ensure a continuation of volunteer recruitment within the city, while providing positive and rewarding experiences; through provision of accredited qualifications and experience, provide accessible routes back into paid employment for volunteers; create opportunities for community-supportive job roles, such as community officers, further events, sports club coaches, and continued growth of the volunteer database.

(Continued)

Box 6.1. Continued.

The success of the MEV has since secured additional funding from central government, alongside interest from international, national and regional bodies. The Games, alongside MEV, have demonstrated a correlation between volunteering opportunities and regeneration, education and employment. In addition, there is also provision for experienced volunteers to train, team lead and mentor new volunteers, thus ensuring a continuation of volunteer support and event sustainability.

Source: Manchester City Council (2009)

Having outlined the HRP process and the role of volunteers within events, the event organization can start the recruitment and selection process.

RECRUITMENT AND SELECTION

Having established the demand for additional HR, the recruitment and selection process starts. Recruitment is concerned with attracting applicants to a job, whereas selection is concerned with choosing the right person among the applicants. Recruiting a person involves several stages (Fig. 6.2).

The job analysis identifies the nature and purpose of the job. A job analysis can be carried out by using focus groups, questionnaires, interviews and similar research among existing employees and managers in order to establish the exact requirements, duties and conditions of a particular job. This forms the basis for the job description and person specification. While the job description explains the detail of the job in terms of duties (such as the job title, tasks involved, work environment, working conditions, reporting relationships, salary and rewards, performance standards), the person specification outlines the ideal candidate that is to be

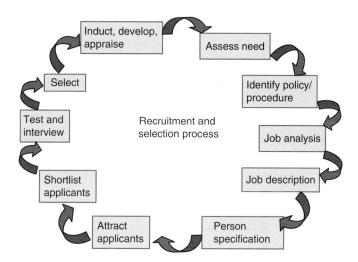

Fig. 6.2. Recruitment and selection process.

appointed to the job. Skills, knowledge, specific competencies and attributes are just a few aspects of which the person specification aims to review. These documents are comparable to marketing materials as the organization seeks to attract the most suitable and qualified employees. Paying attention to detailed information regarding job requirements is also necessary, as a recruitment campaign has to attract the right amount of people suitable for the job. If a job advert is not adequately specific in its requirements for the post, it is likely that larger numbers of potential employees will apply and be selected for interview, resulting in increased time and effort required for the selection process. If, however, the specification is too demanding, the organization may deter desirable applicants. The question of where to advertise a job is equally important, as this will undoubtedly affect the type of individuals applying.

Box 6.2. Oxfam – Shift leader job description.

The Shift leader is stationed in the Oxbox (the Oxfam HQ Portakabin) and is responsible for the smooth running of the shift. Each shift may consist of between 50 and 200 people and you will have a management team of a maximum of 5 people to assist you. Duties include:

- Overseeing shift change over – ensuring there are adequate staffing levels in all locations and that each location has supervision;
- Taking immediate responsibility for the health & safety and welfare of all stewards on that shift;
- Acting as liaison between Oxfam and the festival organisers in the absence of the Stewards Coordinator;
- Dealing with any queries over the radio from the gates/steward locations;
- Coordinating with the Comms team to ensure emergency situations are immediately communicated to the relevant agencies;
- Coordinating with the festival production teams to maintain site (and therefore public) safety (reporting on facilities and services);
- Assisting the Oxfam Stewards Coordinator to manage a response to a major incident;
- Reallocating stewards to other areas to fill gaps and boost steward numbers during busier periods;
- Keeping adequate paperwork – ensuring that all stewards on shift have been signed in/out and recording any changes to the staffing lists, logging radio usage, and signing in/out equipment;
- Managing one or two deputy shift leaders and one or two drivers;
- Ensuring that refreshments – tea/coffee and water – and supplies – hats, ponchos, sun block – are distributed to the stewards' positions;
- Answering queries posed by off-duty stewards, i.e. shift changes, lost tabards/laminate passes, lost property, illness, etc.;
- Recording all incidents/accidents and carrying out any follow-ups required;
- Anything else that may arise (in the nature of festivals!).

In order to carry out this job, you need to:

- Have had extensive experience in festival supervision, and have previously volunteered as a supervisor or deputy shift leader (or shift leader);
- Be flexible;
- Be confident;

(Continued)

Box 6.2. Continued.

- Enjoy strategic planning;
- Have good management skills;
- Have a good memory;
- Feel confident using a radio;
- Cope well under pressure and in stressful situations;
- Be willing to make decisions quickly.

Reprinted with permission from Oxfam (2010)

Acquiring of employees and volunteers can be done through referral by other employees, the Internet (such as the company's own website or online notice boards), recruitment agencies, newspaper advertising, or approaching specific associations and clubs. While the Internet has made job advertisements and applications more accessible, this often adds to issues relating to high volumes of applications. Colleges and universities are useful places to look for eager students wishing to gain work experience during their studies. Events such as the Olympics or the Edinburgh Festival use their websites to call for volunteer applications with much success in attracting interest, whereas the UK charity Oxfam works together with music festivals across the country (e.g. Glastonbury, Leeds/Reading) to recruit volunteers to work as stewards, steward supervisors and similar jobs (see Box 6.3). Generally, local community events experience greater problems attracting suitable volunteers.

Box 6.3. Oxfam application.

Volunteer for Oxfam at festivals – Application form
Personal details
*Please ensure all mandatory fields are filled.

Title:	**Gender*:**	❑ Female	❑ Male
First name*:	**Last name*:**	**Date of Birth*:**	(e.g. DD/MM/YYYY)
Postcode (UK only):		**Address*:**	
Town*:		**Country*:**	
Phone number (Please supply at least one)*:		**E-mail*:**	

❑ **Please tick if you are a competent First Aider**. (This is to allow us to provide First Aid cover for Oxfam stewards, not for members of the public.)

Please provide details of a contact in case of emergency: This should not be someone with you at the festival. We have had trouble contacting people on site, due to poor mobile phone coverage. In an emergency situation, contacting someone off site can be much easier and quicker.

Please provide details of your doctor/GP: This information will only be passed to medical personnel in case of emergency. ❑ I give my permission for Oxfam to store my doctor's/GP's details in case of emergency. I understand that this information will be held confidentially and only used if absolutely necessary.*

(Continued)

Box 6.3. Continued.

Are you connected with Oxfam in any of the following ways:

❑ Oxfam employee / ❑ Shop volunteer / ❑ Office volunteer / ❑ Monthly donor / ❑ Campaigner

Eating requirements: We provide meal tickets during the festival and try to cater for everyone. In order to ensure we meet your requirements, please indicate whether you are a*:

❑ Meat eater / ❑ Vegetarian / ❑ Vegan / ❑ Other (please specify)

Are you colour blind?* ❑ Yes   ❑ No

Please give details of any disability or medical condition we should be aware of.

Equal Opportunities: How would you describe yourself (ethnic origin)?

Do you have any unspent criminal convictions?*   ❑ Yes ❑ No

For information on what constitutes a spent or un-spent criminal conviction, please visit the Nacro Disclosures Service.

Referee Details:

❑ If you have worked at two or more festivals for Oxfam, you do not need to provide a reference – please tick the box and proceed. ❑ If you have worked at only one festival for Oxfam, or have never stewarded for Oxfam, then you need to provide details of a referee. This should be someone suitable who is not related to you, i.e. your employer or college tutor, or someone connected to Oxfam.

First name*:   **Last name*:**   **Referee e-mail*:**

Company*:   **Position held*:**   **Daytime tel.*:**

Your referee will be contacted automatically by e-mail once you have submitted your application. If there is any issue with your reference, we will contact you; you do not need to contact us.

Where did you hear about festival volunteering?* ❑ Word of Mouth / ❑ E-mail / ❑ Website / ❑ Letter / ❑ RAG / ❑ Volunteering organisation / ❑ Other

Training course details: We are providing three-hour training sessions around the country and we encourage you to attend one. If you have never stewarded before, your role will be much easier, so book now to secure your place! We would not expect you to travel more than an hour from your home, so if there is not a session near you, we will ensure that you have all the information you need before you start your stewarding duties. We are offering two different types of stewards training (Glastonbury and non-Glastonbury), and also supervisor training. Please make sure your training session is before your first festival.

Glastonbury Festival details: Please supply details of your availability, travel plans and shift partners.

Availability: ❑ I am available to steward from Tuesday to Monday*

Our stewarding team must be available for the full onsite dates including Monday. If you cannot steward on Monday, please tick this box, but also tick the box below to say you cannot work the late shift so we don't allocate you a shift on Monday or overnight Sunday.

(Continued)

Box 6.3. Continued.

❏ I am not available to work the late shift on Monday.

❏ I would like to arrive on Monday and have my own transport.

Travel information: How will you be coming to Glastonbury?*

If you are driving what is your vehicle registration number:

Children: ❏ If you are bringing a child or children under 18 years of age please tick here.

We will send you the relevant form to complete. If your child or children are aged 13–18 you'll need to register for tickets through normal Glastonbury channels.

Shift Partners: If you wish to work your shifts at the same time as your friends and family, please provide their details below. This does not guarantee you will be working together on the same shift, but we will try to accommodate your requests wherever possible. We can only do this if you provide the following information.* We require your shift partner's date of birth to match you with them. We use this information for no other purpose.

Supervisory role: ❏ Please tick this box if you would like to apply for a supervisory role at any of the festivals you have chosen. Please read the supervisor job descriptions and fill in the form below. Supervisors will be required to work 3 × 8¼ hour shifts.

Preferred role/position at the festivals you are applying for*: (Please be precise as our rostering will be informed by this information, e.g. Glastonbury – Supervisor – Staff camping.) We are keen to allocate supervisory positions to past supervisors or experienced stewards.

Have you previously worked as a Supervisor for Oxfam?* ❏ Yes ❏ No

If Yes, please state your most recent experience first. (Festival/Year/Role/Position)

If No, please detail relevant supervisory experience:

Declaration

Please read 2009 Standards of Behaviour and Volunteer Policy for Festival Stewards.

❏ I confirm that I have read and understood that if my behaviour falls outside of these standards, it will lead to my eviction from site and my deposit being forfeit.

Reprinted with permission from Oxfam (2010)

Questions

- Look at the application form for Oxfam and consider the reason for each question – why are applicants required to provide the information?
- If you were to recruit staff for events – what questions would you ask? Give reasons.

The next stage to consider is the selection process. This may be achieved through a variety of methods, including interviews (individual or group) or numerous other activities performed within assessment centres (Table 6.1). As with recruitment, the approach to selection will reflect the organizational strategy and philosophy towards their employees. The selection process has the main aim of differentiating between the candidates and predicting as far as possible their future performance at work. Decisions are not necessarily based on the qualifications but on the person's attitude and approach to the job. HR Departments usually offer training for anyone involved in the recruitment and selection process, as procedures have to be documented to ensure equal opportunities are adhered to (see below).

Table 6.1. Selection methods.

Selection method	Staff involved
(Un)structured interviews	Line manager
Intelligence and personality testing (psychometric testing)	Senior manager
Work sampling	Functional managers HR staff
Assessment centres (e.g. team-working exercises)	Recruitment consultant
Desk exercise (e.g. letter writing, calculations)	
Presentations	
Group interviews	

Questions

- What skills are being tested by each one of these methods?
- Which one of these methods do you consider to be the most effective for the post of an event manager, event assistant manager and volunteer?
- Considering that events like the Olympics require 100,000 volunteers, how would you organize recruitment on such a large scale?

Considering recruitment and selection of paid employees and volunteers, the process is similar; however, there are some key differences that are to be taken into account. If a hotel is seeking a permanent events manager for their conferencing and banqueting department, the process of doing a job analysis, coming up with a job description and setting up a interview, possibly combined with a presentation, will be much more rigorous, as the appointment will be more permanent and needs to be more focused to make sure that the right candidate is hired. Recruiting and selecting volunteers are more likely to take place on a larger scale as a higher number of staff is recruited for only a limited period.

Whether looking at the short-term recruitment of volunteers or the long-term selection of permanent paid staff, it has to be highlighted that the recruitment and selection process within in any organization is a continuous process, which needs to be adjusted constantly. Redundancies, retirement and more general changes to the workforce have to be considered and result in a rolling programme for recruitment and selection. The more effective recruitment and selection procedures are, the less ad hoc and firefighting approaches are needed, which can waste the manager's valuable time needed for other aspects of events management.

PERFORMANCE MANAGEMENT

Performance management is a strategic and integrated approach that assures the success of an organization. This already starts with the planning as well as the recruitment and selection process as HR must be matched to the organization's overall mission and objectives. However, more attention is paid here to three further essential aspects of HRM, namely motivation, training and development, and appraisal or evaluation. While motivation looks at the theoretical underpinning and how this can be applied to the workplace, training and appraisals give more concrete ideas in how to manage HR effectively. The latter two aspects fulfil different roles in contributing to the overall success of an events company by managing the performance of each individual employee.

Motivation

Motivation is a phenomenon experienced differently by each individual, and can be loosely defined as the reason behind initiating and performing voluntary behaviour. These behaviours are goal-directed and may be divided into two important factors: the primary incentive that created a particular motive (arousal), and the route and intensity with which an individual chooses to engage in a particular behaviour (direction or choice of behaviour). These behaviour choices can be further subcategorized into ends versus means, based on the individual's reasons behind a particular behaviour. Ends refer to an individual performing behaviour for reasons none other than desire to engage in that behaviour; for example, an individual who participates in a running event for the sheer desire and enjoyment of running. Means refer to the participation in a behaviour for its instrumental value; for example, an individual who goes running to increase fitness or train for a specific running event. Motivational theories, therefore, attempt to predict behaviour; and where industry is concerned, theories provide scope for the manipulation of an individual's actions in order to increase productivity, economic returns or the underlying cause of the event itself.

Work-based motivation is a well-researched and highly lucrative phenomenon, whereby theoretical underpinning is extensive and often contested. However, the majority of research falls into the camp of 'content' theories, whereby interest is directed at specific factors that motivate individuals (Bowdin *et al.*, 2006). These may be tangible aspects such as pay, benefits and material goods, alongside intangible aspects including satisfaction, status and development. Because of the reliance on volunteerism and the very nature of the events industry itself, the impact of social factors, desire for affiliation and accumulation of friendship as factors increasing motivation are highly important.

One of the more predominant work-based motivational theories is Herzberg's Two-Factor Theory. Hertzberg theorized that factors causing dissatisfaction are different from those causing satisfaction, terming satisfiers as 'motivators' (such as recognition, achievement, empowerment and growth) and dissatisfiers as 'hygiene' factors (e.g. work conditions, salary and supervision). The word 'hygiene' was used to describe maintenance factors that, when present, avoid dissatisfaction but do not actually lead to satisfaction. Simultaneously, the absence of motivators does not necessarily result in dissatisfaction. Hence, satisfaction and dissatisfaction are not two polar opposites but separate issues independently affected by work-based stimuli. Hertzberg further explained this by describing that humans have two distinct types of needs referred to as physiological needs (fulfilled by hygiene factors such as money, security, food and shelter) and psychological factors (fulfilled by actions that lead to self-development and growth). The absence of one of these factors will not affect the other (Fig. 6.3).

Another useful motivational theory is the expectancy theory by Vroom (Van Der Wagen, 2007), who argues that crucial to employee motivation is the perception of a link between effort and reward. In a very simple way, this link can be thought of as a process that employees first calculate whether there is a connection between effort and reward, and secondly, the probability that high performance will lead to rewards (Fig. 6.4).

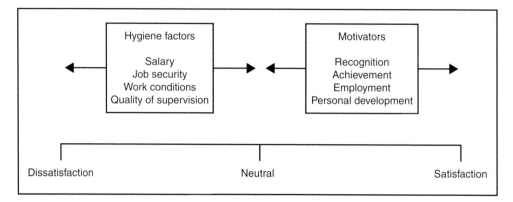

Fig. 6.3. Herzberg Two-Factor Model. Adapted from Bowdin *et al.* (2006).

Fig. 6.4. Expectancy theory of motivation. Adapted from Van Der Wagen (2007).

Questions

- Apply these theories to paid employees and volunteers – what aspects are the predominant motivators for each type of employee? How would you manage expectations?
- Herzberg's model has been developed from Maslow's hierarchy of needs – how has it been expanded? How would you apply Maslow's hierarchy of needs to both paid employees and volunteers?
- See rewards below – what kind of rewards would match which of the hygiene factors/motivators?
- Given the difference between paid employees and volunteers – how important do you consider money as a motivator?

Motivation of volunteers

The unique nature of volunteerism lends itself to alternative reasons for participation that do not encompass monetary rewards. Volunteer motivation has been largely researched within the events industry, leading to numerous identified categories of underlying incentives for participation. Monga's (2006) five-dimensional model identifies the explanatory concepts of this phenomenon, known as: affiliatory, altruistic, instrumental, egotistical and solidary motivations. Affiliatory motivation refers to the individual's affiliation or attachment to the specific event. This form of motivation towards volunteering at an event is often observed in those who have previously worked for the cause for which the event is aimed, for example, a former art director volunteering as an arts festival committee member because of long-term service and genuine appreciation of the arts. Altruistic motivation refers to the individual's uncalculated concern for others or the desire to support societal causes. This form of motivation is often attributed to those volunteering at charitable events, whereby the individual has genuine sympathy/empathy for those the charity strives to aid. Instrumental motivation identifies aspects of self-interest in participation, such as the acquisition of new skills, career progression or learned experiences. This is a very logical and self-oriented reason for volunteering, whereby the individual chooses to volunteer for the purposes of personal gain, for example, an individual aspiring to work within the music industry who chooses to volunteer in a music festival for the purposes of gaining experience, credibility and potentially, training and qualifications. Egotistical motivation encompasses the satisfaction derived from achieving goals and being instrumental in terms of the event's success. These individuals are believed to volunteer out of a desire to be an important part of the event's triumph and the psychological experience of self-worth, ability to achieve and recognition of these achievements. Lastly, solidary motivation refers to the enjoyment of social interaction and engagement among people with similar interests. For example, a keen tennis player may wish to volunteer at the Wimbledon Tennis Championships out of years of tennis enthusiasm and the desire to socialize with those who share that enthusiasm. In the case of a local community event like the Peter-and-Paul-Festival (see Chapter 9) the locals volunteer in the festival because they are interested in their own local heritage, enjoy the gregariousness that comes with the event and develop new skills when representing historical aspects of their city's past.

Labour turnover

Motivation undoubtedly affects not only work productivity but also the amount of staff leaving an establishment, causing the need for replacements. This process is referred to as labour turnover, which is expressed as the number of staff leaving an establishment in proportion to the workforce as a whole. An increased level of labour turnover is an exceptionally unwanted affair, whereby the repeated recruitment and retraining of staff is financially damaging, as well as the effects turnover has on staff morale and overall work productivity. Effective recruitment and selection procedures, alongside motivational strategies are the key to reducing the volume of labour turnover. Conversely, the innate nature of the events industry, through the need for sessional, seasonal and casual staff, lends itself to higher rates of labour turnover. This is simply related to fast-paced creation and termination of perishable job requirements and most certainly is not viewed in a negative way.

For example, the Glastonbury Festival recruits security staff to cater for the safety of consumers throughout the duration of the event. Once the event concludes, there is no longer a requirement for these staff members. Therefore, the events industry may exhibit high rates of turnover that act only as an economic safeguard to unwanted staff costs. Additionally, labour turnover is often seen as a means for recruiting 'fresh blood' into a company, bringing forth enhanced experience and expertise. Consequently, for a company to manage turnover effectively, the financial gains created by new staff must outweigh financial losses incurred by repeated recruitment and retraining these new staff. Labour turnover is often investigated through the use of exit interviews, surveys and opinion polls. These may prove to be useful tools given the information they may bring to managers. Results should be investigated for emerging themes, including the employee's position within the company, length of service, background and correlates of absenteeism/poor timekeeping.

Rewards

Motivation can be increased and sustained through the presence of work-based reward systems. Financial rewards generally take precedence over other incentives; however, advancements in research and theoretical underpinning do not necessarily support such methods. Incremental pay schemes, bonuses and even health insurance have become so popular they are often seen not as a reward, but as employee rights; salary increments may prove to motivate employees only as far as to reaching their next pay increase and not directed at work-based productivity (see motivation, above).

Given the nature of the events industry and its demand for volunteerism, non-financial reward systems are largely required, directed at both paid and unpaid staff. To an extent, the nature of the event may help direct the type of reward offered. A sports event, for example, may pave the way for volunteer workers to receive rewards in the form of sport coaching/operations certification. However, volunteers often suggest that involvement in events of which they enjoy is a reward in itself. For example, volunteering at a music festival would undoubtedly ensure free entry, which may be viewed as part of the reward for work. Festival volunteers recruited by Oxfam for Glastonbury or Leeds/Reading are required to work three shifts of 8¼ h, but also have the opportunity to attend the festival's performances. It is therefore, imperative that managers ensure an enjoyable, friendly atmosphere.

Employees (paid or otherwise) often have a set of needs that require fulfilment for motivation to be present. Recognition and appreciation for completed work tasks, alongside feedback on performance and a greater understanding of organizational objectives, are all intangible rewards with equal or greater performance-based motivation than financial incentives.

Reward systems should aim to satisfy needs that lead to increased motivation. For example, the need for personal growth and development can be satisfied through continuing professional development (CPD), whereby additional training incentives are accessible, leading to promotion, empowerment and enhanced responsibility – all of which contribute to overall work-based motivation.

Managing volunteers

Based on the motivation of volunteers, it is highly important for managers to recognize and satisfy these needs, as their commitment to the event will cease if needs are continually unmet. While statistics have remained relatively stable in terms of volunteer recruitment, poor organization, boredom, insufficient support with volunteer tasks, poor communication and advice, time restraints and lack of recognition and gratitude may compromise the volunteer's commitment. Creating a fun, yet challenging environment whereby volunteers feel empowered within their job roles and surrounded by those with similar interests is an effective way to enhance volunteer sustainability.

Recognizing the barriers to volunteering also demonstrates good practice, as in doing so, managers should attempt to adopt strategies to alleviate these barriers. Deterrents to volunteering are most commonly: lack of time; poor social affiliation (i.e. not knowing any of the other volunteers); and inadequate skills or experience to handle job-related tasks. Managers, therefore need to ensure systems are in place to allow a flexible approach to voluntary working hours that incorporate a supportive network (particularly at the beginning of a volunteer's employment). Clear and specific instructions are often required alongside training and development opportunities and the formation of friendships. Additionally, research indicates that volunteers are more likely to be recruited and committed if they have a genuine interest in the event, alongside sympathy and commonality for those at whom the event is aimed. Numerous surveys reveal that people would be more likely to volunteer if: they were asked directly; their friends were also involved or had strong opportunities to make friends; they had assistance and clear instructions during their line of work; and if the role benefitted their future career prospects. It is suggested that contact information of all volunteers is retained should similar events recur in the future, as these volunteers (if given a previous, worthy experience) are very likely to consider volunteering again. Many organizations create volunteer mailing lists and distribute information via newsletters and future volunteer recruitment opportunities. It is often observed that volunteers at events are younger than volunteers in general, allowing the acquisition of experience in an industry or job role that would not have been easily sought should the individual have been chasing paid employment. As earlier suggested, the accumulation of any work experience (paid or unpaid) aids employability and thus, career development for the young, inexperienced individual.

Box 6.4. Oxfam – 2010 standards of behaviour for festival volunteers.

Please read each of the following statements carefully.

1. I will complete three 8¼-h shifts, at each festival at which I am volunteering. I understand that failing to volunteer on the shifts designated to me, without a valid reason (e.g. a doctor's note), will lead to my deposit being forfeited.
2. I will be 18 years old or over on the first day of the first festival at which I am volunteering.
3. I have read Oxfam's Health and Safety Policy and attended the health and safety training and campaign training (campaigners only) for festival volunteers and I will not do anything to endanger my or other person's safety.
4. I have read all of the Frequently Asked Questions and corresponding answers.
5. Oxfam can pass my data (including personal data) to festival organisers, the police and other checking agencies, as is deemed necessary for the safe and secure running of each festival.
6. I understand that it is expressly forbidden to consume alcohol or take any intoxicants while (or immediately prior to) volunteering as a steward or campaigner at a festival for Oxfam. Oxfam reserves the right to have any steward or campaigner found to be volunteering under the influence of drink or intoxicants, or behaving in a manner which might bring Oxfam's reputation into disrepute, removed from the festival site and their deposit shall be forfeited.
7. I understand that Oxfam is not responsible for the personal possessions of any steward or campaigner volunteering at a festival for Oxfam.
8. I will wear my Oxfam t-shirt/high-visibility Oxfam tabard at all times while on shift at a festival for Oxfam.
9. I will comply with the festival's own policies at all times during my attendance at each festival at which I am volunteering.
10. The festival management reserves the right to conduct searches on entrance and exit to the festival site, whether you are on or off shift.
11. I agree to read the Oxfam Stewarding Guide before arriving on site, in order to be informed on health & safety and my role as a steward or campaigner.
12. I will arrive on the festival site with everything I will need to support myself until I leave the festival site. This includes clothing for all weathers, food, money and general camping equipment.

(Continued)

Box 6.4. Continued.

13. I understand that Oxfam may take photographs of me and use them on its website and other media for campaign, marketing and training purposes. (If you do not wish to be photographed, please let us know at your on-site briefing.)

I have read and understood that if my behaviour falls outside of these standards it will lead to my eviction from site and my deposit being forfeited. (A record of your acceptance of our standards of behaviour volunteering policy will be added to your stewarding record.)

Reprinted with permission from Oxfam (2010)

Training and development

Training should start with an induction to the event, with some organizations expanding this procedure to 'orientation' training of the company. Once paid and voluntary staff are appointed, a structured induction programme is designed to impart a range of different information aimed at assisting the employee within their role. It is advisable to prepare an induction kit in advance so that staff have the necessary information at hand and are then able to use this resource as a referral tool (Table 6.2).

A continued approach to training and development is crucial to employee efficacy, as their skills, knowledge and attributes directly influence the success of the event. Training sessions can focus on specific job skills or knowledge that will result in enhanced staff performance.

Table 6.2. Training at events.

Induction training	Induction kit
Basic information about the event (history, mission, objectives, stakeholders, budget, locations, programme details)	Annual report; welcoming message; event mission statement; sponsor and stakeholder list
Tours of event area, with introduction to suppliers, offices, contact points, information help desks	Map of event area; list of suppliers
Introduction to staff and volunteers	Name badge; staff list with contact details
Introduction to working arrangements and organization, including reporting relationships, performance expectations and responsibilities	Organizational chart; job descriptions
Terms and conditions of employment to inform workforce on probationary periods, grievance procedures, absenteeism, sickness, dress code, security, salary and overtime rates, benefits (meals)	Staff handbook; uniform (T-shirt); meal voucher
Overview of training programmes	Training schedule

These sessions can be on-the-job or off-the-job, in-house (at/during the event) or off-site (before or after the event). For most events, particularly small or mid-sized events, training takes place on-the-job with experienced staff (paid or volunteer) acting as the trainers and advice givers. Common forms of on-the-job training involve learning through observing their colleagues at work, or learning through participation (learning by doing). Such approaches are very cost-effective, with the added benefits of engaging the learner from the initial point of work, offering provision of immediate feedback, encouragement and socialization while shaping the newly formed team. However, on-the-job training can be hard to control, particularly if the person shadowed is not adequately trained or if the new staff member inherits their bad habits, which are more difficult to eliminate at a latter stage.

Mentoring or coaching is a variation of on-the-job training, which involves a more experienced and senior staff member building a one-to-one relationship with the new employee, offering advice and counselling whenever required. This not only benefits the employee, but also gives the senior staff member an opportunity to reflect on work-based processes and procedures. Finally, job rotation involves allocation of different jobs to the new recruit for a limited period. This process allows individuals to acquire a wider range of skills, compassion and understanding of co-worker's responsibilities, alongside an appreciation for the event as a whole. Because of the need to have the right people performing the rights jobs, job rotation training is considered impractical during the actual delivery of the event and thus, should be restricted to preparatory stages of the event.

Events will also require off-the-job training, particularly before the event takes place. This can be achieved through lectures, seminars, workshops, case studies, role-play or simulation. This approach has often demonstrated success as larger numbers of staff and volunteers can be trained simultaneously, hence making it is easier to disseminate information. Bringing together people from different areas and departments can also encourage wider socialization and networking, aiding mutual understanding and appreciation of differentiated job roles within the event organization, as opposed to individuals merely focusing on their job role. However, training can be more generic and therefore not specific or relevant enough. Furthermore, it represents a more passive approach to learning and can jeopardize motivation and concentration.

There are several methods of accurately and efficiently identifying training needs; performance appraisals are one option (see below). Alternatively, job requirements can be analysed through job descriptions, which will state the required skills. A third option is to receive feedback from existing staff.

Professional development in turn is concerned with the acquisition of new skills and knowledge that prepare individuals for future job possibilities, thus having a more long-term view to training. While any event organization should have effective training and policies in place, the very nature of the event makes it difficult to implement and deliver; during the busy delivery of an event, there is often limited time to concentrate on training. Staff and management are consumed with their personal job roles and catering towards the event's delivery. It is therefore, advised that staff training takes places prior to the event.

Appraisal and performance review

Appraisals, evaluations or performance reviews play a central role to both the employer and the employee. Such procedures aim to facilitate the development of an employee as well as their contribution towards increased motivation, thus enhancing performance and the success of the event. It is a two-way discussion between an employee and their line manager, which incorporates the employee's past and present experiences alongside their achievements. This information then forms the basis for an agreement of the employee's future training needs. Naturally, this process not only benefits the employee in terms of continuing his or her professional development, but also the company in that a developed workforce is likely to result in organizational success.

There are several purposes of undertaking a performance review, including: the instigation of management control; a method (in the case of paid employees) that links pay to performance; a means of identifying potential; problem solving; succession planning; and most importantly, the improvement of staff competency in contributing towards the success of an event. A commonly used tool during the appraisal process is goal setting. Goals are jointly set by supervisors and staff, which should be specific to the particular job, but also relate to more generic areas such as technical skills (e.g. communication, problem solving, team working, etc.). It is important that the goals are specific, measurable, achievable, realistic and time bound (SMART), as this assures a consistent and easy way to measure an employee's performance. If the goals are too vague or unrealistic, the employee is less likely to perform well, thus impacting on his or her motivation.

There are various techniques and approaches to appraisals, including written essays, critical incident reports, rating scales, and multi-person comparison through group-order ranking. In terms of approaches, the appraisal is usually undertaken 'top-down' with the direct line manager appraising the employee. Alternative ways for appraisals include:

- Self-appraisals – these have the benefit of lessening an employee's defensiveness and can be more revealing. These create an excellent environment for job discussions between manager and employee.
- Peer appraisal – these are advantageous in that colleagues provide judgement of the appraisee's work performance. Colleagues selected for this task should have daily interactions and observations of the appraise, alongside an ability to objectively critique job-related performance.
- Upward appraisal – employees or immediate subordinates appraise managers.
- Customer appraisal – these are executed through use of customer surveys or mystery shoppers, which provide external feedback on an employee's performance.
- 360° appraisals – these involve a combination of all of the above whereby a full circle of sources is used to gather information and feedback.

In any case, when carrying out an appraisal, there are some general issues as well as some event-specific issues that have to be taken into account. Appraisals can have a significant impact on employee motivation as judgements are made. Depending on the relationship between the manager and the employee, the appraisal may differ in terms of objectivity; if the employee has a good relationship and socializes with the manager, it is more likely that they will receive positive feedback, whereas a strained relationship can affect the appraisal in a negative way. Similarly, friendships and/or animosity can cause bias among workers and impact the peer appraisal process, whereas over-inflated opinions or self-serving biases can impact on the self-evaluation process. Although this should be avoided in any way, prejudices and discrimination (based on gender, age or race) might become clear and result in an uncomfortable appraisal review process. Managers might be uncomfortable with this role and require training specific to the performance review process. As it is a two-way process, the appraisee also needs the right skills (e.g. communication and inter-personal skills).

The criteria for performance review must be established clearly and managers have to decide whether to appraise in the context of work or compare performance with other staff.

In any case, appraising can prove erroneous if irrelevant aspects are taken into account (see SMART goals above for assuring the right aspects are appraised). External factors have to be taken into account as they can affect the organization's overall performance (e.g. economic recession). Appraisals can be very time-consuming and involve considerable paperwork. This often presents difficulties within the events industry; managers might not deem it necessary to carry out appraisals for volunteers who only work for a limited period. At international or large events, managers deal with staff from diverse backgrounds, and hence, cultural differences have to be taken into account. Once the performance review has been considered, outcomes are quite often ignored and the whole appraisal process becomes irrelevant if they are not followed up. As a number of event services are outsourced to agencies, event managers have to rely on suppliers to undertake appraisals and have no control over all staff in an equal way.

Appraising and training volunteers

Such mechanisms are relatively straightforward to implement with paid staff; volunteers, however, are far more difficult to appraise. Time and other resources are required to adequately conduct an appraisal, which, given the perishable nature of the event and voluntary status of the employee, does not appear particularly necessary. Events organizations may often take a more relaxed approach to appraisals with volunteers, adopting more of a 'debriefing' method of evaluation. In turn, volunteers are asked to provide feedback from their experience as an unpaid employee. Collectively, this information forms the basis of requirements for training and development of either existing or future volunteers. Training a volunteer also demonstrates some degree of difficulty, particularly if that training is seen by the organization as compulsory. Any mandatory feature of the job should be made clear in the recruitment and selection phase of employment, and be marketed as a positive component of the volunteering experience; the individual should be made aware of the beneficial nature training and development has to offer their CV, attainment of additional qualifications, improvement of skills and abilities, level of employability and, thus, their future career.

Question

How would you make sure that volunteers at an event are given feedback? Why do you think this is necessary?

WELFARE POLICIES

Every organization is subject to legislation that aims to safeguard the welfare of employees, baring equal importance to both paid and volunteer workers; however, statutory compliance is just one reason as to why companies adopt such policies, and this is often demonstrated through the implementation of various optional policies with similar interests. Promotion of employee welfare has the benefit of ensuring staff feel cared for, less isolated and more secure, which increases satisfaction, leading to motivation. This in turn, reduces the risk of financially draining labour turnover costs. Additionally, such policies have the added benefit of attracting desirable employees to the workforce resulting in competitive advantage.

Throughout the last century, employment law has evolved dramatically in terms of its provision of equal opportunity policies. These include the prevention of discrimination related to age, sex, ethnicity, disability and sexual orientation, but also other categorized community groups that may not immediately spring to mind. Table 6.3 provides an overview of equal opportunity policies to which HR managers must comply.

Stress within the workplace can occur for a number of reasons, including workload, hours of work, physical conditions, access to resources and support, relationships with colleagues, management styles and communication. Because of the hefty costs of stress-induced absenteeism, the frequency of welfare initiatives has increased. Table 6.3 highlights some of the mandatory requirements for guarding against workplace-induced conditions of stress. In addition to legislation, many companies have adopted additional welfare initiatives to reduce workplace stress. The Olympic Delivery Authority (ODA) for the London 2012 Olympic Games, for example, has commissioned a team of occupational health experts to offer free support to all staff, including lifestyle screening and access to healthcare services, all in support of employee welfare. Initiatives such as these are a growing trend within all

Table 6.3. Employment legislation.

Legislation	Description
Race Relations Act (1976)	Prohibits workplace discrimination on the ground of race, colour, nationality, ethnic and national origin
Sex Discrimination Act (1975)	Prohibits discrimination and victimization on the grounds of sex, marital status
Disability Discrimination Act (1995)	Promotes civil rights to disabled persons and safeguards workplace discrimination
Equal Pay Act (1970)	Enforces equality of pay and work conditions between men and women
Rehabilitation of Offenders Act (1974)	Safeguards workplace discrimination of ex-offenders by enabling a policy whereby, in some cases, convictions do not need to be mentioned to employers
EU Directive on Working Time Regulations (1998)	Enforces working time limits (48 hours weekly) and restrictions on night work, and governs rest breaks, overtime, paid annual leave and Sunday work
Employment Rights Act (1996)	Employees are entitled to a contract of employment which establishes the condition of employment
Workplace (Health, Safety and Welfare) Regulations (1992)	Builds on HSWA 1974 (below) that includes regulations for workplace ventilation, temperature, lighting, cleanliness, room space per worker and access to drinking water
Health and Safety at Work Act (1974)	Primary piece of legislation covering all occupational health and safety in the UK
Council Directive 89/391/ EEC (1989)	European directive that enforces minimum standards for health and safety at work, and includes work-related stress

industries, many of which include provision of exercise (through either free gym member-ships or on-site fitness professionals). Concessionary time off has also increased to enable employees to rest and recuperate for work.

Other schemes include the inclusion of health-promoting foods within staff venues alongside nutritional advice. Organizational counselling services for a range of psychological illnesses are another optional method, aiming to enhance the welfare of staff. Even the struc-tural design of a workplace has a role to play in the reduction of stress, whereby office space, equipment, décor and external grounds and architecture are designed to promote a comfort-able, stress-free environment; architects are often required build light, airy work stations with suitable break-time space that is away from their usual place of work, which offers a relaxing and revitalizing environment. In addition, many companies set up teams of new employees aiming to reduce stress and promote healthy working lives for their employees. While many of these services come at an additional cost, the expenditure must be weighed against the losses incurred by stress-induced absenteeism, decreased performance and high rates of labour turn-over, increased accidents and customer complaints.

Because of the highly legislated domain of health and safety plus increased lawsuits and compensatory claims, carelessness towards health and safety at work can be incredibly costly to organizations. It is not unusual for a company to declare itself bankrupt as a result of a con-viction of health and safety negligence. Organizations, therefore, allocate plentiful resources towards the prevention of incidences and on legal compliance.

Questions

- Look at H&S as discussed in Chapter 7 – what applies to staff/employees?
- What training would you provide to employees and volunteers to ensure H&S is achieved at an event?
- How easy do you think it is to implement welfare policies at an event, given the nature of events?

Further areas covered under employment law and welfare policies are grievance and discipli-nary procedures to assure neither the employer nor employee breaches the employment condi-tion or legislation.

CONCLUSION

The chapter has outlined the various elements that form part of the HRM process. As events involve a high level of contact between employees and customers, the management of people is a crucial part of events management. Effective HRM starts with the HRP process and extends to the operational human resource plan, which considers the appropriate recruitment and selection procedures, training plans, welfare policies and management of rewards and employee motivation. The temporary nature of events and the structure of the event workforce (through the use of volunteers) makes HRM a challenging task, which needs to be addressed throughout the management of events on a strategic and operational level to ensure the overall success of the event.

FURTHER READING

Van Der Wagen, L. (2007) *Human Resource Management for Events – Managing the Events Workforce.* Butterworth-Heinemann, Oxford.

REVIEW QUESTIONS

1. What are the key differences and similarities between paid employees and volunteers in terms of HRP, recruitment and selection, training and motivation?

2. Technology has had a major impact on the industry overall – consider at what point in the HRM process this has a direct and indirect impact.

3. Using an event with which you are familiar, assess the HRM practices and suggest ways in which the management of HR can be improved.

ACKNOWLEDGEMENT

The authors are grateful to Oxfam for their contribution to the case studies and information provided in this chapter.

REFERENCES

Bowdin, G., Allen, J., O'Toole, W., Harris, R. and McDonnell, I. (2006) *Events Management*, 2nd edn. Butterworth-Heinemann, Oxford.

Hanlon, C. and Jago, L. (2004) The challenge of retaining personnel in major sport event organisations. *Event Management* 9, 39–49.

Manchester City Council (2009) Commonwealth Games NW 2002 Legacy Programme [online]. Manchester City Council. Available at: <http://www.manchester.gov.uk/info/200079/regeneration/510/commonwealth_games_nw_2002_legacy_programme/2> (accessed 2 December 2009).

Monga, M. (2006) Measuring motivation to volunteer for special events. *Event Management* 10, 47–61.

Nickson, D. (2007) *Human Resource Management for the Hospitality and Tourism Industries.* Butterworth-Heinemann, Oxford.

Ralston, R., Lumsden, L. and Downward, P. (2005) The third force in events tourism: volunteers at the XVII Commonwealth Games. *Journal of Sustainable Tourism* 13, 504.

Van Der Wagen, L. (2007) *Human Resource Management for Events – Managing the Events Workforce.* Butterworth-Heinemann, Oxford.

chapter 7

Marketing Events

Debra Wale and Andrew Ridal

OBJECTIVES OF THE CHAPTER

This chapter introduces and outlines concepts and models of marketing in an events context. It provides explanation, with case studies providing practical illustration, and strategies for marketing events with a particular focus on contemporary e-marketing communications. It will be ideal as a resource for event planners marketing events of any scale in any sector.

This chapter is designed to enable you to:

- understand the process of marketing planning;
- consider and evaluate the marketing environment to develop marketing choices;
- understand how (what is known as) the marketing mix may be used to plan integrated marketing campaigns to communicate products and services to new and existing customers; and
- understand how consumer behaviour, segmentation, targeting and positioning help the event planner to focus marketing activity.

EVENT MARKETING

Event marketing is the function in the event management process whereby marketers create, promote and stage event experiences that satisfy customer needs and that customers choose over other competitors in the marketplace. Utilizing the principles of segmentation and targeting, marketers identify and attract new and existing audiences (by informing them about the event) and work to retain them for future events, a process informed by carrying out market research of the event environment and existing and potential audiences.

Marketing enables event organizers to capture customer data and understand what motivates event attendance; it also allows customers to tell event organizers their dislikes, in order to improve future events.

An event may provide a service (e.g. musical entertainment) alongside physical goods (e.g. food, drink). Services and goods combine to create experiences. It is the experience that the event consumer is buying, e.g. '80s nights (nostalgia), Disney (magic), extreme sports such as bungee jumping (excitement/adrenalin rush), competitions/charity fundraisers (achievement/self-actualization) or a multi-cultural health promotional road show (education, diversity).

Events appeal to different people, and every consumer has their own individual make-up (e.g. attitudes, interests, opinions). Marketers need to gain an understanding of what motivates consumers to attend events in order to create, improve (customer feedback) and market events effectively by selecting appropriate marketing channels and deploying the right marketing mix in the design of an integrated marketing communications campaign. Marketers create the desire to purchase by placing stimuli in marketing communications that appeal to the personal characteristics of the event consumer (Kotler *et al.*, 2010).

MOTIVATIONS AND EVENT ATTENDANCE

Studying motivation with regard to event attendance addresses the key question of why people attend events. It is very important to understand what motivates someone to go to an event in order to be able to market events effectively. Motivation theorists believe that motivation is linked to variables such as intrinsic and extrinsic factors, and these motivate specific buying behaviour; thus motivation plays a key role in the decision-making process that determines which events consumers will attend. In order to examine the motivation for people to attend events, two different approaches can be adopted: extrinsic and intrinsic motivation. Extrinsic motivation results from influences external to the person and requires the analysis of motivation from a sociological perspective, whereas intrinsic motivation includes the personal needs of the individuals themselves, thus taking a psychological perspective to event attendance motivation. The case study in Box 7.1 discusses motivational factors for music festival attendance.

Extrinsic motivation

Within this model, theorists propose three different approaches to explain motivation through the relationship between work and leisure time:

1. Work and leisure in conflict – work time is in opposition to leisure time. Similarly to a holiday, it can be argued that attending an event compensates for the work or even lifestyle, i.e. if an individual has a hectic, demanding job, they need to seek relaxation during their leisure time. The opposite is thought to be true for those with constraining, dull employment, who are more likely to seek excitement, thrills and challenge during their leisure time.

2. Leisure as an extension of work – in contrast to the opposition/compensation model above, the extension model asserts that employment and leisure are intrinsically interlinked and that work patterns and leisure patterns are very similar. This suggests that those individuals with exciting and demanding jobs are more likely to seek stimulation during their leisure time, and that those with dull, rule-constrained employment are more likely to want a more regulated,

---

Box 7.1. Motivations to attend music events.

The festival industry is growing rapidly and, as such, it is imperative that event managers strive to better understand the motives of festival attendance in order to design better product offerings and services and also to ensure sustained development for future growth.

A study (carried out by Gelder and Robinson, 2009) was conducted to compare critically the motivations of visitors who attended either Glastonbury or the V Festival, two of the largest music festivals in the UK, which bring in a combined audience of over 200,000 people annually.

Across the two festivals, but predominantly for Glastonbury, the most consistent and recurring motive was socialization, highlighting the need for event managers to ensure they offer a wide range of ancillary activities to satisfy those to whom the music is less important.

The main motive for attending the V Festival was for the music/artists playing; however, it is equally important to create a fun and festive atmosphere that offers ample opportunity to socialize and have non-musical experiences focusing on social/leisure family togetherness and excitement.

The results of the study also highlighted that multiple motivations come into play; henceforth, festival managers who rely specifically on the music or artists to draw in large crowds can expect to be disappointed with the turnout. Music festival organizers need to use different marketing tactics to broaden the appeal of festivals.

The research also supported the work of Petrick and Li (2006), finding that festivals should be conceptualized as recreation rather than tourism. This suggests a need for more research on event visitor motivation theory.

Study provided by Gemma Gelder

---

less challenging activity during their leisure time. Consequently, changes in the patterns of work will change patterns of leisure and thus event attendance.

3. The third proposition suggests that employment has nothing to do with the chosen type of leisure; hence people who like stimulating leisure time and attending exciting events are equally likely to have a demanding or highly regulated job.

While the leisure–work relationship can be very useful as a basis for analysis, social determinants form another framework for consideration of extrinsic motivation. Social determinants influence the person to attend an event and to make that decision to purchase the ticket. Social determinants can be classified as cultural, social and personal. Specific social determinants are outlined in Fig. 7.1.

All these factors influence motivation and they can influence the decision making process. Social factors are not mutually exclusive; they exert a combined influence, and while one may be more easily identified by an individual, others may work on the subconscious level. These economic, technological, social, cultural and political factors within any society act as determinants that drive or limit who attends events and how often this happens.

Extrinsic motivators are useful to explain general motivations to attend events; however, for a better picture, the psychological, intrinsic factors need exploration, as they make a considerable contribution to the analysis of motivation to attend events.

Social determinants		
Cultural	Cultural background	Black, Asian or Caucasian
	Religion	Christian, Muslim, Jewish, Hindu
	Subculture	Linguistic, aesthetic, religious, political, sexual, geographic
Social	Reference groups	Friends, colleagues
	Family	Traditional family unit, non-traditional family: one parent family, gay/lesbian family
	Roles	Friend, colleague, mother, brother
	Status	Professional standing, educational level
Personal	Age	Segmentation of groups according to age, e.g. baby boomers, silver brigade
	Lifestyle	Family situation, age, preferences
	Occupation	Challenge, level of regulation
	Economic circumstances	Disposable income
	Personality	Introvert, extrovert

Fig. 7.1. Social determinants.

Intrinsic motivation

Some authors assert that motivation is a fundamentally psychological concept and is not socio-logical as discussed above. In the context of the internal factors within individuals, expressed as needs, wants and/or desires, which motivate people to attend events, it is difficult to generalize. Each person is different, they have their own set of attitudes, individual personality, and no two of us are the same. Everyone thus has a distinct and different motivation as to which event to attend, when and where. Thus the study of motivation in the event context is challenging. It is, however, possible to make some generalizations, within the context of the societal values, norms and influences on each individual, which become their psychological needs. There are consequently some overlaps between the extrinsic motivations discussed above and intrinsic 'push' and 'pull' motivation factors (Table 7.1).

Table 7.1. Motivation factors for event attendees.

Push factors	Pull factors
Entertainment	Climate
Excitement	Accommodation
Relaxation	Food and beverages
Escape	Performance/performer
Prestige	
Time with family	
Socialization	
Nostalgia	
Ambiance	
Education	

Push/pull factors

Motivational factors are generally viewed in two main categories, 'push' and 'pull'.

Push factors

These are the factors intrinsic to the individual, which influence the person to make a purchase decision. They are intangible and are the psychological benefits that the person perceives they will gain from attending the event and using the facilities offered. They are internal factors and are person-specific; no two individuals will be the same. The push factors are those that attendees see as a way that they can satisfy a desire or a need, such as a wish to be entertained or to relax, to get thrills or excitement, to experience nostalgia, to escape from day-to-day life, to gain prestige in the eyes of their peer group or to spend time with friends and/or family (called socialization by some authors). Attendees also seek the general ambiance of festivals, which makes the crucial difference between engaging in an activity such as listening to music at home/watching a performance on television and going to an event where it is performed live. Another key factor is the desire to learn, which has led to the preponderance of 'edutainment' at events, satisfying the desires of families to spend time together, while also helping to educate the children.

Pull factors

These refer to the attractions that are intrinsic to the event setting. Pull factors can be described as event-specific attributes or outer motivations. They are the attributes at the event site that are the destination itself or the attractions sited there that are so appealing that they are 'pulling' the individual towards themselves.

They are the tangible factors such as the climate (e.g. snow or sunshine), food and drink in the area, and hotel or camping facilities. They also include the actual entertainment available at the event such as the artists, who will perform, or the play or performance in which they will take part. Attendees find out about these from good marketing materials be they brochures, advertisements or e-marketing campaigns.

In the international context, research suggests that there are broad similarities in motivation between people from most countries, including the USA, Italy, Spain, South Korea and the UK. The key factors for all international event attendees seem to be spending time with family, excitement and socialization (Lee *et al.*, 2004; Richards, 2007; Gelder and Robinson, 2009).

The buyer decision process

By understanding the process a buyer goes through when making a purchase decision (Fig. 7.2), a marketer can design the event experience, and communicate it to match the stimuli associated with the personality traits recognized as the motivator for a group's buying behaviour.

Activity
- Summarize push and pull factors.
- Use the push and pull table (Table 7.2) to list the motivational factors from an event that you have recently experienced.
- Adapt the buyer decision process model to describe your ticket purchasing behaviour for the event you attended.

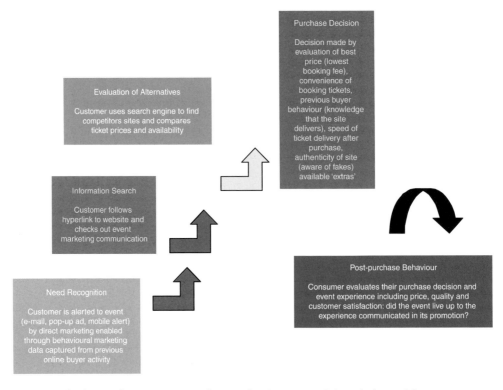

Fig. 7.2. The buyer decision process for purchasing event tickets (adapted from Wale, 2009).

MARKETING PLANNING

The scale and scope of the events industry mean that different events require different approaches to marketing planning. The marketing function for any event starts from conception and continues through to evaluation and preparation for the next iteration. In the case of mega-events like the Olympics where a bidding process allocates management rights to the event, marketing plays a key role in securing the event and can take place years in advance of the actual event, e.g. the London 2012 bidding process started in January 2004 (london2012, 2004) with the bid's official launch. Other one-off events will require a different approach to marketing planning, whether small or large private, public, not for profit (including charity).

A strategic approach to marketing enables event organizers to evaluate the marketing environment, make informed marketing choices, gain competitive advantage, modify plans to cope with environmental changes (see Manchester United Football Club case study, Box 7.2), analyse results and use this evaluation to draw up future marketing objectives. This is demonstrated in the strategic marketing cycle (Fig. 7.3).

Marketing planning involves analysis of the market, the choice of marketing activity, and its implementation through marketing campaigns in order to communicate products and services to target customers. An organization's marketing plan should be based on a market analysis that will provide a strategic direction for the organization. It frames marketer's objectives for achieving the marketing goal and should be drawn up at the feasibility stage of event planning or annually for events operating in the long term.

Box 7.2. Manchester United Football Club postpones Indonesia tour after Jakarta bombing.

Manchester United Football Club cancelled its ten-date Indonesia Tour within minutes of the breaking news of the Jakarta bombing in Indonesia in July 2009. The team's manager, Alex Ferguson, appeared on international television explaining that the risk factor was the reason for pulling out. The impact of this PR bad news story for Indonesia helped to publicize and deliver a warning to tourists that Indonesia was a high-risk tourist destination. Bali, one of the planned dates on the tour, was hit hard by the Jakarta bombings and the cancelled football event; having just recovered from bombings in 2003 and 2005, they had seen their best tourism growth in 2007.

MARKETING ANALYSIS

The macro-environment is researched through conducting a situation analysis of the internal factors influencing, and the external factors affecting, the current, emerging and future marketplace. A PESTEL analysis is a good framework to capture the external factors impacting on marketing decisions (see Chapter 10). This then feeds into the internal dimensions of the SWOT analysis (e.g. strengths and weaknesses) and informs marketing decisions. The strengths and weaknesses are determined through an internal audit of the organization's capabilities.

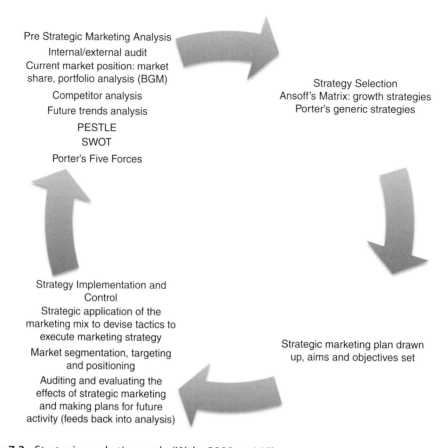

Pre Strategic Marketing Analysis
Internal/external audit
Current market position: market
share, portfolio analysis (BGM)
Competitor analysis
Future trends analysis
PESTLE
SWOT
Porter's Five Forces

Strategy Selection
Ansoff's Matrix: growth strategies
Porter's generic strategies

Strategy Implementation and Control
Strategic application of the
marketing mix to devise tactics to
execute marketing strategy
Market segmentation, targeting
and positioning
Auditing and evaluating the
effects of strategic marketing
and making plans for future
activity (feeds back into analysis)

Strategic marketing plan drawn
up, aims and objectives set

Fig. 7.3. Strategic marketing cycle (Wale, 2009, p. 145).

SETTING MARKETING OBJECTIVES

When an event organization has undertaken an analysis of the market, it is then possible to set marketing objectives to work towards and provide the first steps in the development of a marketing plan. Marketing objectives should be SMART (specific, measurable, achievable, realistic, timed) and based around strategic choice options.

Strategic choice: Ansoff's Growth Matrix

Ansoff's Growth Matrix is a marketing tool, which can be used to determine the direction for marketing strategy; in the current economic environment, the safest strategy is one of consolidation (market concentration) of strengths rather than expansion (extension, diversification) of opportunities. The environment is, however, constantly changing and opportunities present themselves to event organizations. An event organization considering expansion of their business has a number of options to consider:

- **Market penetration or concentration** – existing products in existing markets; the strategy to increase market share and sales.
- **Product development** – new products for existing markets; the key to this strategy is developing the right product to the marketplace before competitors.

- **Market extension or development** – existing products for new markets; in this strategy new markets include international expansion, use of a different marketing channel, e.g. social networking, to a different market segment, e.g. Facebook users.
- **Diversification or innovation** – new products for new markets; this strategy involves vertical forward integration, acquiring intermediaries that form part of the supply chain, e.g. ticket agents; horizontal diversification, acquiring a competitor in the marketplace to extend into, e.g. event suppliers in a different country; or conglomerate diversification, expanding into unfamiliar territory.

IMPLEMENTING MARKETING STRATEGY

The implementation stage sees the translation of event marketing objectives to practice, through strategic application of the marketing mix (7 Ps) in well-planned integrated marketing campaigns to target and capture the chosen market (segmentation, targeting and positioning).

FEEDBACK AND EVENT EVALUATION

The final stage of the strategic process involves collecting and evaluating consumers' event experiences. This can be achieved through feedback forms at the event, or through follow-up direct mail communications (via post, SMS text, telephone or e-mail). The Internet and other forms of digital media are making the evaluation process more and more immediate. Blogs and Facebook provide opportunities for people to discuss their event experiences and consumers are able to text their responses as the action happens at events.

SEGMENTATION

It is a common truism that 'you can't please all of the people all of the time'. It is therefore important for marketers to be able to identify which of the people they can please most, if not all, of the time. This process is called *segmentation*. It is the practice of dividing a population into smaller, easily identifiable groups that will respond to a specific message targeted towards them.

Segmentation variables

There are a number of ways to segment a population. The most common segmentation variables are:

- **Geographic** – assuming that people who live in the same area have similar consumption patterns and needs.
- **Demographic** – dividing a population by age, income, sex, socio-economic status.
- **Psychographic (or Lifestyle)** – identifying people's personality traits, attitudes and opinions.
- **Benefit** – where people are all seeing the same benefit from a purchase but have chosen that product for different reasons. For example, two people will be receiving the benefit of watching the same concert, but one may be there on a date, and the other may be in a corporate box with their company.
- **Behavioural** – identifying people by how they consume a product or frequency of purchase.

Segmentation methods

There are many methods of segmenting customers and the choice depends on which attributes match customers to the product or service that is to be targeted. The *National Readership Survey* (NRS) is a well used segmentation method in the UK, categorizing the population by the socio-economic variables social class and income into the following categories:

- A – Higher managerial, administrative or professional.
- B – Intermediate managerial, administrative and professional.
- C1– Supervisory, clerical, junior administrative or professional.
- C2– Skilled manual workers.
- D – Semi-skilled and unskilled manual workers.
- E – State pensioners, widows, lowest-grade workers.

The case study in Box 7.3 demonstrates how segmentation can be applied to specific audiences to facilitate target marketing.

Regardless of which segmentation method is used, in order for the resultant information to be useful, the chosen segment must be (Adcock *et al.*, 2001):

- **Definable** – You must be able to easily describe your segment.
- **Sizeable** – It is more efficient to talk to lots of people at the same time.
- **Reachable** – Efficient and effective communications and supply channels.
- **Relevant** – The segment must have a desire to purchase your product offering.

The Internet and specialist social networking sites have accelerated the segmentation process as consumers select events of interest through search engines, purchase, registration and membership. Data are captured and individual behaviours are anonymized and aggregated, and audience segments are created enabling behavioural targeting, i.e. Internet users are served ads based on their online behaviour (Nutley, 2009).

Box 7.3. Grand Theatre Wolverhampton pantomime audiences.

With 82 performances over 8 weeks, the Grand Theatre Wolverhampton's pantomime is one of the biggest in the UK. As audiences get older and children 'grow out' of pantomime, the theatre constantly has to generate new audiences. By segmenting the local population, the theatre is able to focus its marketing efforts and target them to the identified segments. The Grand Theatre identifies two key segmensts: (i) Young Families – Iceland Mum; and (ii) 2.4 children – Grandma's Treat:

- Young Families – Iceland Mum
  - Single income
  - Grandparents still working
  - Children aged 1–8 years
  - C1, C2, D, E
  - Don't go to theatre
- 2.4 Children – Grandma's Treat
  - Dual income
  - Retired grandparents

(Continued)

Box 7.3. Continued.
> Children aged 8+
> A, B, C1
> Grandparents like plays

From these segments, the theatre is able to identify what is important to these groups, who the decision maker is, where you find them, how you communicate with them and the important elements in the message.

- Young Families – Iceland Mum
  > Mum is boss!
  > Budget supermarket/on the bus
  > Outdoor media
  > Value and reassurance
  > Message elements: star name, title, fun, family, value added, visuals, re-living childhood.
- 2.4 Children – Grandma's Treat
  > Grandma is key
  > Shopping with friends/tea room
  > Mailing/local newspaper
  > 'Traditional', clean and quality and value perception
  > Message elements: title, traditional, adventure, descriptive text.

TARGETING

Targeting is about selecting the most relevant segments and developing a product offer and communications strategy that will be attractive to the segments. Once relevant segments have been identified, it is important to test the segment – this may be done via focus groups or customer panels. The testing should involve checks to establish the most effective variables for the group. This may be everything from the colour of the promotional material to the key elements of the message or sales proposition or position. There are three targeting strategies.

Undifferentiated targeting

In order to gain competitive advantage, a product or service is mass marketed at a lower cost than the competition. The product is usually a low-end, no frills product, which is cheap to produce, has low overheads and can be distributed to a mass market at a cheaper price than competitors. Marketing tends to focus on promoting low-cost benefits, e.g. selling student nights by promoting cheap drinks.

Differentiated targeting

Marketing based on differentiation focuses on matching features and benefits of a range (categories) of a brand's products and services to attract a range of customers to the brand. For instance, an arts centre will produce a range of products (different events) for different audiences, and these will be available for different age groups and sexes.

Marketing spend is distributed between the different market segments on a cyclical basis. This might follow a seasonal approach, e.g. pantomime.

Niche targeting

Companies with a number of brands or product lines focus marketing spend on products capable of category leadership, e.g. the Crucible Theatre in Sheffield stages the World Snooker Championship.

Activity

- Review the section on segmentation and targeting.
- Construct a table with four columns and ten rows.
- Access the NIA (National Indoor Arena) website at http://www.thenia.co.uk
- In the first column list ten forthcoming events (products).
- In the second column, segment the events according to audience type (use demographic and NRS variables).
- In the third column, consider the messages for each event (use the Grand Theatre Wolverhampton case study to help you with this task).
- In the fourth column, list the possible communication channels for targeting each audience (other than the NIA website).
- Select one of the events on your chart. What hospitality packages are available? How will this add further segmentation and targeting opportunities for the NIA?

MARKETING MIX

The marketing mix, also referred to as the 7 Ps, is made up of the concepts *product, price, place, promotion* (communication), *people, process* and *physical evidence*. Each event is unique and the marketing mix must be manipulated to reflect the marketing environment, competitors and future trends, and get the product to market so that it is the targeted consumers' choice above that of the competition (communication creates the desire for the consumer to consume). Products and services need to be designed and delivered for/to the target market, at the right price, and available to purchase/experience in the right place using the most appropriate communication tactics for the targeted customer in an ever-changing marketing environment.

The marketing mix of services: people, process and physical evidence

Events are made up of tangible and intangible elements. Levitt (1986) proposed that instead of talking of 'goods' and of 'services', it is better to talk of 'tangibles' and 'intangibles'.

Products are manufactured and services are performed, and in performing services, a number of actors are involved: employees, suppliers, shareholders and stakeholders (includes other customers in the service environment). Services have a range of characteristics, which means that they require the services mix: people, process and physical evidence to be employed for the delivery of the event experience. The characteristics of the services are:

- **Intangibility** – the customer cannot see tangible evidence of the product being purchased. The tangible evidence is the ticket/merchandise/photo or recording on mobile phone … a memory of the experience.
- **Inseparability** – production and consumption occur at the same time. An event customer enjoys the event as it is being delivered.

- **Heterogeneity** – maintaining a consistent product is difficult: each individual has a different experience of the event and this can be affected by the location, i.e. view of the event, other customers (drunken spectators) or friendly or unhelpful staff.
- **Ownership** – the consumer does not usually buy the title of the service, i.e. you pay for the event and take home the feeling of enjoyment or dissatisfaction.
- **Perishability** – the event experience cannot be stored. Unused capacity is lost forever. Unsold tickets cannot be stockpiled for the following day.

PEOPLE

Internal marketing incorporates the training systems and ongoing delivery of the service by the stakeholders involved in event delivery. This means that internal systems need to make sure that staff (including volunteers) are equipped (through the HR function) to deliver the level of service required to perform the service – this means that personnel need to be happy enough in their work to buy into the company ethos (reflected in brand values, e.g. teamwork) and portray it at all times in the performance of their job role.

PROCESS

The process of an event incorporates the systems and procedures set up to deliver the event to the consumer. This will consist of operating procedures for each part of the process, e.g. queuing systems, service delivery guidelines for staff, health and safety procedures. Processes need to be communicated to all event stakeholders, and managed and controlled, and are subject to internal audit systems, e.g. checklists, and external audits, e.g. mystery guest. The process part of the marketing mix is brand management.

PHYSICAL EVIDENCE

The physical evidence presents customer-facing communications to customers incorporating signage, transportation, uniforms, website and these all have to be in keeping with the brand image. This is achieved through uniformity in design features, e.g. colours, logos and messages conveyed to consumers by the people involved in their delivery.

PRODUCT

Events, like any product in the service sector are intangible, transient and, by definition, produced and consumed simultaneously. To understand the true nature of the exchange process between producer and consumer, we must first appreciate what the customers are actually buying and how this affects the decision-making process.

Features and benefits

Features – the things that make the product what it is. To take a simple example, imagine a charity fundraising dinner. The features are the venue, the food and drink, the service, the raffle and the after-dinner speaker.

Benefits – what the features give you. Using the example above, the benefits of attending the fundraising dinner are easy to understand: on a very basic level, there is sustenance, social interaction and shared experiences. There are also slightly more complex benefits such as good feelings associated with donating money to charity, the excitement of the raffle and the entertainment of the after-dinner speaker.

Levitt (1986) proposes that as marketers we must understand that people do not buy products for how they do things (features), but rather what they give you at the point of use or consumption (benefits). In short, products are purchased because the benefits of the product satisfy the customer's needs.

The product make-up

It is therefore the case that every product has intrinsic benefits. By breaking the product down into levels, we can more easily identify and understand these benefits, which enable us to communicate these with our potential customers more effectively.

Kotler *et al.* (2010) proposed three levels of a product: core product, actual (or real) product and augmented product. Table 7.2 shows the levels of product for a fundraising dinner.

This is all well and good when applied to an event where the tangible elements are immediately intrinsic to the product such as a dinner, but the same rules also apply to intangible products and services. The following list shows the levels of product for the V Festival, a large music festival established in 1996 that attracts over 85,000 visitors per day over a weekend with over 115 acts, held at Western Park, South Staffordshire:

- **Core product:** the ticket! The piece of paper/barcode/wristband that gets you into the event.
- **Actual product:** over 115 different bands, the venue, the spot on which to pitch your tent, the shops and merchandise, the traffic management, the stewards, the toilets.
- **Augmented product:** the atmosphere, the anticipation, the experience.

While the overall marketing offering is the event itself, many of the elements that make up the overall product have tangible aspects and associated benefits. Using this model, we

Table 7.2. Levels of a product.

Product level	Definition	Features	Benefits
Core product	The central product satisfying the key need with core benefits	Food and drink	Sustenance
Actual product	What the product actually is made up of (usually tangible)	The venue, the raffle tickets, the other guests	Somewhere to sit and eat, social interaction and shared experiences
Augmented product	Additional intangible elements	The service, the speaker, and raffle draw and collection	Excitement, entertainment and positive feelings of giving

can better understand the nature of the exchange process, identifying the key features, benefits and therefore what needs we are satisfying, so we can understand more about our customers. In short, using the model in this way allows marketers to understand the entire product and focus specifically on the needs of the customer, and therefore better meet expectations.

Product life cycle

In the case of an event, the *event development stage* involves a feasibility study to ensure that the event is viable and will break even financially.

- **Introductory stage** – involves heavy publicity to bring the event to the attention of the consumer. An integrated communications strategy will ensure that a communications mix, which takes into account discounting as deemed necessary, e.g. the Internet and social networking, has enabled targeted communication and pre-registration for music festivals in advance of ticket release.
- **Growth** – an event in growth will have manipulated the marketing mix to the best effect and may sell out within minutes of ticket release. The PR machine will be used to communicate this popularity and create the desire for ticket purchase at the next possible opportunity.
- **Maturity** – can be applied to repeat annual events, for example, which may attract a loyal consumer base, fall in and out of fashion (depending on the marketing environment, content, artists/celebrity endorsement). Heavy promotion, e.g. discounting through loyalty schemes, may be necessary to ensure the event sells out year after year.

BRAND IMAGE AND EVENTS

Event tourism is the recognized strategy for cities as a key driver for economic development and regeneration, and the competition to win mega-events has mobilized national and regional governments' marketing function (marketing development agencies) in ensuring that bids win the opportunity to stage sporting, music, arts and cultural events. The knock-on effect (positive or negative) from high-profile events can make or break a local economy. Cities and venues use the kudos from association with events to brand themselves as City of Sport (London; Sheffield), City of Culture (Liverpool) and to gain international recognition, e.g. London 2012, Edinburgh Festival, Glastonbury, Wimbledon, Crucible (snooker).

PRICE

Getting the right price is a balancing act. Charge too much and no one will purchase. Charge too little and you won't cover the costs. Finding the balancing point between what the customers will be willing to pay and how much is required to make the event profitable is a hard job for marketers.

Careful costing is the secret to successful pricing, taking into account all income, including sponsorship, grants and advertising revenue as well as ticket sales and the impact of promotional discounts. In addition to the income, all expenditure must be budgeted for.

Taxes, insurance and licensing costs should obviously be included in the overall budget for the event, but it is also wise to ensure that all aspects of the event are covered from public liability insurance to insurance against losses because of cancellation by a headline act or bad weather, for example.

Once the budget is in place, a baseline price or ticket yield can be set. This is the minimum average price that needs to be levied in order for the event to be feasible. This is obviously dependent on the forecasted ticket sales, which can be estimated using information from the focus groups and other research, the venue's figures and sales patterns for similar events.

This research will also allow marketers to establish the degree of elasticity in the pricing, that is to say the degree to which sales increase or decrease with changes in prices. For Madonna's 2009 concert at Madison Square Garden in New York, tickets were selling for a top price of over £3000, but over 100,000 tickets were sold on the first day. The price of tickets did not matter to the fans and hence the price is relatively inelastic: as the price increases, the number of tickets sold remains constant.

When setting prices for events, it is important to consider all the costs to the customer – this is not just the cost of the ticket, but includes booking fees and travel, for example. There is also the opportunity cost to the customer. This concept, first proposed by Kotler *et al.* (2010) takes into account the cost to the customer of coming to an event in terms of time, and what they cannot do as a result of attending. If that is missing their favourite TV programme, the opportunity costs may be low, but if that is missing their mother's birthday party, the costs may increase.

Armed with all this information, marketers can go about setting their pricing policy. There are a number of types (from Adcock *et al.*, 2001):

- **A penetration policy** may see a deliberately low price set to maximize the sales but at a smaller profit margin. This is a common for newer events where the audience or customer base is not already established.
- **An economy strategy** is for budget events, where costs to customer are low. This could be because costs are low and therefore the price can be, or it may also be a loss leader if there is funding from an external source and the main aim is to have large numbers attending.
- **A skimming policy** sees marketers charging as much as they can get away with for a high margin and low costs. Good for one-off events, but audiences can feel short-changed.
- **Premium policy** where costs to the producer are high, and so are ticket prices, but the value to the audience is proportionally high.
- **Psychological pricing** is about trying to get customers to respond emotionally to prices. Seeing £19.95 rather than £20 can be significant and certainly works as part of all the above strategies except the premium policy. With premium events, customers are expecting the price to be 'reassuringly expensive'. Top price tickets at the Royal Opera House in London are over £220 – more than three times the top price tickets of other theatres in the West End.

Supply and demand

Marketers aim to create the desire to purchase, supply and demand play a part in creating interest and inflating the ticket price for events (see Box 7.4). Positive supply and demand

---

Box 7.4. Supply and demand: Take That's 'Circus' Tour 2009.

Take That's 2009 'Circus' tour became the fastest-selling in UK history, selling 600,000 tickets in 5 hours (*Daily Mail*, 2008). When a second wave of tickets was released, consumers were given no indication of supply and, as dates were released, demand for tickets outstripped supply (and these also sold out in record time). Tickets were immediately available for sale on eBay, selling for larger sums than the ticket's face price. Over the following months, further tickets became available, with tickets released for sale at various venues right up to the concert dates. Ticket sales slowed down as demand decreased, leaving a number of tickets available for purchase. eBay activity ground to a halt as it became apparent that the supply of tickets outweighed the demand; tickets on eBay were eventually sold at a fraction of the original purchase price.

---

is created when a product is desired and demanded by more people than the production can satisfy. Negative supply and demand is created when there is a supply of a product but little/ no demand.

Marketing in the recession

Mintel's 2009 British Lifestyle's report attributes fear of how the recession might affect consumers to their changing buyer behaviour. Spending on nights out declined by 8% in 2008, with 2009 figures projected to show further decline, with consumers cutting back not because they have to but because its seen as the right thing to do in a troubled economy (Brenchley, 2009).

Leisure organizations have been forced to introduce price reductions in order to come through the recession in good shape. Price reductions help to communicate a 'value for money' message to consumers. Football clubs have heavily discounted season tickets, seeing the benefits of rewarding customer loyalty to maintaining retention in the short and long term and riding the recession. Bolton Wanderers Football Club has used the opportunity to grow the market sector 'children', seeing this as a market opportunity to fill empty seats, nurture fans of the future and offer value for money to families purchasing more than one season ticket (Hayman, 2009).

PLACE

Marketing or distribution channels

Events can be sold directly to consumers or indirectly via marketing channels (distribution channels). Marketing channels are made up of intermediaries: sales agents, wholesalers and retailers. Ticket sales for events are often handled by an intermediary, e.g. seetickets.com or Ticketmaster. This enables event operators to buy into the security of a professional outfit to manage ticket sales (including management information to evaluate consumer behaviour and sales data for future events).

Push/pull factors and place

Push and pull are terms used to describe the method by which companies place their products and services within distribution channels (how events are sold to consumers).

Pushing the communication to the customer via intermediaries (ticket agents) makes use of larger networks.

A pull strategy sells directly to consumers using a message designed to inform, remind or persuade, pulling people towards taking specified action, e.g. direct e-mail notification of an event, which gets users to log on to a website.

PROMOTION (COMMUNICATIONS)

Promotion is the part of the marketing mix that uses marketing communication channels to sell products and services to targeted consumers. The communications mix consists of advertising, sponsorship, direct and word-of-mouth marketing, PR, sales and merchandising.

Integrated marketing campaigns use a variety of communications methods and media to create as much impact as possible for a product or service within a specific timescale. The trend for electronic communications has seen the rise in campaigns opting for this medium, but traditional methods are still employed, such as paper brochures, direct marketing by postal mail, and flyers and billposters. Promoting events is key to their success or failure, whether paying or free entry. The skill is to hit as many of the marketing channels appropriate to the targeting strategy as possible, sending repeated communications to build anticipation, excitement and desire to purchase.

Designing and communicating messages

AIDA is the framework most commonly used for designing a promotional message:

- A: Get attention (cognitive)
- I: Hold interest
- D: Arouse desire (affective)
- A: Obtain action (behavioural)

The message on the communication, be it a billposter, leaflet, brochure, direct mail, advert, etc., needs to convey the event accurately and there are a number of factors to consider: relevant and accurate copy; who, what, where, when and why of event; unique selling point (USP) of event; inclusion of quotes from previous reviews; font (size, colour, typeface); and number of words (minimal). Considering visuals, images should represent the target market and the communication should display the logos of the event organization and any sponsors. The process for communicating a promotional message is:

1. Determine target market.
2. Select communication channels considered the best fit (one or more) for the target market depending on the budget.
3. Design a message that will provide the right information to arouse interest in the event and purchase/attendance behaviour (buying a ticket or attending if a free event).
4. Promote features and benefits to target market, e.g. quality/price/size/thrilling experience.
5. Consider an appropriate format to attract attention: position, colour, copy (words), headline or strapline.
6. Message structure: who, what, when, where and why.

Writing a press release

A press release is the biggest PR opportunity available and is used to generate coverage in the media: TV, radio, newspaper and specialist publication (as a news story), to get the event free media coverage. The format for a press release is:

1. **Start** with the words **PRESS RELEASE** (in bold) and put the date for the news to be released.
2. **Headline**: the first ten words of your release are the most important. Briefly summarize the event news. This is used to hook the media, so must be newsworthy. The headline should be specific and sum up the main idea of the press release.
3. **Details of the event**: the who, what, where, when and why of the event. Ensure that the important details of the event are covered.
4. **Main body of the release**: further explanation, statistics, background, or other details relevant to the event. Include quotes and photographs.
5. **Media contact information for the event**: contact person: phone/fax number, e-mail address, website address.

The press release should be written on company letterhead, in the style of the targeted media, as a news report (make the copy press ready) and, after e-mailing to the media, followed up with a phone call.

ADVERTISING

Advertising involves communicating a message to a target market through the most suitable channel that motivates purchase behaviour. Advertising channels include cinema, television, Internet, radio (see BBC Radio One case study, Box 7.5), print, information kiosks (touch screen) and billboards, both static and digital.

There are a number of free listing services that the event planner can tap into to communicate prior notice of events: newspaper, specialist publications, radio, other similar events, noticeboards and through placing posters/banners in the area where the event will take place.

For events such as festivals, the launch event provides a publicity machine and information exchange to a number of audiences: press, target audience and local influential figures who will communicate the message further through word-of-mouth, e.g. taxi drivers and other business figures.

Box 7.5. BBC Radio One at Edinburgh Festival Fringe 2009.

The biggest arts festival in the world – the Edinburgh Festival Fringe (*Marketing*, 2009).

The Scott Mills Show on BBC Radio One took *Scott Mills: The Musical* to the Edinburgh Festival Fringe in August 2009, using his 5–7 pm show to advertise the production over a 6-month period running up to the performance. The show was transmitted live from Edinburgh, giving the Festival profile among his viewing consumers (the appearance at Edinburgh also gave Scott Mills and Radio One profile among the Festival consumer audience). Scott and his team had several Scottish radio interviews prior to the production. The production was posted onto the Radio One Website for listeners to view and on the breakfast show the morning after the first night. Exit feedback (recorded as the audience left the performance) was played.

MERCHANDISE

Events and sponsors of events use merchandising opportunities for high brand recognition.

Merchandise is advertising material containing messages relating to a specific event, e.g. tour T-shirts and memorabilia. Many venues adopt slogans from reviews (good news stories) and display on T-shirts (often worn by staff) to shout about achievements. Point of sale merchandise is used within venues to sell products unrelated to an event, e.g. alcohol.

Merchandise is characterized by its sale at events and through event outlets (stores and online merchandise sites) as well as through intermediaries (e.g. retail outlets, sports and music stores). Merchandise for events is often unique, because of the nature of events as a one-off experience, and can be sought-after as a collector's item, fetching high sums on auction sites such as eBay.

Freebies from sponsors can become the deciding factor for consumers taking part in similar events where there is a choice, e.g. in running events the seasoned competitor may make their race selection through the contents of the 'freebie package' given to all race finishers (the race with the best give-aways is selected), therefore building a comparison table between similar events and then selecting the one with the best features and benefits.

PR

Good news/bad news stories

PR strategy is a balance between using good news stories as a means of promotion and managing bad news stories to deflect negative publicity. Events are often high risk in media terms with health and safety: disasters, event cancellation, supporter behaviour and quality of performers all at the hands of reporters looking for a bad news story to sell. The fashion is to create good news stories from event consumers (see Cancer Research case study, Box 7.6), personalizing events and building loyalty from and relationships with consumers and supporters (Wilkerson, 2009).

SPONSORSHIP

Global sponsorship expenditure for 2009 is predicted to be £26.96 billion with film, theatre, the arts and fashion the growth areas providing sponsors with useful content: videos of performances,

---

Box 7.6. Cancer Research UK's Race For Life.

Cancer Research UK's (CRUK) partnership with Race For life has helped to increase awareness of cancer and to increase charity donations. A recent shift in the charity's brand strategy has seen the use of cancer patients and survivors rather than actors, 'because ... the research that people are surviving, and demonstrating this, increases people's consideration of the charity, encouraging them to donate more ... the use of real people has also deflected the negative responses that charity campaigns can provoke' (Wilkerson, 2009, p. 20). CRUK's partnership with Race for Life is the brand's key awareness activity. Race For Life, which started in 1994, saw 740,000 participants in races across the UK between May and July 2009 (Wilkerson, 2009). CRUK 'Share Your Story' on their website invites participants to contribute personal experiences to help with publicity. Cancerchat enables experience to be shared on a discussion forum.

Source: Cancer Research UK (2009)

music and artworks, which can be used on websites, adverts and customer-only products or services. Sponsors, often referred to as partners, use sponsorship to create awareness, increase brand loyalty, change or refocus the brand image, drive retailer traffic, and stimulate sales, trial or use (Jack, 2009). Sponsorship has moved from its corporate hospitality function with brands signing up to gain the use of valuable content, push a message or entertain clients.

Sponsorship deals are moving from celebrity sponsorship to growth areas such as cause-related marketing (Jack, 2009). Associating a brand with a charity or responsible product can help an event to reposition itself as socially responsible and attract consumers with associated buying behaviour. Brands that have been criticized for less scrupulous corporate social responsibility (CSR) practices are keen to associate with events that will help them establish and build consumer perceptions that they are environmentally and socially responsible. McDonald's has had its share of bad publicity for its CSR practice, e.g. McLibel. McDonald's has used sponsorship deals with major events such as London 2012 to create good news stories in an attempt to negate the bad ones.

Products will pay a premium to associate themselves with events and the image of the product will be strongly aligned with the image of the event and portray the characteristics of the participants. At the Trinidad Carnival in February 2009, two beers were represented as official sponsors: Carib and Stag. Very similar in taste, they were positioning themselves to two different markets. Both had equal exposure and utilized merchandising opportunities: free cups, headscarves, T-shirts and other paraphernalia. Stag's advertising was blatant in its masculine message: 'Stag Lager beer – A Man's Beer'.

ATMOSPHERICS

Atmospherics is about understanding how the environment and physical attributes of a venue or surroundings can affect the customer's behaviour and enjoyment, both on a conscious and sub-conscious level. Whether they know it or not, customers will respond differently to different colours, different floor coverings, different music and different lighting. It is therefore important that marketers understand these changes in behaviour and use them to maximize the impact. Live events use atmospherics to stimulate the audiences' senses and convey the mood of an event, e.g. rousing/sad music, fireworks and special effects, such as strobe lights, stage floor lighting and 3D effects like snow. The idea is to give an experience to satisfy expectations and ultimately ensure repeat purchasing behaviour. Sometimes atmospherics are used to control an environment, as can be illustrated in the Theatre Toilets case study in Box 7.7.

Box 7.7. Theatre toilets.

The Coronation Hall, in Ulverston, South Cumbria, UK was like many other theatres and concert halls, especially when it came to the queue outside the ladies' toilets. The marketing staff had noted that a significant number of comments and complaints referred to this problem. The Council therefore began to investigate plans to extend the toilets and increase the number of cubicles. At the same time, the marketing team discreetly studied the behaviour of the ladies in the toilets and in doing so discovered that it was not the lack of cubicles that was the problem, it was the people stood around chatting that were causing bottlenecks.

Having discovered this, the marketing manager suggested redecorating the ladies' toilets. The soft carpet and subtle lighting were replaced with industrial but stylish lino and

(Continued)

Box 7.7. Continued.
hard, bright lights. The walls were painted a bright white. The changes turned the toilets from a warm, cosy area to a hard, clinical, clean and sterile area.

Following the changes, the effect was evident. People were moving through the toilets much more quickly, and the queues were significantly reduced. As a result, the plans to extend the toilets were ... flushed!

E-COMMUNICATIONS

Significant drives to improve broadband and Internet availability and accessibility over the past 10 years has created a 24/7, low-cost and interactive media that has revolutionized the marketers' toolbox, not to mention the massive potential of e-commerce operations even to small organizations – see the Arena Theatre online booking case study in Box 7.8. Using websites, e-mail and social networking sites as part of an integrated communications strategy is key to developing deeper, richer and more meaningful interaction with existing and potential customers (see V Festival case study, Box 7.9).

Social networking websites and the ease with which users can generate their own content including video, is creating huge on-line communities, where users can upload pictures, videos and directly share their experiences about events. This enables marketers to not only reach customers easily, cheaply and in a very focused way, but also offers a semi-tangible legacy to an event days, weeks, months, years after the event has taken place.

With faster and faster broadband speeds, online video is the fastest growing area in e-marketing. According to *Marketing Week* (2009), 4.7 billion online videos were viewed in the UK in April 2009 alone. While the potential of this is difficult to harness, the growth in organizations that are creating video specifically for online circulation is significant. A massive viral campaign, where the users themselves disseminate videos and other content is an incredibly powerful medium. We have all received e-mails from friends and colleagues inviting us to 'check out this funny video', which we then pass that on to a network of our friends and colleagues. This rapid dissemination of content is, according to de-construct (2009), a digital marketing and communications agency, three times as effective as traditional media including television for enabling customer recall (*Marketing Week*, 2009).

Box 7.8. Arena Theatre Wolverhampton online booking.
The Arena Theatre in Wolverhampton launched its online booking system in November 2008. While this is a number of years after similar systems have been available, other venues including the Grand Theatre Wolverhampton, which has had online booking for over 3 years, average about 20% of their sales online. The Arena Theatre has, however, in the space of a year developed the online sales to the point that 40% of sales come from online bookers, with a significant majority of transactions being conducted outside of the Box Office opening hours. Through the development of an integrated communications strategy, that places 'buy now' links in all e-mails and throughout the website, customers can view content and be able to buy tickets within a couple of clicks.

Box 7.9. V Festival.

The V Festival's website has over 200,000 registered users. The festival organizers appointed de-construct as their digital agency in June 2009. According to Dawn Woodhouse, V Festival coordinator, the festival aims to build 'a content-rich digital festival destination' (V Festival, 2009). From forums and live Twitter updates, to exclusive videos and performances, users can interact with and relive the festival long after the last tent has come down. Of course, all of this content sits besides links to the online merchandise shop and links to the ticket distributors.

VIRAL MARKETING (SOCIAL MEDIA MARKETING)

Based on the concept of word-of-mouth marketing (person-to-person communication), viral marketing involves spreading a message across multiple media making it reach more people. It relies on people using various elements of social media to forward the message (Charlesworth, 2009). Examples of social media include Facebook, Bebo, Twitter, SMS texting, mobile phones and YouTube. The case study in Box 7.10 demonstrates the immediacy and impact of social media to the success of artists and events.

Box 7.10. Viral marketing: *Britain's Got Talent* live shows.

Susan Boyle's appearance on *Britain's Got Talent* created PR frenzy when she became an 'unlikely global Internet star' (Holmwood, 2009). Described as the biggest viral marketing campaign, it broke viewing records with viewings of her video clip on YouTube leaping from 1.5 to 5 million in under 24 h. By April 2009, assorted clips of Boyle's performance had been viewed more than 11 million times (Holmwood, 2009). Celebrity chatter on Twitter and Facebook by Hollywood actors including Demi Moore helping to increase global awareness of this overnight success. Reality television shows have been criticized by event marketers as marketing vehicles for their live shows. *The X Factor* sold out before the TV series had aired the final, and Susan Boyle was front-page news internationally following her appearance, featuring on International news and gaining extensive media coverage in America including the Oprah Winfrey show. Michael Jackson viewed *Britain's Got Talent* contestant Shaheen Jafargholi on YouTube and he was invited to duet with Jackson on the singer's 30-date comeback London concerts at the O2 Arena (Timesonline, 2009). Following Michael Jackson's unexpected death in June 2009, Shaheen was elevated to the international stage with his performance at Michael Jackson's Memorial Concert.

Questions

Consider a recent event that you have experienced.
- What marketing communication channels did they use to promote the event?
- Which channel was the most effective to get your attention?
- What information was communicated in the promotion? Consider images and words.
- Using the information provided in the promotion section, suggest alternative methods that could have been used.

POSITIONING

Positioning is used by marketers to understand customers' perceptions (psychological responses) of events in order to correctly place the communications of products or services so that they will be in choice position, above the competition. Positioning follows different conventions.

- **Positioning against a competitor's offering**, also referred to as comparison marketing (Thomas, 2009) – here an aggressive position is taken to play the competitor at their strengths; often the competitor is named in communications with their weaknesses highlighted.
- **Positioning the benefits of the event**, e.g. value, unique experience. To determine the benefits, the consumer's profile needs to be analysed (segmentation) and the marketer has to be able to predict the most likely variables to appeal to the targeted consumer. Marketing intelligence data from focus groups and other feedback mechanisms is used to determine variables.

Competition on price-focused advertising as a result of the recession has spurred competition, and price perception strategies have been used to communicate price position to customers.

REPOSITIONING

Repositioning strategies are used to change/expand the target market. This may be decided because of a growing market segment determined by market intelligence, e.g. Mintel future trends, which will indicate changing demographics such as a decrease in the market. Repositioning may involve the inclusion of a demographic not previously represented, e.g. the inclusion of BMX in the Beijing 2008 Olympics was a strategy to engage the youth market.

Repositioning strategies are used to communicate a chosen image to consumers. This may be necessary to enter different markets, e.g. international markets.

Box 7.11. From the inside out, City of Birmingham Symphony Orchestra.

The City of Birmingham Symphony Orchestra, under the baton of Sir Simon Rattle, became one of the premier orchestras in Europe over the 18 years of his tenure. The international reputation of the Orchestra was cemented with the opening in 1991 of the 'acoustically perfect' Symphony Hall, Birmingham (thsh, 2009). This 2200-seat behemoth in the heart of the England's second city is 'a concert hall which any city in the world would be proud to own' (thsh, 2009).

Sir Simon left the City of Birmingham Symphony Orchestra in 1998, and immediately the impact on sales and attendance was seen. According to Sarah Gee, then Director of Communications, 'the perception was that quality had slipped – think of Virgin without Richard Branson' (Morton Smyth Ltd, 2004). With the appointment of Steven Maddock as Chief Executive, and facing 'a challenging situation', the Orchestra embarked upon a major repositioning operation based on audience research but with the addition of a healthy dollop of instinct!

(Continued)

Box 7.11. Continued.

In 2001, the major elements of repositioning were complete. Gone was the stuffy City of Birmingham Symphony Orchestra image, as CBSO became the main brand with its associated colourful and dynamic 'splat' logo. But this change was more than skin deep. According to consultants Morton Smyth Ltd (2004), together Gee and Maddock transformed the organization, challenging attitudes and working practices within the company ensuring that firstly, the entire operation became much more focused on the customer (as opposed to audience) and secondly, the culture within the organization was positive and able to adapt and adopt the developments to the product and marketing offering. These developments in the offering were 'significant, but not rocket science' (Morton Smyth Ltd, 2004). By adopting a more informal, chatty and unashamedly enthusiastic and emotional communications strategy, CBSO re-connected with their audience – making the audience realize that the Orchestra felt the same way about the music as they did – as well as opening up doorways to new potential customers, whom previously may have felt excluded by the perception of elitism (Morton Smyth Ltd, 2004).

Realizing the importance of this new, larger potential audience, the CBSO developed a series of several new programming strands to augment their existing product offering. At the forefront of these new strands were two initiatives:

- **Sunday afternoon family concerts** that dispensed with the stuffy traditions, where everything is clearly explained by familiar presenters from television and radio, who introduce the pieces and make the concert enjoyable to people of all ages.
- **Rush hour concerts** – typically concerts would start at 6 pm and last about an hour. These concerts included a wide range of music from film scores to more challenging work by composers such as Stravinsky.

Both of these strands included attractive pricing strategies, usually with tickets ranging from £5 to £10. This was part of a broader pricing policy that saw the introduction of 'Student Standby' tickets at £1.50 as well as a range of season ticket deals and other rewards for regular attendees.

The effects of the repositioning were significant. On top of a 17% increase in audiences in the first full year following the programme, there was a 25% increase in fundraising income and corporate sponsorship, securing the financial position of the Orchestra. The most considerable change, and the most important according to Sarah Gee, is the significant increase in both families and 16–25-year-olds attending concerts. She says, 'It is these people that will form the audiences of the future' (Morton Smyth Ltd, 2004).

SUMMARY

The chapter has outlined concepts related to the marketing of events. Regardless of sector, admission price or audience, the ideas can be used to aid the event marketing planner. The strategic planning process captures the marketing cycle and provides a framework to help the reader to make informed marketing decisions.

Case studies and models have been provided to help students and industry professionals to understand marketing further and to provide practical examples that can be used as an aid to marketing planning.

FURTHER READING

Important periodicals include *Marketing Week* and *Marketing*. The Mintel database is a good resource for market intelligence.

For general reading:

Fisk, P. (2008) *Marketing Genius*, 2nd edn. Wiley Capstone, Mankato, Minnesota.

Kotler, P., Roberto, N. and Lee, N. (2002) *Social Marketing: Improving the Quality of Life*, 2nd edn. Sage, London.

McCarthy, F., Ondaatje, E., Zakaras, L. and Brooks, A. (2004) *Gifts of the Muse – Reframing the Debate about the Benefits of the Arts*. Rand, Santa Monica, California.

Rein, I.J., Kotler, P. and Shields, B. (2006) *The Elusive Fan: Reinventing Sports in a Crowded Marketplace*. McGraw-Hill, New York.

Saget, A. (2006) *The Event Marketing Handbook: Beyond Logistics and Planning*. Kaplan, Chicago, Illinois.

REVIEW QUESTIONS

Select a forthcoming event of your choice: sport, theatre, music concert.

1. Analyse the event using the marketing mix (7 Ps).
2. What marketing communication methods are being used to promote the event?
3. What is the message being communicated e.g. features and benefits/strapline?
4. How are competitors marketing the same/similar product: What marketing channels are they utilizing?
5. How does the promotion of your product fit with the marketing environment?
6. Who has the market share for your product service?
7. Who is the targeted consumer?
8. Using the information from this chapter, how could the marketing of your chosen event be improved?

REFERENCES

Adcock, D., Halborg, A. and Ross, C. (2001) *Marketing Principles and Practice*, 4th edn. Prentice Hall, Mahwah, New Jersey.

Brenchley, S. (2009) Consumer caution. *Leisure Management* Issue 3, 34–35.

Cancer Research UK (2009) Available at: www.raceforlife.org (accessed 13 August 2009).

Charlesworth, A. (2009) *Internet Marketing: a Practical Approach*. Butterworth-Heinemann, Oxford.

Daily Mail (2008) Take That sold 600,000 tickets for their European tour in just five hours today. Available at: http://www.dailymail.co.uk/tvshowbiz/article-1082158/Take-That-sold-600-000-tickets-European-tour-just-hours-today.html#ixzz0ZTEbUXFV (accessed 14 August 2009).

de-construct (2009) Available at: http://pressitt.com/smnr/de-construct-appointed-as-v-festivals-digital-agency/165/ (accessed 14 December 2009).

Gelder, G. and Robinson, P. (2009) A critical comparative study of visitor motivations for attending music festivals: a case study of Glastonbury and V-Festival. *Event Management* 13, 181–196.

Hayman, P. (2009) Staying strong. *Leisure Management* Issue 3.

Holmwood, L. (2009) Susan Boyle's Britain's Got Talent Performance a Hit for ITV Website. Available at: http://guardian.co.uk (accessed 16 April 2009).

Jack, L. (2009) Brands looking for partners in buyers' market. *Marketing Week*, 6 August 2009.

Kotler, P., Bowen, J.T. and Makens, J.C. (2010) *Marketing for Hospitality and Tourism*, 5th edn. Prentice Hall, Mahwah, New Jersey.

Lee, C.K., Lee, Y.K. and Wicks, B.E. (2004) Segmentation of festival motivation by nationality and satisfaction. *Tourism Management* 25, 61–70.

Levitt, T.M. (1986) *The Marketing Imagination*, expanded edn. Free Press, New York.

london2012 (2004) Prime Minister We Won't Let You Down. Available at: http://www.london2012.com/news/bid-phase/prime-minister-we-wont-let-you-down.php (accessed 14 August 2009).

Marketing (2009) Fringe benefits for Sponsors. 5 August 2009.

Marketing Week (2009) Available at: http://www.marketingweek.co.uk/beyond-the-screen/3003085.article (accessed 14 December 2009).

Morton Smyth Ltd (2004) Not For The Likes Of You – Arts Council England 2004. Available at: http://www.takingpartinthearts.com/content.php?content=942 (accessed 14 December 2009).

Nutley, M. (2009) Better targeting lies in the public interest. *Marketing Week*, 30 July 2009.

Petrick, J.F. and Li, X. (2006) A review of festival and event motivation studies. *Event Management* 9, 239–245.

Richards, G. (2007) Culture and authenticity in a traditional event: the views of producers, residents and visitors in Barcelona. *Event Management* 11, 33–44.

Thomas, J. (2009) Supermarkets stick by comparison strategies: price focussed ads fuelled by the recession are under scrutiny. *Marketing*, 5 August 2009.

thsh (2009) Available at: http://www.thsh.co.uk/page/symphony-hall-birmingham/history-of-symphony-hall (accessed 14 August 2009).

Timesonline (2009) Michael Jackson captivated by Shaheen Jafargholi on YouTube. 8 July 2009.

V Festival (2009) Available at: http://www.VFestival.co.uk/about (accessed 14 December 2009).

Wale, D. (2009) Marketing. In: Robinson, P. (ed.) *Operations Management in the Travel Industry*. CAB International, Wallingford, UK.

Wilkerson, B. (2009) Back to reality. *Marketing*, 5 August 2009.

chapter 8

Managing a Quality Event Experience

Ade Oriade

OBJECTIVES OF THE CHAPTER

This chapter stresses the importance of the management of service quality in the events industry. It examines the nature of event products and the role of service quality in enhancing event attendees' experience. The chapter examines how service quality influences satisfaction and repeat visits to events, in the context of concepts and theories of quality management. Theoretical perspectives on perceived quality, value and customer satisfaction are explored and theories such as gap analysis and Kano's theory of attractive quality are highlighted to provide frameworks to enhance students' understanding and assist practitioners in evaluating and managing service quality in the industry.

The objectives of the chapter are to:

- examine the nature of the event product and the role of service quality in enhancing event attendees' experience;
- appraise quality issues that influence events management;
- analyse elements of the quality management process for events planning and organizations; and
- explore and apply quality management concepts and theories in understanding the contexts in which events are held and event organizations operate.

INTRODUCTION

Consumer perceptions of service experiences are central to the viability of organizations, be they service or manufacturing. Service organizations providing event experiences are no exception and the enjoyment and satisfaction of event visitors is shaped by the complex inter-actions of consumers, the event programme, the setting of the event, its management systems, staff and volunteers, and other visitors. It is this interaction that gives rise to quality percep-tion. The word 'quality' means different things to different people and has, over time, become a vital management focus, especially in the service sector. People may find it hard to define or articulate quality, but know when a product or service is not of satisfactory quality. Given the above, researchers and writers have done a tremendous amount of work to shed more light on the definitions and management of quality. To be able to manage quality in a professional way, managers need to understand the nature of quality and appreciate the basic principles underlying its management.

THE NATURE OF THE EVENT PRODUCT

The event product is experiential, consisting of both tangible and intangible elements (see Fig. 8.1). It is essentially a service consisting of an intangible experience of limited duration within a tran-sitory, managed environment. By its nature, and like any other service, the production and con-sumption of events are inseparable. An attendee of an event will have to be present at the point of production for the experience to be consumed. The implications here for managers are twofold: often there is little opportunity to correct mistakes before consumption; secondly, once the prod-uct has been produced it has to be consumed otherwise it will perish, as the event product is difficult, if at all possible, to store. Another characteristic of the event product is the variability of its nature. No two episodes of an event are the same, as the process of production (participants'

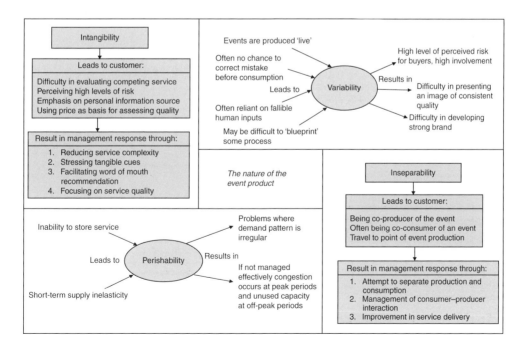

Fig. 8.1. The nature of the event product.

performance, service provider attitude) and production outcomes (experience) are most likely to differ from one episode to the other and from one attendee to another. For event visitors, depending on involvement, some level of risk perception emanates here. Event attendee's sense of negative variability is likely to create a high level of perceived risk and subsequently it is difficult for an event, or attraction, or destination hosting an event to develop a competitive brand.

It is safe to assume that all destinations planning and hosting events aspire to develop strong brands because often the aim of event planners and managers is to deliver attractive event programmes that will appeal to the event attendees and encourage repeat attendance. While the emphasis on the content of the programme will ensure optimal performance of participants and engagement of the spectators, there is also a need for attention to be focused on service performance, exemplified as the extra 'features' that make an event special.

THE MANY FACES OF QUALITY

The word 'quality' means different things to different people. While there may be some variations in the way quality is being defined, there are two main approaches employed in defining quality. These are the manufacturing industry approach and the service industry approach. Defining quality using the manufacturing approach ensures that the focus is on 'the totality of features and characteristics of a product or service that bears on its ability to meet a stated or implied need' (ISO, 1994). To this end, quality writers like Crosby (1979) defined quality as 'conformance to requirements' and Juran (1988) as 'fitness for use'.

On the other hand, quality in the service sector focuses on customer experience and based on this, Engel *et al.* (1986) view quality as a function of the customer's experiences and the personal values that govern their expectations. The common conceptualization of service quality is the one put forward by Parasuraman *et al.* (1985), denoting service quality as the gap between customers' (visitors') expectations and performance of service received. Based on this perceived quality is the extent to which an event attendee's expectations and perceptions of service delivered are similar or different. Given this view, expectation becomes a major influence in the way the characteristics of service will be perceived and consequently influences the resultant level of satisfaction derived from the event. The implication is that quality in the events industry is predominantly assessed from the human dimension, which is mostly intangible and consequently hard to measure in contrast to physical products.

Aside from these two approaches, and to understand the quality context fully, Garvin (1988) listed five categories of criteria that can be used to define quality. They are:

- Transcendent/judgemental criteria: superiority or excellence; an image that is variable in the minds of customers.
- Product-based criteria: a function of specific, measurable variables where differences in quality reflect differences in quantity of some product attribute.
- User-based criteria: fitness for intended use.
- Value-based criteria: the relationship of usefulness or satisfaction to price.
- Manufacturing-based criteria: conformance to specifications: the desirable outcome of engineering and manufacturing practice.

The user and value-based criteria, arguably, can be said to be more applicable in an event context. However, other bases are useful in explaining attendees of events definition of quality. For instance, an attendee may use the transcendent basis to judge an event or number and variety (product-based) of activities/exhibits/shows in an event to arrive at the overall judgement of quality.

It is not uncommon when people are discussing events they have attended to hear expressions like 'there is nothing much to see there' or 'plenty to see and do' or 'you can't see everything in one visit'. Expressions like this are often followed by other views such as 'it is not value for money going by the number of activities' or 'you need to see for yourself', respectively. It is safe to conclude that visitors to events, as a consequence of their perception of the quality, value and feeling of satisfaction, may recommend the event, revisit or never attend again. (See the section on related and intermediary concepts for further explanation.)

In evaluating quality, expectation plays a major role in the way the characteristics of service are perceived. Customer expectations of a product may be built on past experience, recommendations from friends and relatives (like the illustration above) and/or promotional/organization communication to the customer, which informs the basis of customer judgement of the service provided. The judgement, most of the time, is based on rational evaluation and reflection; at other times, there is ample opportunity for customers to judge without rational evaluation. Audiences judge service from both subjective and objective perspectives. They evaluate quality from a number of dimensions which range from tangible to intangible aspects of the product. The area of quality dimension has been widely researched in services management generally and event and leisure related studies in particular. In view of these efforts a number of theories and models have been developed to improve our knowledge of the construct quality as well as how to manage it.

Question

Think of a recent event you attended, and define and evaluate your quality perception using the different criteria suggested by Garvin (1988). What was your experience? What sort of behaviour did you exhibit afterwards?

CONCEPTS AND THEORIES OF QUALITY MANAGEMENT

Quality management emanates from the manufacturing industry. The majority of concepts and theories of service quality are developed from quality management in manufacturing. However, it has been proved that quality in the service sector cannot be managed like the manufacturing sector because of the characteristics of services (intangible, perishable, inseparable, etc.). To this end, the customers' viewpoint is the mainstay of service quality exploration. The use of the customers' viewpoints in exploring service quality is exemplified by two schools of thought: the Scandinavian school and the US school, otherwise known as Nordic and American perspectives of conceptualization of service quality. Both of these are based on the confirmation/disconfirmation paradigm. This is an approach to studying customer satisfaction based on the assumption that visitors, before attending an event, have a set of expectations against which the performance of the event will be judged. The expectations are either confirmed (when the expectations match with performance) or disconfirmed (negatively – lower performance or positively – higher performance than expectations).

The American school of thought sees customers (event attendees) as information processors and employs the confirmation/disconfirmation paradigm to operationalize service quality. This school of thought, arguably led by Parasuraman *et al.* revising their 1985 work, defines service quality in terms of five service characteristics – empathy, tangibility, assurance, responsiveness and reliability. While the Parasuraman *et al.* conceptualization has been widely used in services management studies and practice, including events management, the dimensions they proposed have been found not to be applicable in some service sectors. Figure 8.2 presents a diagrammatic expression of Parasuraman *et al.*'s conceptualization of service quality as the discrepancy between expectations and service performance.

On the other hand, the Scandinavian school emphasizes a more holistic idea based on technical and functional dimensions, customer relationships and organization image (Grönroos, 2000). The technical aspect of quality according to Grönroos (1982) represents *what* the attendees receive, measured objectively by event attendees. The functional quality denotes *how* the service is delivered, which is mostly evaluated subjectively by the customers (event attendees). The *how* dimension places much emphasis on volunteers'/employees' behaviour and relationships with attendees in terms of courtesy, attentiveness, friendliness and so on. Grönroos subsequently expanded his 1982 theory of functional and technical quality to a more holistic model of *Total Perceived Quality* (Fig. 8.3), which incorporates and considers the effect of external factors on expected quality. Williams and Buswell (2003) submit that this model can be employed and is appropriate in the tourism and leisure contexts, which includes many events.

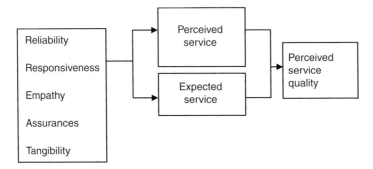

Fig. 8.2. Perceived service quality. Source: adapted from Parasuraman *et al.* (1988).

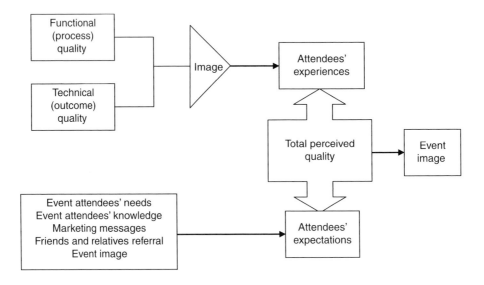

Fig. 8.3. Total Perceived Quality model. Source: adapted from Grönroos (2000).

While most writers concur with Parasuraman *et al.* and Grönroos, that customers (event attendees) categorize into dimensions the characteristics of service, it must be noted that no study is yet able to present a set of dimensions capable of capturing features of quality in all service sectors. Oriade (2008), in agreement with other writers' views, submits that quality is context specific; hence, managers need to identify dimensions that are applicable in their sector. Managers not only should be able to identify appropriate quality features that are the basis of attendees' quality perception formation, they also need to know their implications for service delivery and how to manage them. Researchers in the field of service quality have delineated both conceptually and empirically the identification and management of important quality features in various sectors. One such effort can be found in Kano's theory of attractive quality.

Kano's theory of attractive quality

Kano's theory of attractive quality has been widely applied within quality management, product development and services management. It has commonly been used in product development and service development processes to study the role of various quality attributes in customers' perceptions of quality. The theory of attractive quality focuses on the correlation between the performance of a specific quality attribute and customer satisfaction with that quality attribute.

The principal aspect of Kano theory of attractive quality is the classification of quality into five categories of attributes:

- One-dimensional (Satisfier) attributes – a symmetrical relationship between the degree of functionality and satisfaction.
- Attractive (Exciter) attributes – characterized by heightening levels of satisfaction in relation to increased functionality.
- Must-be (Non-negotiable) attributes – their presence in products prevents perception of inferior quality.
- Neutral attributes – the functional state that neither brings about satisfaction nor dissatisfaction.
- Reverse quality – characteristics that bring about negative impacts or dissatisfaction. The main idea here is to identify what these features are and avoid investing on or creating them.

These categories can be employed by event managers to identify opportunities for service differentiation and can help managers to understand when event attendees are employing compensatory principles when making choices. Kano (2001) contested the customary belief that better performance of services will lead to more satisfied customers; a view that is prevalent in the events industry. Kano (2001) posits that attributes of a product (event) will be perceived differently by individual attendees and each attribute has a different level of influence on customers' (event attendees') satisfaction.

In applying Kano's principle in managing the quality of an event, imagine employing a survey method to elicit responses from the attendees of an event – not the conventional customer satisfaction survey! Managers need to ask a set of two opposing questions (in terms of sufficiency or insufficiency) for each identified quality attribute of your event – for example car parking. The questionnaire will read thus:

1a. If the event has adequate car parking facilities, how would you feel?
1b. If the event does not have adequate car parking facilities, how would you feel?

Assume the respondent's answer to 1a is *neutral* on a three-level scale featuring dissatisfied, neutral and satisfied (Kano, 2001, revised scale); and the answer to 1b is *dissatisfied*. Note the term 'sceptical' (Fig. 8.4) is used to denote a response where the clarity of the question to the respondent cannot be ascertained. In this case, the car parking facility is a must-be attribute of your event for that attendee or all attendees in his/her category.

Question

How would you design a questionnaire for an event of your choice to identify different event attributes?

Event managers can employ a simple survey instrument to explore the attributes of their products and utilize the Kano methodology to further develop and refine their events in order to optimize customer satisfaction.

Kelley and Turley (2001) investigate the importance of service attributes used by sports fans when evaluating the quality of their service experience at sporting events. The result of their research carried out at a major athletic conference revealed nine factors deemed as important by fans who attended the sporting event. The interpretation of these factors leads to the following labels:

1. Employees
2. Price
3. Facility access
4. Concessions
5. Fan comfort
6. Game experience
7. Showtime
8. Convenience
9. Smoking

It must be noted that attributes will differ from event to event; similarly the nature of the attributes according to Kano (2001) metamorphoses from one category to another over time.

Physical state		Functional		
	User perception	Dissatisfied	Neutral	Satisfied
Dysfunctional	Dissatisfied	Sceptical	Must-be	One-dimensional
	Neutral	Reverse	Indifferent	Attractive
	Satisfied	Reverse	Reverse	Sceptical

Fig. 8.4. Three-level Kano methodology.

> **Question**
>
> Assuming you are a consultant, how will you advise a planner of a hallmark event who seeks your service on how to identify the important features of the event?

RELATED AND INTERMEDIARY CONCEPTS

It would be incomplete to write about quality without mentioning the other important concepts that contribute to the total experience of attending and hoping to revisit an event. Such concepts include perceived value, visitors' satisfaction and behavioural intentions, and all of these constructs are discussed in the following subsections.

Perceived value

Value has been defined and conceptualized in various ways – from the unidimensional measure (Zeithaml, 1988) to the multi-dimensional scale (Bolton and Drew, 1991). Zeithaml (1988, p. 14) suggests that 'perceived value is the customer's overall assessment of the utility of a product based on perceptions of what is received and what is given'. Value is considered to guide the retention decisions of customers. In view of this, the conceptualization of value as a 'benefits–sacrifice' construct appears to be a key factor in event experience, judging from the fact that attendees give up their time and pay a price for a ticket in order to obtain some benefits, which may be knowledge, opportunities to socialize, relaxation, needs for new experiences or opportunities to see specific teams or bands perform.

The trade-off models have been criticized as too simplistic in explaining service experiences, as they ignore the multi-dimensional nature of service experiences. The multi-dimensional scale is said to be able to overcome the validity issues raised. Value has been viewed as a complex construct with traditional functional dimensions like perceived risk, quality, benefits and price, interacting with socio-psychological dimensions such as prestige, novelty and hedonism. However, multi-dimensional models are very useful in explaining an event attendee's perceived value as people seek to satisfy socio-psychological prestige, novelty and hedonism needs as well as sacrificing money and time as they attend events.

To this end, value becomes a key concept to consider in managing an event attendee's experience. Quality influences customer perceptions of value and in turn perceived value is an important antecedent to visitors' satisfaction and behavioural intents.

Visitor satisfaction

Consumer satisfaction has been defined by various authors in service marketing and in leisure-related disciplines. Notable among them is Oliver (1996, p. 87), who defines consumer satisfaction as 'a judgment that a product or service feature, or the product or service itself, provided a pleasurable level of consumption-related fulfilment'.

Crompton (2003) adapts Herzberg's hygiene and motivator conditions of job satisfaction and suggests that the same conditions contribute to explaining the level of visitor satisfaction with an event. To this end, Crompton (2003) proposes that hygiene attributes are the general infrastructural features that form the basis of the development of an event. If the quality of these generic features falls below a given limit, then dissatisfaction sets in. However, the presence of these features does not significantly result in visitor satisfaction even though they must be present. The motivator attributes represent the unique features of events and Crompton (2003) suggests that these are the chief attractor of visitors to events; the visitors' interaction with these features results in satisfaction. This idea can be viewed alongside Kano's classification of attractive quality.

Often, the principal aim of a manager is to gauge visitors' level of satisfaction with a given event. This they do in view of retaining loyal customers (more about customer loyalty will be discussed in the next subsection) and subsequently optimizing an organization's profit through sustaining and improving the organization's market share.

Behavioural intentions

A number of studies have found a close relationship between quality, satisfaction and behavioural intentions. Behavioural intensions are indicators that show whether a customer will remain loyal to a provider or defect to another. Behavioural intentions could be positive where a visitor will engage in *word of mouth* – saying good things and recommending an event to families and friends, and expressing cognitive loyalty to a service provider. Loyalty depicts the tendency for an attendee to revisit and make an event his/her first choice among alternatives when making a purchase decision. On the other hand, behavioural intentions could be unfavourable resulting in the visitor complaining, making negative comments to others and not returning to the same event. It is a known fact that satisfied visitors are likely to spread the word about an event thereby providing free publicity.

Box 8.1. Quality management at the Festival International de Lanaudière.

The Festival International de Lanaudière takes place in Joliette, Quebec, each year and had, with the support of Tourisme Quebec, developed a quality management programme to ensure the delivery of a high-quality event. This quality programme is holistic in its nature and covers every aspect of the event's management. Examples of the quality policy include:

- Human Resources: evaluation of training and delivery of special 'Clients Plus' training.
- Procedures: written and oral communication, emergency plans, helping less able visitors and environmental practices.
- A requirement for event suppliers, concessions and subcontractors to adhere to the event's standards of service.

The festival organizers comment that they are 'committed to welcoming our visitors in a professional and courteous manner so that they have a pleasant experience at the Festival. Our visitors will be well informed about our activities and services as well as about any changes that might occur. We assure our visitors that they will have a comfortable stay at the Festival, and that we will do our very best to accommodate people in need of adapted services. Your satisfaction is important to us, and we will respond within a reasonable length of time to any comments you may wish to send us.'

This focus on quality management is essential to ensure that visitors to the Festival have a good time, and it also encourages repeat visits. The organizers have also become involved in a certification scheme to recognize the high standards of quality that visitors have come to expect.

Sources: Various

KEY PROCESSES IN MANAGING SERVICE QUALITY IN EVENTS

In managing quality, particularly in the service sector, it is recommended that managers need to be conversant with two things: (i) the way in which customers evaluate quality; and (ii) how to manage quality in a systematic manner. So far, the chapter has explained how event attendees judge the quality of an event by looking at different ways in which quality can be defined, supported with models and theories that can help in making this clear in different contexts. The second aspect of the focus of the chapter is to examine ways to manage quality in events.

The management of quality is said to have gone through four stages. The evolutionary stages are found to be: inspection, quality control, quality assurance and Total Quality Management (TQM) (see Fig. 8.5). Inspection as a quality management method employed measuring, gauging and sorting. The quality control era involved the use of statistical process control. The quality assurance stage witnessed the establishment of standards administered and assessed both internally and externally. Common quality standards and systems found in the event and leisure related industry include the Visitor Attraction Quality Assurance Scheme (VAQAS), ISO 9000 family, Investors in People (IIP) and Michelin Stars among others. The final stage is TQM. Dale (1999) sees the movement as progressive in nature, whereas Garvin (1988) considers it a chronological evolution of quality management where new organizations join at the later stages.

Inspection		Quality Control	
Primary concern	Detection	Primary concern	Control
View of quality	A problem to be solved	View of quality	A problem to be solved
Emphasis	Product uniformity	Emphasis	Product uniformity with reduced inspection
Methods	Gauging and measurement	Methods	Statistical process control
Role of quality professionals	Inspecting, sorting, counting and grading	Role of quality professionals	Troubleshooting and statistical method
Whose responsibility	The inspection department	Whose responsibility	Manufacturing and engineering department
Orientation and approach	'Inspect in' quality	Orientation and approach	'Control in' quality
Quality Assurance		**Total Quality Management**	
Primary concern	Coordination	Primary concern	Strategic impact
View of quality	A problem to be solved productively	View of quality	A competitive opportunity
Emphasis	Entire production chain	Emphasis	The market and customer needs
Methods	Programmes and systems	Methods	Strategic planning, goal setting and mobilization
Role of quality professionals	Quality measurement, planning and programme design	Role of quality professionals	Goal setting, education and training; teamwork and programme design
Whose responsibility	All departments with minimal top management involvement	Whose responsibility	Everyone; management provides strong leadership
Orientation and approach	'Build in' quality	Orientation and approach	'Manage in' quality

Fig. 8.5. Evolution of quality management. Source: adapted from Garvin (1988).

The lesson from the quality evolution/movement is that quality management has moved away from being a predominantly internal orientation to employing and combining different methods and techniques for measurement. Again, the notion of quality evolution indicates the departure from the ideas of quality management being the responsibility of one department or a set of people; for quality to be effectively managed, it must be seen as an organization-wide affair with a change in culture and visionary leadership. The following subsections explore the key processes in quality management based on a TQM philosophy.

Establishment of quality strategy

For any quality effort to be fruitful there must be a strategic base. Event organizers and managers need to base their quality management on achievable and cost-effective strategies. The main focus should be on attendees' needs and the pitfall of *overquality*, which would lead to excessive time consumption, high labour cost and exorbitant prices, must also be avoided. Efforts should be made to marry the quality of programming with the service delivery mechanism to ensure consistency. The strategy should consider competition, product design, organization competencies, suppliers and means of implementation with the event attendees as the central focus. Finally, the quality strategy must fit in with the overall organization strategy.

Question

How can you design a quality strategy for an event and ensure that it is implemented by everybody involved in the event?

Quality planning

Quality has to be planned and well documented to provide a focused orientation towards an effective and manageable improvement process. Planning is concerned with aims and objectives – defining these and how they are to be achieved. A typical quality planning process will follow the pattern below:

- situation analysis;
- identification of quality mission;
- putting in place a quality policy;
- goal setting;
- formulation of action plan;
- implementation of plan; and
- monitoring, evaluation and review.

The essential feature that distinguishes quality planning from general management planning is its focus on improvement. Just as quality needs to be matched with the organizations overall strategy, quality planning can be seen as an extension of strategic planning (see Chapter 10).

Leadership and management of change

Leadership is about demonstrating an ability to influence and manage people. Hence it must be visionary and inspirational to bring about quality improvements. The leader must be capable of bringing about a change of culture, particularly where the existing practice needs improvement in terms of quality orientation. Leadership does not end with influencing and managing people, but also includes personal accountability. This requires education, competence and commitment on the part of the workforce and senior management. Commitment to quality should be top-down when transforming the vision of an event into a reality. Poor quality may result from a lack of commitment on the part of managers.

Team building and teamwork

The need for people to work together to achieve a common goal cannot be overemphasized in quality management, particularly in events where a myriad of activities are carried out by a diverse range of professionals and non-professionals alike. Oakland and Morris (1998) identify three basic elements of teamwork:

- Task needs: the common purpose agreed by team members. This requires a shared sense of identity which may be visible both within and outside of the group.
- Team needs – the need for the team to make a concerted effort in the same direction to achieve a common goal. This may bring about some sort of formal or informal interaction and structure. The team must agree on the methods and instruments to be employed in accomplishing a task in order to succeed, so group cohesiveness becomes a factor.
- Individual needs – the need for each member to know what to contribute to the team effort and be willing to play their part.

Good teamwork is essential for effective delivery of any event, particularly with the customer–supplier relationship that permeates a typical delivery mechanism. However, teams take time, commitment and other resources to develop. Teambuilding facilitates the development of healthy relationships among members and this in turn enhances performance, and events rely heavily on 'teams'.

Communication

Communication is an essential conduit, which links all the three principal groupings in an event together: the internal groups (members of an organization), the third-party groups (suppliers and other stakeholders, e.g. the police, local authorities) and event attendees. There is a need for effective communication between all units to convey the explicit stance that will advance integration and performance. For instance, imagine the conflict and perception of quality of experience that will arise from communication breakdown between event security operatives and attendees; between waiting staff who are laying up for dinner and technicians who are getting the function suite ready by pulling and drawing cables around the room; and a manager who got the event order wrong and staff who got the revised event order late from the manager.

Communication between the organization and the customer is vital and could take many forms and dimensions. This could be achieved through marketing and promotional materials or through interaction between an individual event attendee and server during the 'moments of truth', the times when customers come into contact with people in the organization. Effective communication helps inform event attendees of the nature of the service offering, thereby helping to shape and manage their expectations. Powerful words, such as *convenient, safe, happy, comfortable, value* and *love*, connect to emotions that can help event attendees develop mental images of good feelings and positive experiences. Attractive words, like *breathtaking, captivating, classic, contemporary, charming* and *timeless*, are the icing on the cake, especially when selling event products, and particularly for celebration events such as weddings.

The exchange of ideas and information between the other two groupings, or within each group, is also crucial in enhancing integration and performance. Communication between an organization and its suppliers is essential to drive up quality. It is suggested that the kind of relationship developed here should be a *partnership* to enhance effective and mutual exchanges of ideas. Most of the time the focus of debate in terms of communication and quality management within an organization is the direction of the flow of information, which is usually top-down. It is a known fact that frontline servers who regularly come in contact with event attendees are a good source of information of customers' needs and expectations. Astute organizations that intend to succeed and/or maintain their market share must tap into the opportunities presented by the frontline staff to promote bottom-up communication. Forums for employees to voice their ideas and contribute to policy formation and decision making should be created. One common method of involving employees in problem solving and decision making is the use of *quality circles*, particularly where there are quality issues to be resolved.

Education and training

The development and involvement of people is vital in managing event quality. There is a need to optimize employees' contributions and poor quality often results from a lack of awareness of quality and/or employing the wrong systems for quality improvement. As a result, learning becomes a vital ingredient in quality management. As most event organizations depend on volunteers or seasonal casual workers, learning is compromised. This means that most people come into the workplace with diverse cultures. Williams and Buswell (2003) argue that there is a reciprocal connection between an organization's training programme and its quality culture. Contrary to what is generally obtainable in the industry, seasonality and volunteerism should not hinder staff training. A good example in the industry is Cancer Research UK's approach to recruiting and training volunteers and seasonal staff for Race for Life events (see Box 8.2).

Box 8.2. Cancer Research UK.

Apart from the regular training programmes for volunteers, Cancer Research UK also has in place a 12-week internship scheme that is aimed at undergraduates, graduates and people who want to change career paths. Interns get the opportunity to work on a specific project that enables them to develop skills and work experience that are valued in industry. Training programmes like these help Cancer Research UK to shape volunteers' customer orientation and at the same time instil the organization's culture and values in the minds of its workers.

Scientific decision making

Managers need to interpret data from internal and external sources to facilitate timely and effective decisions for planning, directing and controlling event activities. Events consist of a set of interdependent and interrelated systems, process and facts. To this end, managers must make use of tools that are capable of helping them to make effective decisions in terms of operations or overall event strategy.

To do this, managers must make use of the old tools (flow charts, checklists, control charts, bar graphs, Pareto charts/analysis; fishbone diagrams/cause–effect analysis and scatter diagrams/regression analysis) and the new tools (affinity diagrams, interrelationship diagrams, tree diagrams, matrix diagrams, matrix data analysis, arrow diagrams and process decision programme charts), some of which are discussed elsewhere in the literature (see James, 1996). These tools are capable of helping managers to make effective decision in terms of operations or overall event strategy. Accurate measuring devices for identifying opportunities for improvement and for measuring performance against internal and external standards should be used.

Process control

Process denotes a set of interrelated and interacting activities, which transform inputs into outputs (see Chapter 5). There is a need to ensure that each process transforms inputs effectively into the desired outputs. All activities that are undertaken for an event and within an event organization need to be controlled (i.e. organized, monitored and measured). Control is not just about measuring progress; it is about preventing and rectifying what has gone wrong. What most managers want to deal with, or better still minimize, is variation. Variation is the difference in the reproducibility of a particular action; the difference between a particular action and the target outcome. There are two main classes of causes of variation – common and special causes. Common causes are the result of the design of the system. Special causes arise from external sources and are not inherent in the process. It is imperative that managers identify and recognize the implications of causes of variation on their events in order to control event delivery processes.

A control process will set standards, measure performance, compare results with standards and initiate corrective action as required. Standards of performance need to be clearly stated qualitatively or quantitatively, and these standards must be represented in outcomes and/or impacts. The measurement of performance depends upon relevance, adequacy and timeliness of the event. When comparing actual performance against target performance, a number of techniques and tools may be employed. For instance, an approach of taking action when variation is substantial may be adopted. Such variation may be detected by the use of a control chart or other similar tools.

Continuous improvement

The term *continuous improvement* refers to the constant enhancement of the event delivery process and the provision of customer satisfaction, involving all operations and work units. The drivers for continuous improvement include the changing needs of the customer, survival of organizations in the increasingly competitive business environment and changing technology among many other factors. There is no doubt that managers and planners of events endeavour to meet the regularly changing needs of their audiences, as they ensure this continuous improvement inevitably becomes the main quality objective.

Continuous learning is inevitable if an event aims to remain competitive. The organizers and planners must be ready to challenge the status quo by being innovative. Corporate social responsibility is increasingly gaining ground and has become an important factor for consumers in the events sector (see Chapter 9). The implication here is that event organizations and organizers must be seen to be improving their efforts to minimize any adverse effects their events have on people and the environment while maximizing the legacy benefits (see Chapter 11). They must be seen to be exceeding the minimum regulating framework in which the organization operates and be striving to understand and respond to the expectations of society.

Sustainable event and quality

Event attendees' expectations and requirements are always changing. One of the major influences of changing expectations and perception of quality is the consideration for the environment and the society as a whole. These days, organizations are using sustainability agenda to differentiate themselves. Although this is not conventional quality management per se, guidelines provided by organizations such as the International Organization for Standardization, (ISO), the European Foundation for Quality Management (EFQM) and Standards UK encourage event organizers to consider the impacts the events they hold have on the environment and society by directing their attention to the reduction of carbon emissions, elimination of wastage, improvement of resource efficiency and engagement in activities that benefit the local community. Examples include efficient resource use and reduction of wastage, which are in line with quality management principles. Organizations taking up certification are audited against specific standard requirements. The audit ensures that the candidate organization's management systems are in line with the set requirements, mirroring the needs of both the organization and the event.

Notable standards that can be employed that provide guidance and help enhance the delivery of sustainable event include BS 8901 and ISO 14001. These standards utilize similar management principles employed by the ISO 9000 family of quality standards incorporating Deming's PDCA (plan–do–check–act) approach. ISO is in the process of developing an International Standard specific to promoting sustainable management of events – *Sustainability in events management* ISO 20121. This initiative is aimed at standardizing the events industry's global attempt in addressing the challenges posed by the negative impacts events have on the environment. A new ISO project committee, ISO/PC 250, is charged with developing the standard and a number of countries are already engaged as participants or observers in the process. The development of ISO 20121 is expected to be completed in 2012 to coincide with the London Olympic Games.

Box 8.3. The Argungu Fishing Festival.

Argungu Fishing Festival historically predates the 'Conquests' of Kanta of Kebbi in the early 16th century, when it was mainly in the form of religious rites. Today the festival has taken centre stage as one of the foremost cultural events in Nigeria. The modern-day festival dates from 1934 and marked the end of centuries of hostilities between the Sokoto Caliphate and the Kebbi Kingdom.

The event takes place in Argungu, a small village in the north of Nigeria, and has developed into a major cultural event that is a key element in the regions tourism strategy.

It is now achieving a remarkable position in the list of global events, with nationals of 21 countries witnessing the 2009 event, which lasted for 4 days. Over that time, according to the Nigerian Tourism Development Corporation, a total of 262,386 visitors witnessed the famous event. Newspaper reports suggest that there were up to 10,000 fishermen taking part, although some estimates were rather more conservative, suggesting 1000 participants.

The event is not without its problems, which have included cheating, issues around crowd control and fishermen refusing to wait for the official start of the competition.

As an event like this grows and develops, the management of quality becomes important, and the problems tend to increase making this a challenge. As a tool for

(Continued)

Box 8.3. Continued.

attracting tourism, any event has to deliver a level of quality synonymous with the broader destination brand. Areas that the event organizers have targeted for improvements in 2010 include the use of managed arenas, accommodation provision and crowd control. Included in 2010 preparations is the training of local staff from the state ministry of tourism.

Alhaji Abubakar Ladan, the Director General Argungu International Fishing and Cultural Festival, said 'We are discussing with the Nigerian Tourism Development Corporation and the federal ministry of tourism to see how we can organize training for the locals and some of our staff to become experts tours guards'.

These approaches to internal developments for the delivery of an event all add to its profile, thereby increasing future audience numbers and international recognition.

Sources: Various

Questions
- What are the quality attributes of the Argungu Fishing Festival?
- What are the major quality issues in the festival?
- How can the quality issues be managed?

SUMMARY

A mission of achieving organizational objectives by being viable and competitive is not an easy one. Over the years, managers have employed differentiation and continuous improvement strategies to achieve this. The management of quality has become the major focus of many event organizations, particularly those in the service sector. Although quality can mean different things to different people, there are some basic principles that underpin its management. The event manager needs to be conversant with these basic principles to deliver successful and continuous events. It is common knowledge that quality is determined by customers; hence, the knowledge of how customers evaluate quality becomes imperative for event managers.

In addition, the nature of events as a product needs to be fully understood in order to manage quality. The event product is essentially a service that consists of intangible experiences that are produced and consumed simultaneously. Coupled with the inevitability of knowing the way that customers evaluate quality, the nature of the event product and methods of managing quality, it is also essential that event managers understand the position of quality within the context of overall organizational strategy and effectively incorporate quality management in to this. The compatibility of both strategies must be ensured – the overall organization strategy must serve as foundation upon which quality strategy is built.

FURTHER READING

James, P. (1996) *Total Quality Management*. Prentice Hall, Hemel Hempstead, UK.

REVIEW QUESTIONS

1. List five reasons why you think managing event quality is important.
2. How related is sustainable event planning to quality management?
3. What advice would you give an event organizing subcommittee to develop quality policies for a recurring major event?

REFERENCES

Bolton, R.N. and Drew, J.H. (1991) A multistage model of consumers' assessment of service quality and value. *Journal of Consumer Research* 17, 375–384.

Crompton, J. (2003) Adapting Herzberg: a conceptualization of the effects of hygiene and motivator attributes on perceptions of event quality. *Journal of Travel Research* 41, 305–310.

Crosby, P.B. (1979) *Quality is Free: the Art of Making Quality Certain*. McGraw-Hill, New York.

Dale, B.G. (ed.) (1999) *Managing Quality*. Blackwell Business, Oxford.

Engel, J.F., Blackwell, R.D. and Miniard, P.W. (1986) *Consumer Behavior*. Dryden Press, New York.

Garvin, D.A. (1988) *Managing Quality: The Strategic and Competitive Edge*. Free Press, New York.

Grönroos, C. (1982) *Strategic Management and Marketing in Service Sector*. Marketing Science Institute, Cambridge, Massachusetts.

Grönroos, C. (2000) *Service Management and Marketing: a Customer Relationship Management Approach*, 2nd edn. John Wiley & Sons, Chichester, UK.

ISO (1994) *ISO 9000: 1994 Quality Management Standard*. International Organization for Standardization, Geneva.

James, P. (1996) *Total Quality Management*. Prentice Hall, Hemel Hempstead, UK.

Juran, J.M. (1988) *Juran on Planning for Quality*. Free Press, New York.

Kano, N. (2001) Life cycle and creation of attractive quality. *Proceedings of the 4th QMOD Conference*, Linkoping, Sweden, pp. 18–36.

Kelley, S.W. and Turley, L.W. (2001) Consumer perceptions of service quality attributes at sporting events. *Journal of Business Research* 54, 161–166.

Oakland, J. and Morris, P. (1998) *Pocket Guide to TQM: a Pictorial Guide for Managers*. Butterworth-Heinemann, Oxford.

Oliver, R. (1996) *Satisfaction: a Behavioral Perspective on the Consumer*. McGraw-Hill, New York.

Oriade, A. (2008) Delivering the total visitor experience: shouldn't we know how visitors form their perception of quality? *Attractions and Events as Catalysts for Regeneration and Social Change*, *Proceedings of the EUTO Conference*, 24–25 September, University of Nottingham, Nottingham, UK, pp. 150–163.

Parasuraman, A., Zeithaml, V.A. and Berry, L.L. (1988) SERVQUAL: a multiple-item scale for measuring consumer perceptions of service quality. *Journal of Retailing* 64, 12–24.

Parasuraman, A., Zeithaml, V.A. and Berry, L.L. (1985) A conceptual model of service quality and its implication for future research. *Journal of Marketing* 49, 41–50.

Williams, C. and Buswell, J. (2003) *Service Quality in Leisure and Tourism*. CAB International, Wallingford, UK.

Zeithaml, V.A. (1988) Consumer perceptions of price, quality and value: a means-end model and synthesis of evidence. *Journal of Marketing* 52, 2–22.

chapter 9

Sustainability and Events Management

Sine Heitmann and Lóránt Dávid

OBJECTIVES OF THE CHAPTER

This chapter discusses the sustainability of events. Events have different impacts that range from political and economic to socio-cultural and environmental, and while negative impacts should be minimized and positive impacts should be enhanced, the management of these impacts can be difficult. The chapter first outlines the various impacts that events can have on the economy, environment and society, before introducing ideas on sustainability and showing what initiatives are available to event organizations to assure the sustainable management of events, such as environmental management policies, legislation, communication policies, and certifications, codes of conduct, inclusion policies and crowd management. Closely related to sustainability is the concept of corporate social responsibility (CSR), which is increasingly adopted by event organizations.

The objectives of the chapter are to:

- illustrate the economic, environmental and socio-cultural impacts of events;
- explain the concepts of sustainability and sustainable events management; and
- identify and apply tools and techniques to events and event organizers to minimize any negative impacts, while enhancing positive impacts.

INTRODUCTION: THE IMPACTS OF EVENTS

Impacts are essentially the outcomes of an event. If planned, the outcomes are closely related to the objective of an event; however, not all impacts can be planned for and events might have impacts that have not been anticipated. Planned or not, outcomes and impacts have to be taken into account during the planning process and should be measured and evaluated. Because of the temporary nature of an event, most impacts are intense and short-term. Throughout the previous chapters, many different events have been introduced, and depending on the nature and scale of the event, not all impacts are quantifiable or visible, and differ in their degree of intensity. The following gives an overview of key impacts of events.

POLITICAL IMPACTS

Overall, the relationship between politics and events is twofold – whereas events can have political impacts that influence the economic, socio-cultural and environmental impacts (as outlined below), events will always reflect and interact with their political circumstances and environment (see Box 9.1).

Governments realize the ability of events to raise profiles, and many national governments and city councils are keen to host international mega-events as the international prestige improves the profile of the region or nation. The attraction of mega-sport events is highlighted by the strong competition among cities to host the Olympic Games and among nations to hold the FIFA World Cup. Similarly, competition among European cities is strong to become Capital of Culture. Events enhance the promotion of the destination as an attractive place for tourists and subsequently attract further investment (see Economic Impacts, below). Edinburgh has established itself as the Festival City through a range of events, such as the Edinburgh Fringe Festival during summer and Hogmanay at New Year. Events may change or legitimize political priorities in the short term, and in the long term, events have the power to legitimize political ideologies and change socio-cultural reality (see Socio-cultural Impacts, below). On a smaller scale, local community events can be used as a vehicle of communication for a particular political or societal message and contribute to the well-being of the social structure. The development of administrative skills that are associated with staging an event is also considered a benefit for hosting an event. On the other hand, the risk of event failure can have severe impacts on the nation/region holding the event. Misallocation of funds can lead to a lack of trust in the government or local councils. The Sydney 2000 Olympic Games were advertised as the 'People's Games', but controversies surrounding the allocation of tickets emerged when it became public that the Organizing Committee had made a private deal with a wealthy businessmen's club, securing the best seats for its members and leaving the wider public without their preferred tickets. If an event has no clear organizational structure, there can also be a lack of accountability. Using an event as a communication tool, there is a risk of a (political) event being misused for propaganda purposes and legitimizing an ideology not necessarily shared with every stakeholder.

Box 9.1. Political issues at mega-events: Olympic Games 2008 in Beijing and FIFA World Cup 2010 in South Africa.

Beijing Olympics 2008

Before the Olympics took place in Beijing, a range of concerns were expressed over China hosting the Games: violation of open media access, as the government allegedly issued guidelines to local media with instructions to downplay most political issues that were not directly related to the Games (e.g. pro-Tibetan independence and East-Turkestan movements); human rights violations (e.g. forced resettlement of communities, banning

(Continued)

Box 9.1. Continued.

of ethnic Tibetans from working in Beijing, religious prosecution as well as electronic surveillance of internationally owned hotels); China's continuous support of repressive regimes (e.g. Zimbabwe, Myanmar, Sudan and North Korea); potential threats from terrorist groups and violent protests from pro-Tibetan groups; and air pollution in the city and neighbouring regions.

After the Games, the 2008 Olympic Games were generally accepted as a logistical success. No terrorist attack or major public protest happened and the air quality was not as bad as anticipated. The Chinese government considered the Olympic event a great source of national pride, and domestic support for the government and its state communist policies has risen. The influx of tourists has benefited the economy while some manufacturing sectors have lost revenue, as industrial plants had to close down to support government efforts to improve air quality.

FIFA World Cup 2010 in South Africa

In May 2004, South Africa was awarded the rights to host the FIFA World Cup 2010, the first on the African continent. In addition to the construction of new and the improvement of existing stadiums across the country, the South African government also put measures in place that would improve the public transport infrastructure and implement policies to ensure the safety and security of tourists. Throughout the preparation and planning, international critics have expressed doubts about South Africa's ability to plan and organize the event. Further controversies surrounding the event were connected to evictions of shack-dwellers as part of the 'beautification' process of the urban landscapes. South Africa was further hit by protest of communities who demanded access to basic services, jobs and adequate housing, and accused the government of diverting public funds away from social issues to build stadiums and upgrade airports.

Questions
- Both events are situated in less developed countries – compare these events with Olympics and World Cups that took place in more developed countries. To what extent have there been similar concerns before the event?
- Can you think of other events, international or local, that have sparked similar controversies before or during the event?

ECONOMIC IMPACTS

In most cases, events are staged for their economic potential and these are closely connected to tourism. If the event is managed properly, an event can result in high yields and net incomes to the region. When referring to economic impacts, we have to consider different types of impacts – direct, indirect and induced. Direct economic impacts are those impacts that occur before (e.g. investment in infrastructure) and during the event (including increased number of visitors and tourists to the area and their spending at the event). Direct impacts also include the additional employment created through the event. Examples for indirect impacts are the spending of visitors in businesses that are connected to the event (e.g. accommodation, hospitality, excursions, entertainment, etc.). On a larger scale, as the event raises and improves the profile of the region, further indirect impacts can result in investment and development of businesses and further job creation. A knock-on effect here would be the increased tax revenues and income to the national or local government. Coupled with the potentials in tourism development, events are used as a strategy to promote the region as a destination, extend seasonality and length of stay of visitors. Induced economic impacts include the increased spending within the economy as a result of the jobs created and the increased spending power of locals, showing the multiplier effect of events. For example, Edinburgh has positioned itself as the Festival City, but now attracts many visitors outside the festival season, whereas Barcelona and Sydney are still benefiting from the tourism development as a result of hosting the Olympic Games in 1992 and 2000, respectively. On a smaller scale, local events have similar effects, such as the Peter-and-Paul Festival in Bretten (see Box 9.7), which has attracted business development to the city as a result of the annual festival.

Box 9.2. Exporting Germany's Christmas markets.

German Christmas markets are very popular and Frankfurt has used this opportunity to export its Christmas market. In 1997, the first Frankfurt Christmas market took place in Birmingham as a one-time-only twin-city promotional event. As a result of the success, the market is now an annual event and is the largest German Christmas market outside Germany, attracting more than a million visitors. In 2008, the turnover was almost £70 million. The majority of workers are travelling from Germany, but more and more Eastern European immigrants are used to support the workforce. Since its first export, the Frankfurt Christmas Market now takes place in six cities across the UK.

Question

What (direct, indirect and induced) economic benefits does the Christmas market have for Birmingham? What kind of benefits are in it for Frankfurt and Germany?

On the negative side, the risk of event failure poses the threat of negative economic impacts. Financial mismanagement can have adverse effects as high opportunity costs are involved with staging an event and if not managed adequately, the financial burden and potential loss can put pressure on the local government. Montreal hosted the Olympic Games in 1976, but the government was still paying off the debts until the fiscal year of 2006. If not controlled and planned properly, misallocation of funds and lack of accountability can lead to damage to the reputation, both within the region and to the customers (see Box 9.1 on political impacts). Even if successful, an event can result in negative economic impacts such as inflated prices, which have knock-on effects on the local community.

Box 9.3. Economic impacts of events (UK Sport).

UK Sport works closely with the national and regional governments to support bids for hosting sporting events of international importance within the UK. It also commissions research into the economic impacts of events, with the latest reports highlighting key benefits to the nation and regions.

(Continued)

Box 9.3. Continued.

Event	Location	Year	Economic impact (£)
Flora Marathon	London	2000	25,458,187
1st Cornhill Test Match	Birmingham	1997	5,061,768
World Rowing Championships	Berkshire and Buckinghamshire	2006	3,268,703
World Indoor Athletics	Birmingham	2003	3,160,000
World Badminton	Glasgow	1997	2,221,130
European Show Jumping	Hickstead	1999	2,196,298
Euro' Eventing	Oxfordshire	2005	2,116,699
Women's British Open Golf	Berkshire	1997	2,068,663
World Judo	Birmingham	1999	1,943,715
World Cup Triathlon	Salford	2003	1,666,398
UEFA U19 Football	Northern Ireland	2005	752,776
World Half Marathon	Bristol	2001	584,000
Rowing World Cup	Berkshire and Buckinghamshire	2005	583,899
World Indoor Climbing	Birmingham	1999	398,000
ISAF World Youth Sailing	Weymouth/Portland	2006	349,374
IAAF Grand Prix	Sheffield	1997	200,000
Women's Cycling	Wales	2005	56,413

Source: UK Sport (2009)

Questions

- What do you think are the key determinants to the differing economic impacts of those events?
- Using the Internet, access the various reports on economic impacts of the Olympic Games – how do the financial management and the economic impacts differ between cities like Montreal (1976), Los Angeles (1984), Barcelona (1992), Sydney (2000) and Athens (2004)? What can future host cities learn from these?

SOCIO-CULTURAL IMPACTS

Wider impacts on the society level have been briefly mentioned above, but there is a wide range of socio-cultural impacts on a micro-level (Bowdin *et al.*, 2006). The enjoyable shared experience of event visitors encourages social cohesion. Whereas the 1990 FIFA World Cup in Italy with Germany winning the cup contributed to the reunification process by enhancing national pride shortly after the fall of the Berlin Wall in 1989, the 2006 FIFA World Cup in Germany has received much praise for providing an enjoyable and peaceful atmosphere in the streets during match days. As many festivals are used as platforms to promote cultural heritage, the revitalization of traditions or the introduction of new and challenging ideas, people and customs has a positive impact on the communities. The Notting Hill Carnival in London started to introduce the Afro-Caribbean immigrants' culture to Britain and now attracts millions of visitors each year, whereas St Patrick's Day is now celebrated all over the world, despite being the Irish National Day. Events not only give ethnic or cultural minorities the opportunity to raise their profile, but can give other minority groups a way to validate themselves, as exemplified by Christopher Day street parades and Gay Pride festivals all over the world each year. Successful events result in increased community participation and give both communities and visitors a chance to expand their cultural perspectives and provide a platform for cultural exchanges. Some events raise awareness and leave a legacy for increased participation in sporting activities. On the other hand, events can give the community a feel-good factor, most notably the vast range of charity events happening at local or national level. Furthermore, events and festivals present a showcase for new ideas and skills (see Box 9.7).

However, as successful events attract a large crowd of visitors, negative socio-cultural impacts can be observed through anti-social behaviour, alcohol-fuelled negative behaviour and substance abuse. Hooliganism is a particular problem associated with football events. Crowd mismanagement and associated problems present further problems to event organizers. For example, several thousand gatecrashers at the Glastonbury 2000 festival contributed to the decision to cancel the 2001 festival for security and safety concerns, whereas the Birmingham Christmas Lights Switch On event in 2009 had to be cancelled halfway through after four times more visitors than expected turned up to the free event, resulting in multiple cases of injuries related to lack of safety. More severe cases include multiple deaths at the Roskilde Festival 2001 in Denmark, or the deaths of hundreds of Muslim pilgrims in Mecca in 2004. Other negative socio-cultural impacts can occur if events are imposed on a local community and the local input is neglected or the event is manipulated and exploited. Local communities can become alienated and (passively or actively) resist the event. In other cases, if the event becomes too successful, the event risks losing its authenticity and appeal to local communities. In relation to environmental impacts (see below), damage to local amenities and the pressure on and disruption of local infrastructure can affect community life in a negative way. Events can have far-reaching negative impacts, which result in bad press and publicity and damage to the event, the community and other stakeholders.

Box 9.4. Consultation on sex work and the 2010 Soccer World Cup: human rights, public health, soccer and beyond.

In the lead-up to the FIFA 2010 World Cup, sex workers from across South Africa came together at a meeting organized by the Sex Workers Education and Advocacy Taskforce (Sweat) in Cape Town, which was also referred to Consultation on Sex Work and the 2010 Soccer World Cup: Human Rights, Public Health, Soccer and Beyond. Several local and international stakeholders raised various concerns surrounding their trade, such as police harassment and abuse ahead of the tournament as well as threats by police to arrest them for the duration of the competition. Because of the scale of the event, sex workers feared stiff competition from outsiders and organized crime (human and child trafficking) during the football spectacle. Further concerns were raised that the country could run out of condoms during the soccer competition, which would be a backlash in the fight against

(Continued)

Box 9.4. Continued.

AIDS. As some workers argued that the Bill of Rights allows anyone to do the job they want, sex workers have called for the decriminalization of their trade and the creation of a safer working environment. According to the workers, this will ensure an increase of their fees. Plans also include dumping the rand in favour of the US dollar when foreign fans and tourists are targeted. One sex worker said that 'if the buyer keeps buying, we will keep selling. The government said the World Cup would benefit all of us. We all want to be rich. We want to treat our clients from abroad with dignity so that they will come back again.'

Source: Sowetan (2009)

Question

What do you suggest as a possible solution considering South Africa's culture and society?

ENVIRONMENTAL IMPACTS

Finally, environmental impacts are important. When considering the environment, we look at impacts on the natural environment (e.g. natural resources, flora and fauna, landscape) or the man-made environment (e.g. the built environment, which includes heritage buildings). Events can be a showcase for the environment and provide models for best practice. In this case, events increase environmental awareness both within the community and among visitors. The infrastructure is improved through developments in both transport and communications, which can also lead to urban transformation and renewal if an event legacy is managed appropriately.

However, an event can also cause environmental damage and pollution of air, water and landscape through littering, erosion and carbon dioxide emissions through the travelling involved to and from an event. Furthermore, an event will inevitably use considerable energy (water use and heating of accommodation and catering facilities, lighting and sound energy use), which will put considerable pressure on local resources. Through the overuse of facilities and the pressure put on local facilities, the infrastructure suffers and heritage might be destroyed. Furthermore, noise disturbance and traffic congestion affect the local community.

Box 9.5a. Sziget Festival of Budapest.

During a week in August each year, the Sziget Festival in Budapest and its green island in Óbuda attracts students and young adults from Europe and other corners of the world with nearly a 1000 programmes and 60 venues. Sziget is not only a festival, but also a week-long opportunity to camp out in the temporarily built festival city where, besides basic facilities, posting and banking services, restaurants, pubs, shops and a number of other amenities provide comfort and entertainment. During the years, the number of visitors was continuously on the rise (from 43,000 in 1993 to 371,000 in 2007).

Sixty per cent of visitors are from Hungary, mainly from Budapest; 85% of the visitors are under 30 years of age, and higher education graduates are heavily over-represented despite the comparatively low average age. Almost half of the 37,000 foreign visitors come from Germany and France, and almost 90% of the foreign visitors are 30 years of age or younger.

(Continued)

Box 9.5a. Continued.

Two-thirds of the foreigners come either by air or by car. While most domestic visitors (52.6%) slept outdoors on the island, 42.1% commuted from home, 5.8% stayed at friends and only 0.5% booked accommodation in a hotel, guesthouse or campsite. The vast majority (94%) of the foreign visitors named the 'Island' as their accommodation during the festival. A mere 6% of the foreigners stayed at commercial accommodation (hotel, guesthouse or campsite).

During the Sziget Festival in 2006, approximately 2200 m^3 of waste accumulated. This is roughly equal to the amount of rubbish that the residents of a ten-storey building mount up in 9–10 years. The festival venue is situated near busy main roads and the concentration of pollutants is generally very high. For example, the extra CO_2 emissions made by those who arrive by car can grow by as much as 30% during the festival (The Clean Air Action Group, 2007, in Dávid, 2009). Combined with parking problems, the effect of dust generated by visitors also causes the deterioration of the air quality during the festival. Visitors' treading leads to soil compression and as visitors are not using toilets, a chemical soil pollution is noticeable. The threshold limit of noise generated by any free time activity is maximized at 45 decibels during the day between 07.00 and 20.00 h, and at night between 20.00 and 07.00 h this limit is 40 decibels. During the practice sessions and at the actual event, the limit was exceeded by well over 25 and 23 decibels, respectively. Busy traffic on the main roads adds to the noise pollution. One of the greatest problems of the festival is sewage treatment. There are a growing number of bio-toilets on the island; none the less, the number of the more easily cleanable and illuminated container-toilets – because of the lack of sewerage pipeline – could not really be increased. In addition, energy use rises greatly during the festival because of the light and sound requirements (because of the growing number of visitors and demand for public lighting, it was further improved on the island; in 2007, more than 4.5 km of road was illuminated during the festival).

Source: Dávid (2009)

While it is easy to list a range of negative impacts, it should not be forgotten that many negative impacts are temporarily tolerated in exchange for the feel-good factor that the event provides. Furthermore, impacts should not be seen in isolation but in conjunction with each other, as they have knock-on effects. In some cases, impacts are not as straightforward as they seem or easy to evaluate from an ethical or cultural point of view (see Box 9.4).

Impacts can vary in their intensity and can be both short-term and long-term. The very nature of events results in most impacts being rather intense within a short-term period; however, they can have lasting effects. To assure the harmony within the local community and the overall sustainability of events, impacts have to be managed and kept to a minimum. Therefore, the next part of the chapter looks into the concepts of sustainability and CSR to assess how events can be sustainably managed and organized.

SUSTAINABILITY IN EVENTS

For the past few decades, sustainability/sustainable development has become a priority, not only on a local level, but nationally and internationally. The relationship between sustainable development and events is twofold. Destinations have adopted events as a strategy for sustainable tourism development, as they extend the visitor season. At the same time, however, instead of taking events as an instrument in achieving sustainable development, events should also be managed and planned in a sustainable manner. One key driver for a change in philosophy and attitude was the Rio Declaration in 1992, when 180 governments signed an agreement to work collaboratively on a sustainability agenda. 'Sustainability is about meeting the needs of the present generation (of businesses, consumers and communities) without compromising the ability of future generations to meet their needs' (World Commission on Environment and Development, 1987). In other words, sustainability is essentially about minimizing the negative impacts of events while enhancing the positive impacts. Sustainable events will not only consider the environment, but also the economic consequences, the legacy and the community, thereby following the 'triple bottom line' of economic prosperity, social progress and environmental quality. Applying the principles of sustainability to events results in defining sustainable events as events that minimize negative impacts while enhancing positive impacts, thereby assuring the economic viability for the event organization or government, the safeguarding of local culture and heritage, the protection of the natural environment while at the same time providing both the locals and the visitor with an enjoyable experience. While other industries had begun to adopt sustainable measures earlier, the events industry has been relatively late to recognize the importance of sustainability and there is little published material on the extent to which events have engaged with the principles of sustainable development. None the less, event organizations based in countries that have signed the Rio Declaration are encouraged to pursue a responsible approach towards event planning and organization. The FIFA World Cup 2010 provides a platform to advertise the issue of sustainability in events as the world's first international Tourism, Sport and Mega-events Summit is held in South Africa just before the football tournament takes place. At the forefront in adopting sustainability are the Olympic Games, which have developed a sustainability agenda and are actively using their events to promote sustainability. As part of the preparation for London 2012, the London Olympics Organising Committee has designed a detailed action plan on five key areas: climate change, waste, biodiversity, inclusion and healthy living (Fig. 9.1).

The London Olympics Action Plan is only one example, but further sustainable event policies and plans have been developed. At a governmental level, DEFRA (UK) has produced a Sustainable Events Guide (DEFRA, 2007), Environment Canada has produced a Green Meeting Guide (ECEAD, 2007) and the BMU (Germany) has published Guidelines for the Environmentally Sound Organisation of Events (BMU, 2008). At the industry level, SEXI: The Sustainable Exhibition Industry Project (MEBC, 2002) has been developed in the UK, whereas the Convention Industry Council's Green Meetings Report provides guidelines for US-based convention organizers (CIC, 2004). The Sustainable Music Festival – A Strategic Guide presents an international collaboration (Brooks *et al.*, 2007). Furthermore, many individual event organizations are taking the philosophy behind sustainability on board and are producing sustainable events management guidelines or CSR reports (see below). These guidelines and plans show that the events industry has been quick in adopting sustainability principles and is keen to address the key issues surrounding sustainability.

Locating events into the wider context of sustainability and addressing the sustainability of events, there are several key issues that need to be addressed:

- controlled use of resources and assuring the optimal and controlled management of natural, social and cultural resources;
- restriction of over-consumption and reducing the amount of waste to avoid costs in repairing long-lasting environmental damage, and to carry out environmental impact analyses within event concepts;
- conservation and assuring the natural, social, and cultural diversity is a precondition for restrained and controllable events; and
- involving events in long-term developmental concepts: to integrate events in higher-level (national, regional, local) strategies.

Programme element	Climate change	Waste	Biodiversity	Inclusion	Healthy living
Architecture and urban design	Environmentally efficient and climate-proofed design and construction		Creation of new habitats on and around buildings	Using architecture and urban design and regeneration	
Procurement	Sourcing materials with low-embodied carbon	Minimizing waste at source, promoting use of secondary materials	Policies on ecologically sensitive materials: e.g. timber, food	Ethical procurement and fair employment	Sourcing healthy materials and ensuring health and safety on site
Sponsorship	Sustainability section included in invitations to tender, evaluation criteria and partner agreements. Commercial partners will also be required to follow London 2012's sustainability policies on material, packaging and ethical trading. They may also 'activate' their sponsorship by taking on a variety of special projects to support and promote the 'one planet' projects programme				
Venue operations	Venue environment management plans to include resource use (energy, water, materials), waste management, pollution monitoring (water and air quality) and impact on natural environment.			Accessibility standards, language services, signage, accommodating faith groups	Health and safety
Transport	'Public Transport Games' Freighting materials by rail and water Re-use of materials on-site to reduce off-site transportation Low emission vehicles			Games Mobility Service	Active Spectator Programme, low emission vehicles
Technology	Remediation of contaminated land Utilizing technology to reduce carbon emissions and waste Environmental monitoring			Maximizing connectivity – Games for a Connected World	Environmental monitoring equipment
Food	Using food with lower greenhouse gas impacts	Reduced packaging and food waste, and recycling waste (composting)	Sourcing food from environmentally responsible farming	Ensuring local suppliers can contribute and develop sustainable businesses	Providing opportunities for healthy eating
Outreach and education	Promoting Olympic and Paralympic values, including respect for environment, through the One Planet Education Programme			Promoting Olympic and Paralympic values, including respect for others and friendship	Promoting Olympic and Paralympic values, including fair play, healthy living and personal excellence
Legacy planning	Planning across Government and the GLA Group to ensure that the inspirational vale of the Games is used to promote sustainability across London and the UK, including the publication of Government's 'Promise for 2012' and the development of legacy action plans, which will set out key programmes to spread the benefits and leave a sustainable legacy across the UK.				

Fig. 9.1. London 2012 Sustainability Plan (London Organising Committee of the Olympic Games and Paralympic Games, 2007).

The central ideas of sustainability are that there is a holistic and long-term approach to the management of events, and the collaboration and partnerships of all stakeholders (e.g. event organizers, local/national governments, supplier businesses, local communities and event visitors) is essential. The following gives an overview of several initiatives that are already in place and that event managers can adopt to assure the sustainability of their events.

CSR – THE COMPANY'S PERSPECTIVE ON SUSTAINABILITY

Closely related to the concept of sustainability is CSR. While sustainability and sustainable development practices are considered at political level, CSR can be considered the business perspective of sustainability. Similarly to sustainability, businesses have started to adopt CSR policies as a reaction to either the increasingly ethically minded and socially aware customers or as a reaction to legislation. While most companies now have a CSR policy in place to satisfy their stake- and shareholders, CSR has not always been widely accepted. Originating from the 1950s, the idea was opposed because: (i) it was perceived to be an unfair and costly burden to the managers and to shareholders; (ii) would conflict with the business's overall purpose to make money; and (iii) managers did not have the right skills or expertise to deal effectively with social problems. However, these concerns were gradually removed as CSR contributed to the wider organizational goals such as stakeholder management and the argument that proactive environmental management eliminates the risk of potential regulatory and legal actions while improving competitive advantage for businesses through improvement of reputation and a positive influence on the financial performance. Furthermore, it would only be in a business's interest to protect the surrounding environment and society, as otherwise they would lose their critical support structure and customer base – as consumer awareness of environmental and ethical issues is increasing, CSR can safeguard the corporate image (Lee, 2008). Adopting CSR as part of the business strategy can result in economic benefits to event organizers and event facilities – financial savings or avoiding costs can be achieved through the use of re-usable items and thereby reducing/eliminating disposable charges. Finally, there is a growing body of environmental interest groups and events industry environmental bodies (such as AGreenerFestival.com, Green Meetings Industry Council, IFEA), which are pushing the agenda of sustainability and CSR and influencing event organizations to adopt environmentally friendly and socially responsible practices. Similarly to sustainability, CSR addresses mainly environmental aspects (e.g. recycling, waste management, carbon emission control, etc.), but it has been increasingly widened to incorporate social and corporate governance issues (supporting charity work, outreach programmes, employee well-being, etc.).

Box 9.6. CSR at Super Bowl (USA).

The Super Bowl is organized by the National Football League (NFL), which has adopted CSR policies by working with local organizations on a range of projects on youth outreach, health and wellness, arts, education, business advancement for racial and gender minorities and community rebuilding. The 2006 Super Bowl took place in Detroit, a city that faced major problems with poverty, crime and poor education, as well as the city's financial hardship, which had led to reduction in police forces and firefighters and the closure of local community centres. As part of the Super Bowl wider programme, a range of initiatives was implemented:

(Continued)

Box 9.6. Continued.

- *Emerging Business Program* (to provide women and minority owned businesses with the opportunity for participation in the Super Bowl business process;
- *Super Makeover* (an initiative to enhance the city by picking up litter, painting over graffiti and removing weeds in pedestrianized areas);
- *Project 'Green'* (planting 2500 trees and plants to offset carbon emissions);
- *One World, One Detroit* (cultural and diversity related events such as a teen conference on tolerance, and Rock My Soul event with African American art, dance and music);
- *Super Reading Program* (to encourage children in Detroit schools to read and use local public libraries);
- *Youth Education Town* (creation of educational and recreational centres for youth in at-risk neighbourhoods in Super Bowl Host cities, including tutoring, mentoring, career training, computer education, and athletics; YETs are physical legacies of the Super Bowl);
- *SuperBuild* (building 40 homes for families displaced by Hurricane Katrina);
- *Rebuilding Together* (1-day activity of home improvements for families, the elderly or disabled homeowners);
- *Super Bowl NFL Charities Bowling Classic* (proceeds to benefit Detroit Youth Education Town);
- *NFL Experience* (opportunity for families to have a 'Super Bowl experience' from interactive exhibits, clinics, and autograph signings – proceeds to the Detroit Youth Education Town);
- *Taste of the NFL* (to raise money and awareness for the hungry).

Source: Babiak and Wolfe (2006)

Questions
- What sustainability initiatives is the Super Bowl implementing as part of their CSR strategy?
- Compare the Super Bowl's CSR strategy with London 2012 plan – what are differences, what are similarities?

ENVIRONMENTAL MANAGEMENT POLICIES

When referring to sustainability and responsibility within events, most attention is paid to environmental impacts and thus environmental measures and strategies to minimize those impacts. The main impact on the environment is caused by the participants' and visitors' journeys to and from the event, and further impacts are caused by transfers at the venue. As a reaction to this, the idea of climate-neutral mobility has gained currency and offsetting measures are used to compensate for the greenhouse gases and CO_2 emissions. Other initiatives include the use of low-emissions vehicles and encouraging the use of public transport as much as possible through the creation of incentives (e.g. by offering combined tickets – entrance tickets to the event also include free-of-charge travel to and from the venue by public transport) or opportunities to use bicycles at the venue. Apart from being environmentally friendly, it provides an additional service to the visitors. Various events in Germany have implemented a range of measures such as Park & Ride systems at the Munich Oktoberfest, free public transport tickets at the German Protestant Church Congress or establishing arrangements with Deutsche Bahn (German national railway) to make use of their Call a Bike service. The organization of a shuttle service or car-share scheme for travel between the hotel, conference venue and/or point of arrival/departure (railway station, airport) can also contribute to the climate-neutral implementation of events.

Further consideration should be given to questions relating to energy supply (e.g. renewable energies, green power and heat–power cogeneration) and energy consumption when selecting event venues and hotels. In this respect, environmental labels can be used for guidance (see below). Both venues and their suppliers should implement efficient practices to save and minimize the use of water and energy, which can range from using environmentally friendly technology (e.g. water-saving fittings, low-consumption light bulbs) to all members of staff contributing through small actions (such as turning off lights when leaving a room, turning computers off, etc.).

The provision of effective recycling and waste management policies is essential to avoid pollution and can easily be achieved through installation of waste collection points for the separate collection of different waste and the use of ecologically advantageous packaging, e.g. using recyclable and compostable food and beverage containers. Another option is to ask visitors to pay a deposit for dishes or glasses – they receive it back when returning the dish/glass, or they can keep it as a souvenir. Taxation can be effective as well – if non-reusable dishes are used, vendors have to pay a higher licence or visitors are charged more for their food and beverage. To the event organizer, this has additional benefits of increased income, reduced waste logistics and saving money on the waste disposal, as the individual suppliers are responsible for disposal of waste and handling material.

Wider issues should be taken into account when new venues are constructed, as environmentally friendly design and architecture can be implemented at the earliest stage.

Box 9.5b. Sziget Festival of Budapest.

In order to tackle the environmental problems at the Sziget Festival (see Box 9.5a), the government and event organizers have implemented a range of measures to assure a more environmentally sensitive festival:

- Visitors are encouraged to approach the festival venue by means of public transport.
- Temporary car park during the festival at abandoned gas works sites.
- Increasing number of mobile toilets and creation of toilet centres at the most frequented places of the island, using a new technology that does not require a pipeline system, but sewage flows into a large tank from where it is transported away.
- Stages are erected and fitted with noise insulation material and automatic volume-control devices at the problematic places, which continuously measure the noise level and adjust the volume below the threshold limit without human interaction.
- Selective waste collection combined with road-show teaching on environmental consciousness to popularize selection among the 'island dwellers'. In addition, gifts (like pass-holders, textile bags, writing pads, soft drinks, caps and T-shirts) are provided in exchange for beer bottles, PET bottles or cans, and as an initiative to engage in recycling activities.

Source: Dávid (2009)

Questions

- Compare the initiatives with an event that you are familiar with: how are they tackling environmental impacts? What initiatives are in place that the Sziget Festival could also implement?
- How important are technological changes and advances to minimize environmental impacts?

LEGISLATION AND REGULATION

Government legislation plays a central part in minimizing impacts as event organizers have to comply with legal requirements. As outlined above, government can play an active role in planning for events, but they have also the power to implement measures that actively encourage environmentally friendly practices. On an international level, there are EU environmental legislations such as the Sixth Environmental Action Programme, which reviews environmental policies affecting transport. Seaside events are also subjected to the European Flag Scheme, as beaches might be designate to comply with environmental guidelines. EU Employment and Social Policy includes the EU Working Time Directive and the Community Charter of Fundamental Social Rights of Workers to encourage the harmonization of employees' rights (including event organization). A range of further European policies facilitates operation of businesses across national boundaries, which provides opportunities for international events and cultural exchange. Further international regulation can come from UNESCO, which is responsible for designation of World Heritage Sites – this has an indirect impact if these sites are used for events, but the 2003 Convention for the Safeguarding of the Intangible Cultural Heritage now protects events and festivals around the world (such as carnivals in Belgium, Bolivia, Colombia, Croatia and Hungary, as well as religious processions and festivals in China, India, Japan, Mexico and Korea) to assure the upkeep, maintaining and authenticity of important local traditions (UNESCO, 2009).

At a national level, there is a range of further environmental, employment and anti-discriminatory legislation, which contribute to the sustainability of events and events management practices (e.g. see health and safety legislation in Chapter 5, and employment legislation in Chapter 6).

LABELLING AND CERTIFICATION

Eco-labelling and certification schemes have also been on the rise. The European Eco Management and Audit Scheme is an initiative to improve organizations' environmental performance, which recognizes and rewards companies that go beyond the minimum legal compliance and continuously improve their environmental performance. A public environmental statement reporting on the performance is a requirement and the accuracy and reliability is independently checked by an environmental verifier. Similarly, ISO 14001 provides specific requirements for an environmental management system, which enables a company to develop and implement environmental policies and objectives, taking into account legal requirements and other requirements as well as information about significant environmental aspects.

Green Seal is a label that looks specifically at environmentally friendly operations management, whereas the Green Globe is an initiative aimed at the tourism industry but also applicable to events organizations.

More specific to the industry is the certification of BS8901, the British Standard for sustainable events management, which was introduced in 2007 and provides a useful starting point for event managers to assess the sustainability of their events. In order to gain BS8901, event organizations follow the model of planning, implementation and feedback. During the planning phase, the supply chain and the event's stakeholders are assessed, including all communications, to identify how the sustainable message is filtered down. During implementation, it is crucial to assess how effective sustainable measures are carried out and are checked against the standard. Collating feedback is a vital part of the process to learn lessons for future events. BS 8901 has not been universally accepted by the events industry – nevertheless, it provides a uniform approach that is scalable and applicable to both large and small events and has been endorsed by high-level organizations (e.g. London 2012 Olympics), which act as high profile ambassadors for the sustainability of events.

Related to labelling and certification are awards given by industry associations. The Green Meetings Industry Council (USA) presents the 'Green' awards to recognize environmental commitment within the meetings industry (e.g. Green Meeting Awards, Green Supplier Awards, Green Exhibitor Award and Commitment to the Community Award). The Association of Events Organisers, together with its sister organizations the Association of Event Venues and the Event Supplier and Services Association, presents the Excellence Awards, which recognize business performance and standards of best practice.

COMMUNICATION, INFORMATION AND EDUCATION

As mentioned above, events are often used as a platform to spread messages, and hence events can be a useful tool for providing information on sustainability issues. Public education programmes as part of the event have been established to raise the awareness of environmental problems and solutions to a wider audience. However, communication and information at events are also essential to facilitate the sustainable management of events. As early as the planning phase, the goal of staging an event in a sustainable manner and the importance of sustainable practices needs to be communicated across all stakeholders, including staff, suppliers, communities and visitors, which involve comprehensive public relations and internal/external marketing work. Forwarding of information on the environmental concept to all participants with their invitations and information on local public transport at the conference venue are just some examples for the importance of effective communication as a facilitator for sustainable events management. Transparency is an essential part of sustainable events management. As outlined above, certification schemes require organizations to produce reports on their environmental performance, whereas communication with the wider community is also important to minimize any potential conflicts. If event organizers encourage a transparent communication policy on all aspects of their event operations and management, and provide accessible publication of the organization's practices and behaviour, it leads to greater accountability and fewer opportunities for potential mismanagement.

Closely related to a public and transparent communication policy is the involvement of the community. As the community is the first one to notice the impacts, it is important to work with the local community through the establishment of advisory committees and forums in order to safeguard the cooperation of the local community and minimize any potential hostility from this stakeholder. Free or discounted tickets, giving preference to local businesses, providing employment to locals, involving local charity groups and including projects that involve the local community are all initiatives that can help the event to be favourably looked upon, increase the reputation and avoid any conflicts, thereby minimizing potential negative impacts on the local community. However, actively involving the community sounds easier than it is, particularly when we are referring to large-scale events (imagine how difficult it would be to involve all citizens of London in decisions for the London 2012 Olympics). Furthermore, locals might not have the knowledge and skills to be able to participate successfully in the decision-making process. Public participation can become a placation without any actual open discussion.

Box 9.7. Peter-and-Paul Festival, Bretten (Germany).

The Peter-and-Paul Festival in Bretten, Germany, is an annual heritage festival, during which the local community celebrates the history of their city. Over the years, the festival has attracted up to 125,000 visitors. The main focus is the medieval history and a range of activities and smaller events that showcase medieval aspects take place over the 4 days of the festival – jugglers and music performances, theatre plays, medieval dances, and many more. Most of these are performed by local entertainment and theatre groups, but some outsider groups are invited to perform as well. None of these groups receives money, but they collect 'tips' from the audience afterwards. The highlights of the festival are the parade of all participating groups, the fireworks and the re-enactment of a battle that took place in 1504.

One of the key parts of the festival is some 3000 locals who wear medieval costume and form groups with a specific medieval theme, such as archers, sheepherders, lancers, gypsies and many more. Of more than 50 groups, most are local, but several international medieval interest groups (from Poland, Italy and the UK) are invited to camp during the festival. Each group sets up a camp in which members of the group spend most of their time – cooking, socializing or displaying their newly acquired skills to visitors and fellow locals (see Fig. 9.2). Some groups are also selling drinks and food to visitors, although external vendors set up their stalls as well (against a fee and as long as the design and concept fits with the overall medieval theme).

Visitors are not allowed in the camps, but are merely allowed to glimpse into the camps and observe activities. Only if dressed in a medieval costume is access to camps allowed, and while locals welcome the visitors to observe, the separation between locals and visitors is very strict. 'Sometimes you do feel like an exhibit'; 'If I am in the camp they don't disturb me. I mean there must be some parts, where tourists are not allowed to go.' The medieval dress plays a very important role, as these locals explain: 'We do not dress up or put on costumes, we say we want to live our history. To us, it is not a carnival, or a costume party, that is why we say vestments and not costumes.' 'I don't feel costumed; I felt good right from the beginning, because it is practical and comfortable, not like carnival.' 'That gives a feeling of closeness and openness.' 'When I went to the dance, it was weird to see people without vestments, you feel uncomfortable. In the camps it is cosier.'

(Continued)

Box 9.7. Continued.

Fig. 9.2. (a) Sewing new leather bags. (b) Washer women's camp. (c) Skirmish between English and Germans. (d) Chain maille vest maker.

Photos by Sine Heitmann

Questions

- What socio-cultural impacts can you observe?
- How important do you think is the separation of visitors and locals to assure sustainability?
- If a famous national brand was to express interest in sponsoring this event – what would be the arguments for and against this?

CODES OF CONDUCT

Codes of conduct are effective, as they can convey messages to both tourists and the events industry in short and understandable ways and can influence changes in visitor behaviour and business practices. They have the potential to initiate conversation between the stakeholders and parties involved, raise awareness, assist in establishing partnerships and encourage cooperation between stakeholders.

At large events, it can be problematic to get every visitor to sign it, particularly if it is a free event. In cases where admission has to be paid, the code of conduct can be made conditional at time of purchase. However, unless asked to sign, codes of conducts are voluntary and not necessarily binding, and hence their usefulness and effectiveness as a form of education is questioned. Codes of conduct might be seen as rules that restrict behaviour and a visitor might have an adverse reaction and/or refuse to sign or adhere to them.

PARTNERSHIPS AND SUPPLY CHAIN MANAGEMENT

When trying to manage an event sustainably, the initiatives should not be isolated and left to the event organizers, but should be carried out throughout the supply chain and in partnership with all stakeholders concerned. If an event is to be sustainable overall, the suppliers and service providers need to include sustainable policies in their business practices as well, as otherwise all efforts from the event organizer are futile. Preferences should be given to organically and locally sourced, as well as fair trade products and therefore only caterers meeting predefined criteria should be selected. The use of seasonal foods automatically leads to reduction of transportation routes and second-tier environmental impacts of events. Event organizers can implement a procurement policy for suppliers and clauses in contract that bind suppliers and providers to adhering to sustainable practices. Extending the practices of labelling and certification (see above), only suppliers that have undergone certification processes are accepted to be contracted for the event. In order to foster links with the local community, local renewable power companies can be supported by inviting them to provide energy on a discounted rate in exchange for publicity. Close participation with travel and transport providers is also vital, and schemes such as tickets including free public transport (see above) are a result of this. Choosing a venue with easy public access results in sustainable chain management, as environmental impacts are limited and inclusion policies (see below) are achieved. Partnerships can also be effective for sustainable events management by allying with competitors and lobbying local and national government and energy companies for renewable energy.

CROWD MANAGEMENT

Effective crowd management can lead to a reduction of negative behaviour. As many problems are associated with alcohol, an effective bar management policy is needed. From experience in football stadiums, limiting tickets has proved to be successful to avoid large groups coming together and causing disruption. The ban of eccentric costumes has also resulted in avoidance of negative behaviour. Finally, many large-scale events have increased security to manage large crowds.

> **Question**
> Look at Chapter 5 on health and safety management – what measures can help to minimize negative impacts?

INCLUSION

Many events have now adopted inclusion policies, which facilitate the widest participation possible, particularly encouraging people from disadvantaged backgrounds or ethnic minorities to participate (as visitors or employees). This way, effective inclusion policies can also help with the relationship with communities, as traditional owners (i.e. indigenous people) can be included in the events (e.g. opening or closing the ceremony, traditional performances).

Inclusion also extends to disabled visitors. Barrier-free access to events for wheelchair users wherever possible with wheelchair-accessible toilets wherever possible are essential considerations. Where necessary, implementation of measures that facilitate the participation of people with other disabilities (e.g. visually and hearing-impaired people). The use of sign-language interpreters roaming the site as help for the sight/hearing impaired can make a significant difference to visitors. Gender-neutral written and oral formulations are also an essential part of inclusion and anti-discrimination policies.

Questions

- Using Fig. 9.1, investigate each of the individual projects (Public Transport Games, One Planet Education Programme, Promise for 2012, Games for a Connected World) and identify which specific impacts they are targeting and how. How successful do you think these projects will be? What potential problems can you think of?
- Compare London 2012 with a previous Olympic Games (Beijing 2008, Athens 2004, Sydney 2000) – how has the importance of sustainability changed? What projects have other cities used to achieve sustainability, and what problems have they encountered?
- Rio de Janeiro will be the next Olympic venue in 2016 – what can Rio learn from London?

SUMMARY

The chapter has provided an overview of the key political, economic, socio-cultural and environmental impacts of events. While outcomes of events can be planned and inform the event planning process, there are further unplanned impacts that can be observed but have to be taken into account. The management of these impacts are important to assure the sustainability and sustainable management of events. In order to achieve sustainable events management, all stakeholders have to be included and work together. The chapter has outlined a variety of management practices and initiatives that are already in place, and there is evidence that both sustainability and CSR are central to event organizations. Yet, the events industry is still in its infancy when it comes to applying sustainable events management and further initiatives will be emerging and adopted in the future.

FURTHER READING

Raj, R. and Musgrave, J. (eds) (2009) *Event Management and Sustainability*. CAB International, Wallingford, UK.

REVIEW QUESTIONS

1. Consider the other chapters in this book – if an event manager follows the principles of sustainability, how does it feed through the event planning process?

2. Identify event companies and assess their CSR policies. What measures and practices are they implementing?

REFERENCES

Babiak, K. and Wolfe, R. (2006) More than just a game? Corporate social responsibility and Super Bowl XL. *Sport Marketing Quarterly* 15, 214–222.

BMU (2008) Guidelines for Environmentally Sound Organisation of Events, Federal Ministry for the Environment, Nature Conservation and Nuclear Safety (BMU), April 2008. Available at: http://www.bmu.de/files/pdfs/allgemein/application/pdf/broschuere_leitfaden_umweltgerecht_en.pdf (accessed 24 March 2010).

Bowdin, G., Allen, J., O'Toole, W., Harris, R. and McDonnell, I. (2006) *Events Management*, 2nd edn. Butterworth-Heinemann, Oxford.

Brooks, S., O'Halloran, D. and Magnin, A. (2007) The Sustainable Music Festival – A Strategic Guide. Available at: http://www.naturalstep.org/sites/all/files/MusicFestivalsGuidebook.pdf (accessed 24 March 2010).

CIC (2004) Convention Industry Council's Green Meetings Report, March 2004. Available at: http://www.conventionindustry.org/projects/green_meetings_report.pdf (accessed 24 March 2010)

Dávid, L. (2009) Environmental impacts of events. In: Raj, R. and Musgrave, J. (eds) *Event Management and Sustainability*. CAB International, Wallingford, UK.

DEFRA (2007) Sustainable Events Guide, Department for Environment, Food and Rural Affairs. Available at: http://www.defra.gov.uk/sustainable/government/advice/documents/SustainableEventsGuide.pdf (accessed 24 March 2010).

ECEAD (2007) Environment Canada's Green Meeting Guide, Environment Canada – Environmental Affairs Division, August 2007, Version 2.0. Available at: http://www.greeninggovernment.gc.ca/F5B1C0BC-741C-4493-B4B7-B0D56BBE6566/Green_Meeting_Guide_07.pdf (accessed 24 March 2010).

Lee, M.P. (2008) A review of the theories of corporate social responsibility: its evolutionary path and the road ahead. *International Journal of Management Reviews* 10(1), 53–73.

London Organising Committee of the Olympic Games and Paralympic Games (2007) London 2012: Sustainability Plan – Towards a One Planet 2012. Available at: http://www.london2012.com/documents/locog-publications/london-2012-sustainability-plan.pdf (accessed 24 March 2010).

MEBC (Midlands Environmental Business Company) (2002) The Sustainable Exhibition Industry Project. Available at: http://www.mebconline.com/Portals/0/PDF/Sexi.pdf (accessed 24 March 2010).

Sowetan (2009) Decriminalise our trade, Sowetan, 27th November 2009. Available at: http://www.sowetan.co.za/News/Article.aspx?id=1092157 (accessed 24 March 2010).

UK Sport (2009) eventIMPACTS. Available at: http://www.uksport.gov.uk/pages/events-research/ (accessed 24 March 2010).

UNESCO (2009) Intangible Cultural Heritage – ICH, United Nations Educational, Scientific and Cultural Organization. Available at: http://www.unesco.org/culture/ich (accessed 24 March 2010).

World Commission on Environment and Development (1987) *Our Common Future*. Oxford University Press, Oxford.

chapter 10

Business Planning and Strategy

Dimitri Tassiopoulos and Crispin Dale

OBJECTIVES OF THE CHAPTER

This chapter aims to explore strategic management concepts and theories within the context of the events industry from a macro- and micro-scale perspective. Some strategies are more appropriate for large events organizations and destinations, while the majority of events businesses, which can be assumed to be largely small and medium-sized businesses, often require a more appropriate approach to meet the strategic imperatives of their smaller-sized events business or project.

The chapter acknowledges the interrelationships between the different management functions and analyses business situations and strategic options. The chapter will initially introduce the deliberate and emergent nature of strategic management and its impact upon event strategy and planning. Approaches to analysing the external macro- and microenvironment will be discussed with an understanding of the factors that may impact upon events and event operators. Consideration will then be given to concepts and theories that address the strategic options and methods of event operators. Approaches to understanding the implementation of strategies to events as part of the strategic management process will then be addressed in terms of the key knowledge domains of events management. To enhance understanding of the material, the chapter will apply the theories and concepts to 'live' mini-case studies of events and event operators.

The objectives of the chapter are to:

- analyse elements of the strategic management process for events and event organizations;
- explore how strategic management concepts and theories can be used to analyse the strategic context of events and events organizations; and
- discuss strategic issues that influence large, small and medium-sized events and events organizations.

INTRODUCTION

Strategy is a crucial aspect of event planning and management. Strategic decisions will be influenced by factors in the external and competitive environment, the direction that the events organization wishes to pursue and how any chosen strategy can be effectively implemented. The chapter aims to introduce those aspects of strategic management that events operators and organizations should consider when developing and staging events. This will include an analysis of strategic management concepts and theories, as they apply to both large-scale and small-scale events. Case studies from across the globe will be used to support an understanding of the theory.

For the purpose of understanding the application of the theory, it is important to define initially what is understood by strategy. Strategy is a term, according to Antoniou (2008) and Chell (2001), which comes from the Greek *strategia*, meaning 'generalship'. Military strategy often refers to the manoeuvring of troops into position before an enemy in battle. In the events context, there is unlikely to be death and destruction in the same way that occurs on a battlefield. Nevertheless, factors including outmanoeuvring the opposition (i.e. other event operators) and deploying your resources effectively are consistent with a military perspective. Strategy, in short, is thus a term that refers to a complex web of thoughts, ideas, insights, experiences, goals, expertise, memories, perceptions and expectations that provides general guidance for specific actions in pursuit of particular objectives. There are many definitions of strategy. A number of these are illustrated in the following questions.

Questions

Strategy is the direction and scope of an organization over the long term, which achieves advantage in a changing environment through its configuration of resources and competences with the aim of fulfilling stakeholder expectations (Johnson *et al.*, 2008).

Corporate strategy can be described as the identification of the purpose of the organization and the plans and actions to achieve this purpose (Lynch, 2005).

Strategy is the means by which individuals or organizations achieve their objectives (Grant, 2008).

1. What are some of the common keywords that emerge from these definitions?

2. To what extent are these definitions relevant in an event context?

3. Develop your own definition of strategy that also embraces your understanding of events management and planning as it applies to both large and small event enterprises.

Strategy drives performance and an effective strategy results in a good performance. A business's strategy is multifaceted and can be viewed from a number of directions, depending on which aspects of its actions are of interest. There is a basic difference between the content of a business's strategy, the strategic process that the business adopts to maintain the strategy and the environmental context within which the strategy must be made to operate. The strategy content relates to what the business actually does while strategy process relates to the way the business decides what it is going to do. The strategy content has three distinct decision areas: the products to be offered, the markets to be targeted and the approach taken. Mintzberg and Walters (1985) differentiate between deliberate and emergent forms of strategy. Deliberate strategies have a rational intention. The events operator will proceed through a number of logical steps in pursuit of a clearly defined strategic direction. With an emergent strategy, the events operator will learn from external and internal factors, and from the actions of those in the events business. The events operator, therefore, needs to be flexible to change to embed strategies that may emerge from within.

Small business planning behaviour, according to Sexton and van Auken (1982) and Kiriri (2005), could be described as unstructured, irregular and incomprehensive. This characterizes small and medium events enterprise (SMEE) strategizing as incremental, sporadic and reactive. Over the last few decades, strategic management has become an important field of study. Despite its relevance to all organizations, most research is focused on larger organizations and has virtually ignored SMEEs. Such neglect creates the impression that strategic management is for businesses listed on the stock exchange only. Most SMEEs have further given credibility to such generalizations as they believe strategic management is not relevant to them and that many SMEEs are ignorant of the value of anticipatory decision making. Owners of SMEEs create the impression that they are not aware of the potential of strategic planning and do not appreciate the value of spending time and effort on such activity (Tassiopoulos, 2010b). Although research focusing on SMEEs has increased substantially in the last decades, the approach remains fragmented in the study of strategy formulation of SMEEs.

STRATEGY FOR THE EVENTS BUSINESS

In the domain of strategy, numerous concepts are used. It is argued by Bridge and Peel (1999) that since smaller enterprises tend to apply informal processes to enhance planning effectiveness, formal measures (for example, written documentation) may be inappropriate for such businesses. It is noted that the effective planning systems for SMEEs do not emphasize the need for written documentation and formal procedures. Some authors' view is that it is tactical and operational decisions that dominate.

SMEEs operate under conditions that contrast sharply from those of large events organizations and destinations. They are not just smaller versions of large organizations. Typically, SMEEs face different strategic options, as they operate under severe resource constraints, lack specialized managerial expertise (in many cases) and often have different and less aggressive objectives. Most SMEEs confine their strategic options to focusing on the events market opportunities in which they have sufficient resources to compete effectively. SMEEs often have no formal, written statements of strategy or those that are specified are in very general terms. The actual strategy may sometimes have to be deduced from evolving patterns of behaviour and resource allocations. It may, or may not, be intentional and frequently emerges through a series of incremental adjustments to the opportunities and threats that confront the SMEE.

The research by Schindehutte and Morris (2001) found that it is far more important for the entrepreneur to have a concept that loosely fits the opportunity, then to adapt things proactively as they evolve, than to lock the SMEE into specific commitments that limit the business's future options. SMEEs are furthermore not renowned for their strategic thinking and business planning, states Chell (2001); the strategy is at best embedded in the actions and decisions taken but these tend not to be explicit strategy, laid down and rigidly adhered to. It can be indicated that founders of new SMEEs mostly follow some strategy to reach their goals, although these strategies are not always rational or explicit. Research on business strategy frequently differentiates types of strategy by content and process characteristics. Content specifies which kind of strategy is used, for example low cost, differentiation or focus/niche. Alternatively, process refers to how the strategy content is formulated and implemented.

Large events businesses, according to Tassiopoulos (2010b, p. 64), tend to look at:

> the strategic aspect of their business such as globalization, digitization and geographic dispersion of the value chain, more intense competition, outsourcing, faster decision-making, and obsolescence/ innovation. In contrast, small to midsized companies are concerned with more tactical decisions and issues, such as growth, retaining qualified employees, government regulations, cost containment and customer relations.

SMEE owners tend to place greater importance on day-to-day operational issues. Furthermore, although the SMEE owners realize that while growing their businesses is important, managing the growth of their SMEEs is more important because of the limited resources available for business growth.

STRATEGIC PLANNING AND MANAGEMENT

Johnson *et al.* (2008) distinguished between three different levels of strategy that, to some extent, can be applied to events enterprises. This includes corporate, business and operational strategies. Corporate strategy relates to the holistic context of the events organization and how value can be added throughout its component parts. Business level strategy is concerned with how the different component business units of the events organization should develop strategy to gain a competitive advantage in their respective markets. Large events organizations will often be structured around a number of strategic business units (SBUs). These business units act as a basis for developing more clearly defined strategies and may be focused on distinctive market groups. Operational strategy is related to how the corporate or business level strategy can be embedded throughout the events organization in the delivery of its goods and services. This will also comprise strategies that are embedded within the events organizations individual functions such as marketing, human resources, finance, information technology and so on.

As the majority of events organizations are small, it is not unusual for all three of these activities to be undertaken by the owner-manager. SMEE entrepreneurs combine visionary, logical and possibly intuitive skills to pursue a particular strategic direction and position. He/she will need to inspire and persuade customers, partners, employers and suppliers in the delivery of the strategy. The delivery of the strategy also entails two further aspects. First, the entrepreneur will need to play a charismatic role in empowering and motivating employees, and secondly, an architectural role where systems and structures for the delivery of the strategy will need to be developed and embedded. Central to this activity is exploiting opportunities and countering any external or competitive threats. As part of the events planning process, strategic management is often illustrated as a number of stages. This process is illustrated in Fig. 10.1.

First is the strategic analysis of the external events environment. This encompasses both the micro- and macro-environment. This stage acknowledges those external factors that may impact on the event or events operator. This includes an understanding of other events and events operators to exploit opportunities and circumvent threats. Strategic analysis also entails the review of the internal activities of the event so it is aware of its strengths and weaknesses. A review of the event/events operators' internal resources and competences can enable it to decide on its strategic direction. Second is strategic formulation. This stage is concerned with the selection of strategic options that will enable the event/events operator to gain an advantage over competitors. This entails strategically positioning the organization to offer, or seem to be offering, something that provides value to the customer. Strategic positioning is

Fig. 10.1. The strategic management process. Source: adapted from Henry (2008).

the process of identification and exploitation; prioritization of customer needs, and creating value. Strategic positioning, according to Bolton and Thomson (2004) and Kirby (2003), is a convergence between the events business environment (for example, attendees, suppliers and competitors) and events business's resources. This is where the events business possesses strategic (or core) competences to enable it effectively to identify the relevant environmental key success factors. The event/events operator may position themselves relative to competitors or from the effective utilization of their resource strengths. Third is strategic implementation and the successful embedding of the strategic options. Strategy implementation is the process of finding the resources required, and understanding and managing the risks involved. This may involve the management of change. Strategic change is about ensuring that there is creativity and innovation in the business (Bolton and Thomson, 2004). Thus, the team and organization building become increasingly significant within the SMEE. Success is maintained by innovation and strategic change, which keeps an SMEE perpetually a few steps ahead of its competitors.

The chapter will draw further upon the strategic management process as a basis for understanding strategy in events and events planning. Though planning plays a central role in the process, it is the actual implementation of the idea that is planned, rather than the idea itself, which may have been realized opportunistically, largely reliant on the entrepreneur's attentiveness and insight of the market, which is important. This planning is seen to be flexible rather than rigid, as implementation is a learning process with ideas refined with experience.

EVENTS AS STRATEGIC DEVELOPMENT TOOLS

Strategic management is concerned with environmental fit and it is important to achieve congruence between the environment (the source of opportunities and threats), values (and culture) and resources (the strengths and weaknesses, strategic competencies and capabilities, which match or fail to match the environmental needs) for the existing and potential future products and services of the business – the so-called E–V–R (environment–values–resources) congruence model (Thomson, 1999). The environment can be seen as the windows of opportunity that a business has, the resources are representative of the organizational competences and capabilities. Irrespective of whether the events operator is large or small, the owner has the duty to ensure that the resources are developed and changed, and, to exploit the windows of opportunity that the business is presented (Thompson, 2001).

> **Box 10.1.** Festivals and events strategy, North East Tourism.
>
> In 2005, following the launch of the North East Tourism Strategy 2005–2010, partners across North East England began to develop a strategy for festivals and events.
>
> The purpose of the work was to clarify the role that festivals and events play within key economic and social agendas, identify future development requirements and clarify the strategic relationships with regional and sub-regional economic programme activity.
>
> The process has highlighted the wide range of motives for organizing festivals and events and the many purposes, including economic and social, that festivals and events can fulfil.
>
> Led by One NorthEast, this strategy sets out how partners can improve primarily, the economic but also the social impact of festivals and events in North East England and provides a strategic context for coordinated investment in festivals and events activity. This strategy acknowledges existing regional strengths, provides clarity as to the roles and responsibilities of regional and sub-regional partners, and begins to address gaps in the range, quality and geographic spread of activity.
>
> Source: North East England (2009)

FUTURE PLANNING OF EVENTS

A programme of events or a portfolio of events when viewed over the medium to long term can be considered an asset to a region according to O'Toole (2010). Although the results of the asset are intangible, the way that it is created or procured, maintained and eventually disposed parallels the management of physical assets such as roads, machinery and buildings. A large part of the current events management literature, states O'Toole (2010), concerns the management of a single event at a single time.

A strategy, states O'Toole (2010), is a long-term plan of coordinated action designed to achieve a major goal of an organization. Large organizations have strategic plans that may have 3-, 5- and 10-year cycles. Government tourism bodies, for example, have these cycles and need a strategy to enable the effective allocation of their resources. The size of the organization often corresponds to the complexity of its tasks.

A strategy enables the organization to align the tasks into processes that can be delegated to departments, divisions and, finally, individuals. Events can pass their 'use-by' or 'sell-by' dates. The events support process thus does not include the actual internal development of the event. It is concerned with the support for the event. The development of an event involves the interventions by the events owner. In common product development decisions, it involves these alternatives:

1. Grow.
2. Consolidate.
3. Devolve.
4. Cancel.

This development has been compared with the 'product life cycle' (PLC). However, the PLC is a descriptive model and not a prescriptive or predictive one. There are some events that have lasted thousands of years and others that are over in a day. The Olympics is an example of a product that has returned. It would be, however, almost impossible to predict their place in the product life cycle with any accuracy that has financial consequence (O'Toole, 2010).

STRATEGY AND THE LEGACY OF EVENTS

The importance of staging events has increased in a number of destinations; more and more destinations are beginning to realize the potential benefit of using events as a strategic development tool according to Tassiopoulos (2010a). Specific events dominate certain destinations – it could be indicative of certain destinations developing events niches as well as clear branding and positioning. Some destinations have given themselves events-related titles to accentuate their tourism strategy, for example, positioning themselves as 'Sports or Cultural Events Cities'.

The evaluation of events, states Getz (2007, in Tassiopoulos, 2010a), often have to consider the long-term, indirect and often subtle impacts of such events. 'Legacy' applies to all that remains, or is left over, from the events as a positive inheritance, or as challenges to deal with, by future generations. Mega-events are usually sold to the public on the basis of their many benefits plus the creation of a permanent legacy and according to Casey (2008, in Tassiopoulos, 2010a) act as a catalyst for economic regeneration or some other social, environmental or political imperative of the destination. Benefits of events are usually exaggerated while costs are usually underestimated or underemphasized.

Box 10.2. The legacy of the 2010 FIFA World Cup, South Africa.

Throughout its bidding process, South Africa placed an emphasis on 'making it [the 2010 FIFA World Cup] an African event, one that would help spread confidence and prosperity across the entire continent'. 'South Africa stands not as a country alone – but rather as a representative of Africa and as part of an African family of nations' and 'the successful hosting of the FIFA World Cup in Africa provides a powerful, irresistible momentum to [the] African renaissance'.

In constructing it as an African Cup, the South African Government stated that the event was intended to have a clearly defined legacy and social impact:

'An event that will create social and economic opportunities throughout Africa.' In fact, South Africa's hosting of the event as an African event is strongly supported by the African Union (AU), which 'seeks to promote sport as an instrument for sustainable economic development and poverty reduction, peace, and solidarity and social cohesion'.

'To ensure that one day, historians will reflect upon the 2010 World Cup as a moment when Africa stood tall and resolutely turned the tide on centuries of poverty and conflict. We want to show that Africa's time has come.'

In November 2006, the African Legacy Programme, a joint responsibility of the Local Organising Committee (LOC) and the South African government, was announced. For the South African Government, 'one of the main inspirations behind South Africa's preparations for 2010 FIFA World Cup™ – that being to leave a legacy for the African continent'. The objectives of the African Legacy Programme are to:

- support the realization of the objectives of the African Renaissance such as the programmes of the African Union's New Partnership for Africa's Development (NEPAD);
- ensure African participation in the event;
- develop and advance African football; and
- improve Africa's global image and combat Afro-pessimism.

(Continued)

Box 10.2. Continued.

Furthermore, the South African Government maintains that the legacy of the 2010 FIFA World Cup™ will be 'different from that typically associated with other large sporting events for three main reasons:

- The legacy benefits are not to be confined to the host country.
- The host country itself has made an undertaking to make the continent-wide legacy one of the core focus areas of preparations for the event.
- The African Union is actively involved in ensuring that the 2010 FIFA World Cup™ legacy agenda is owned continent-wide.'

Source: Van Wyk and Tassiopoulos (2009)

Legacy planning, according to Casey (2008, in Tassiopoulos, 2010a), needs to start from the very moment of deciding to bid – usually 10 years before the event is planned to be staged. It needs to start with a philosophical base – 'why is a destination bidding?' Casey (2008, cited in Tassiopoulos, 2010a) concludes by stating: 'Through effective legacy planning, we are all entrusted with the outcome of the Games for generations to come'.

CONTINUED GROWTH

International indicators show that over the past few decades there has been a substantial growth in events; all indications are that this growth will continue. Countries with developing economies have much to gain from this trend if they participate in the development of events products. Unfortunately, there are few reliable statistics and few research findings are available. Few destinations have attempted to monitor the trends and classifications necessary to quantify events growth according to Tassiopoulos (2010a).

In developing economies, such as South Africa, India or Brazil, there is a greater interest in issues such as the life cycle of events and the possibility of market saturation of events within a destination. It seems unlikely that there is an upper limit to the number of events that can be organized, given the diversity and benefits of events; however, within a given event, type or destination, saturation could occur. New events products entering a mature event marketplace would have to be innovative. Research evidence seems to indicate that events products can continue to grow as attendance and budget sizes have been increasing in many categories of events.

In the past, bidding for events was usually restricted to cities or destinations in developed economies. Such cities usually possessed the necessary resources, skills, expertise, facilities and infrastructure to bid for and stage events and may have had previous experience in this regard. Consequently, events owners trusted the capacity of these cities to host events as they may have had successful track records.

Destinations in developing countries are also broadening the concept of legacy from that of mere physical infrastructure provision to include the benefits experienced in preparation of a new vision for a destination city or town.

Developing country destinations are, however, increasingly learning to bid and win the right to host events in order that they may also take advantage of the multiple direct and indirect benefits of hosting events. They are studying the past experiences of other cities, both successful and unsuccessful, and are learning to become more internationally competitive (Tassiopoulos, 2010a).

STRATEGIC ANALYSIS: UNDERSTANDING THE EXTERNAL ENVIRONMENT

Event/events operator strategies have to be receptive to factors in the external environment. These factors can be dynamic and ever changing, which can make events planning particularly hazardous. The events operator has to position itself so it is able to react to changing environmental forces and competitive activities. The external environment can be analysed from both a macro- and micro-perspective. The macro-environment is the far environment that the event/events operator functions within. The event/events operator will have minimal control over these factors. The micro-environment is the near or competitive environment and is made up of competitors, markets, industries and sectors. Figure 10.2 illustrates the external macro- and micro-environment in diagrammatic form.

In understanding the macro-environment of the event/events operator, a number of models can potentially be used. Though it has its limitations, the PESTEL (Political, Economic, Social, Technological, Environmental and Legal) model is a framework frequently adopted for the purposes of analysing the macro-environment. The model is used to consider those factors that may have an impact on the event/events operator. The event organizer/operator can then develop strategies that counter challenges and maximize opportunities. Political factors such as the government in charge, international relations, conflict, civil unrest and terrorism all have the potential to influence events and events operators.

Fig. 10.2. The external environment (Dale, 2009).

Box 10.3. Terrorism and the Indian Live Earth Event.

The Indian Live Earth event was scheduled to take place in Mumbai on 7 December 2008. However, the event was cancelled because of a terrorist attack that took place a week earlier at the Taj Mahal Palace Hotel, killing over 150 people. A number of major artists were due to appear at the event, including will.i.am of the Black Eyed Peas, Jon Bon Jovi and Pink Floyd's Roger Waters. Live Earth events had been the inspiration of Kevin Wall and the former US vice president Al Gore. The focus of Live Earth events is to raise awareness of climate change and had previously taken place in Sydney, Tokyo, Hamburg, Johannesburg, Rio de Janeiro, New Jersey and London.

Source: Hannaford (2008)

Economic factors including fluctuations in interest rates and taxation can have an impact on personal disposable income (PDI). This can influence consumer expenditure on event goods and services including attendance and related merchandise.

Box 10.4. Recession and event cancellation.

The Heavenly Planet festival was due to be staged in Reading, UK, on 10 and 11 July 2009. However, as a result of the UK recession, the event had to be cancelled. Following initial poor ticket sales, the organizers decided to make the event free of charge. Nevertheless, the impact of the credit crunch had generated challenges for the festival organizers in continuing to support the event. The event was being organized by Reading Borough Council, festival organizer Melvin Benn and WOMAD's former artistic director, Thomas Brooman.

Source: eFestivals (2009)

Social factors such as demographic changes have the potential for generating new market opportunities for events operators. For instance, the growth in the 50+ population across western countries has encouraged many music event operators to schedule 'heritage acts', which appeal to the needs and tastes of an older generation. Technological factors such e-commerce and online distribution has enabled many events operators to market directly to customers. This can act as a basis for cutting costs related to not having to provide for physical box office premises or having to pay commission to ticket distributors. Online distribution can also provide customers with the potential choice of their seating allocation at the event.

Environmental factors such as climate change have empowered many events operators to consider strategies that minimize the negative impacts of their activities upon the wider environment. In this respect, a number of events operators have positioned their goods and services towards an environmental philosophy. For example, in October 2009, the Lovebox and Bestival music festivals in the UK pledged to cut their carbon emissions by 10% during 2010. From a legal perspective, event/events operators have to consider the legal context in which they are operating. The events industry is a global phenomenon and legal frameworks will differ from country to country. The discussion has noted a number of factors that can have an impact upon an event/events operator. It is important for the events operator to be aware of those factors that act as threats and those that are opportunities. Furthermore, the events operator should prioritize those factors that it perceives as being of the highest importance.

> **Activity**
>
> Using PESTEL, identify the factors within the macro-environment that are currently affecting an event or events operator of your choice. Identify which factors are of the highest priority and distinguish between those factors that are opportunities and threats.

Following this is an analysis of the micro-environment. This embraces an analysis of the event/events operator's competitors, markets, industry and sector. Such an analysis enables the events operator to understand who they are competing against and in what context. This can be influenced by the stage in which the market, industry or sector is in its lifecycle and the number, type and strength of competitors.

COMPETITOR ANALYSIS

Porter's model of competitive structural analysis (Fig. 10.3) presents five forces that influence competition in an industry or sector. It is the collective strength of these that determine the profit potential of the industry. By determining the relative importance of each of these forces, an organization can identify where to position itself to take advantage of opportunities and overcome or circumvent threats (Porter, 1980).

An organization, states Porter (1980), should be aware of the threat of new entrants and the barriers to entering into an industry. This can include the ability to gain economies of scale, the accessibility of distribution channels, the amount of capital required for entry, the ability to differentiate goods and services and the extent of government regulation in the industry. Staging an event requires significant capital resources and, as the Heavenly Planet example illustrated earlier, in the context of a recession this can be challenging for new entrants to

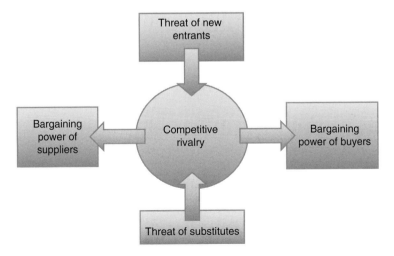

Fig. 10.3. Competitive structural analysis. Source: adapted from Porter (1980).

the industry. This is particularly the case when they are competing against more established events operators in the field who have acquired the reputational resources and potentially have a niche in the market. A further force is the bargaining power of suppliers. This will be influenced by the extent to which suppliers and substitutes are few in number, the costs of switching to alternative suppliers, whether there is the threat of forward integration from suppliers or the degree of differentiation of suppliers' products. Suppliers to events may come in the form of concert promoters and performance companies. These promoters and companies may have acts that give them a distinctive edge in the marketplace. They therefore may be able to negotiate a better contractual deal for the staging of the artist at the event. Alternatively, there is the power of buyers. Buyers will be powerful if they are few in number and are able to switch easily to other alternatives, there is the potential threat of backward integration or products are relatively undifferentiated. Events venues such as Wembley Stadium in London or the Sydney Opera House, Australia, have a recognized presence in the industry. This is based upon their brand recognition, their access to capital resources and their iconic distinctiveness in the minds of consumers. This can therefore influence the level of power that they have over events promoters wishing to distribute their services. The threat from substitute goods and services, which can fulfil a similar need, is determined by the switching costs involved from one brand to another or the degree of motivation that the buyer has to substitute products. The claim on discretionary leisure expenditure may, for example, determine whether a customer decides to take a weekend break or go to an event. Similarly, the propensity for a customer to buy a DVD or watch an event live on television may influence the extent to which they may purchase a ticket for the event. The final force, competitive rivalry, is influenced by the amount, size, diversity and intensity of competition, the rate of industry growth and the relative exit and entry barriers to an industry.

Box 10.5. Live Nation and Ticketmaster.

The competitive model in the global music industry has changed from being based on revenue produced from the sales of recorded music to cash that is generated through the staging of live music concerts and events. Live Nation, which came to being in 2005, and was previously known as Clear Channel Entertainment, is based in Los Angeles. The company operates on a model of vertical integration owning artists, venues and distribution networks. It signs artists, including Madonna, Jay-Z, U2 and Coldplay, as a record label but without owning their music or future recordings. It therefore acts predominately as a music promoter. From a UK perspective, it owns and operates a number of events and venues; this includes the Download, Wireless and Hard Rock Calling events and the operation of venues such as Wembley Arena and Liverpool Empire. By entering into a number of joint ventures and ownerships, the company has also gained access to a number of additional events and venues. This includes having a stake in Festival Republic, which operates the Reading, Leeds and Glastonbury Festivals. With Gaiety Investments, it also acquired a stake in DF Concerts, gaining access to T in the Park in Scotland. It distributes its tickets through its website LiveNation.co.uk and in early 2009 attempted to merge with Ticketmaster. However, the proposed merger was referred by the Office of Fair Trading in the UK to the Competition Commission. This resulted in the deal being blocked on the result that it would generate unfair competition and potentially increase prices.

Sources: Various

Porter's model does have its limitations and has been criticized for analysing industries holistically and within a bounded context (Dale, 2000). Industries and industry sectors are not static and over time alternative forces that influence competition may emerge. For example, when applied to the UK tour operating sector, Dale (2000) has argued that a number of alternative forces are apparent, which include the threat of new entrants, the threat of customer expectations, the influence of synergistic alliances, threat of regulation, threat of alternatives and the influence of digital information technology and organization reinvention. 'Complements' is also forwarded by Grant (2008) as an additional force. Complements are those goods and services that, in contrast to substitutes, can actually increase value.

Questions

1. Using Porter's five forces model, analyse the competitive forces influencing an event/events operator of your choice.
2. To what extent are Porter's five forces a true reflection of competitive activity influencing the industry of your event/events operator. Are alternative forces at play?
3. What strategies should be considered by the event/events operator when attempting to influence those forces, which may act as threats or opportunities?

STRATEGIC GROWTH

An array of strategy models, according to Lussier *et al.* (1998) and Athanassiou *et al.* (2002), have been formulated for use by small business owners in the development of strategy. Better-known models include: the Boston Consulting Group Matrix; Michael Porter's 1980 Generic Competitive Strategies Model; Miles and Snow's 1978 Adaptive Strategy Typology; Lumpkin, Shader and Hills's 1998 Entrepreneurial Orientation Construct; and, Sonfield, Lussier, Greene, Corman and Frazer's 1997 Entrepreneurial Strategic Matrix. Each of these models is supposed to relate various independent variables of organizational situation and strategy, to organizational performance.

To illustrate, Porter (1985) argues that competitive advantage is based upon three generic strategies: cost, differentiation and focus. As illustrated in Fig. 10.4, Porter argues that these strategies can take either a broad or a narrow focus in scope.

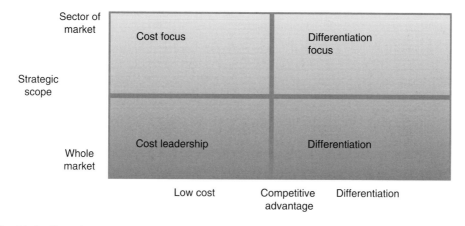

Fig. 10.4. Generic competitive strategies. Source: adapted from Porter (1985).

Cost leadership argues that the events organization can become the lowest cost producer in the industry and thus gain higher profits. Cost leadership can be achieved through gaining economies of scale, reducing the costs of resource inputs or having more efficient distribution systems. Events businesses often attempt to reduce their costs through the distribution and sale of tickets online, thus not having to pay commission to ticketing agents. Though competitors may attempt to achieve an advantage through cost leadership, it should be noted that there can only be one true cost leader. Differentiation strategy is when events businesses offer something unique and sell it a premium price. Differentiation may therefore come through better quality service, brand reputation, better design and so on. To ensure differentiation can be achieved, the events business will need to add value to its product and/or service range. If this added value is perceived by customers as being superior to competitors' offerings, then the events business can command a premium price. In the broadest sense, these two generic strategies can be targeted across the whole market. However, the events business may wish to focus on a particular niche sector of the market based upon, for example, demographic or need variables. In this respect, the events business can pursue a strategy of cost focus or focus differentiation. Cost focus is when the business focuses on a sector of the market, which may be particularly price sensitive. Differentiation focus is when the business differentiates the product to meet the needs of a niche market. Porter argues that a business needs to be clear about which generic strategy it is following otherwise it will become 'stuck in the middle' and have no clear basis upon which to gain competitive advantage.

Questions

1. Analyse different sectors of the events industry and review the generic strategies of events businesses that make up that sector.
2. How are these businesses achieving these strategies?
3. What are the differences between the generic strategies of large and small events businesses?

The events business should determine its strategic direction. Quadrant analysis tools such as the Ansoff Product/Market Growth Matrix may assist with these decision states (O'Toole, 2010). Ansoff's (1968) directional matrix (Fig. 10.5) offers four different strategic directions, which the business can pursue. These directions are based upon its markets and product range, and include four alternatives.

Market penetration is when a business attempts to grow its market share by focusing on its existing markets and product range. Essentially, the business is looking for its customers to purchase more of its current products. Market development is when a business decides to enter into new markets using its existing products. This can be based upon identifying and targeting new market segments or entering into new geographical regions where markets can be exploited. Product development is when a business develops new products for existing markets. This can be a consequence of changing consumer tastes and the business therefore has to tailor and update its products to meet the needs of its existing markets.

Diversification is when the events business enters new markets with new products. This can be on the basis of related or unrelated diversification. Related diversification is when the events business enters into a new market with a new product, which is related to its core business activity. Events businesses can become vertically integrated, owning each part of the

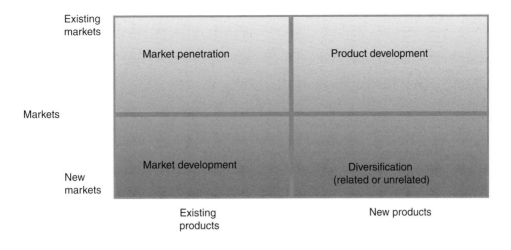

Fig. 10.5. Directional matrix. Source: adapted from Ansoff (1968).

Box 10.6. Market penetration and market development in Ibiza.

Ibiza is one of the Balearic islands, just off the east coast of Spain. In 2008/9, clubbing venues in Ibiza were hit by the global recession with a downturn in trade among a younger demographic. To increase the ratio of customers and penetrate the existing customers more deeply, clubs used incentives such as free bus transfers, early bird discount tickets and drinks offers. This acts as a basis for growing market share while countering the negative effects of the external environment. The island has also developed a strategy of market development by staging the Ibiza Rocks festival. With bands such as Keane, the Ting Tings and The Enemy, the festival appeals to a market that may not automatically see Ibiza as a holiday destination.

Source: Topping (2009)

---

channel of distribution from the supplier to the retailer. Events businesses can also horizontally integrate by merging or acquiring a competing events operator. Unrelated diversification is when the events business enters a new market with a new product that is unrelated to the core business.

Questions

Read the Live Nation example in Box 10.5 and answer the following questions:
1. How has Live Nation developed a strategy of diversification and become a vertically integrated firm?
2. To what extent is the diversification related or unrelated?
3. What are the advantages and disadvantages of the proposed merger between Live Nation and Ticketmaster?

STRATEGIC FORMULATION

Events around the world provide an outstanding platform for economic development and social regeneration with many cities, regions, countries and businesses, now committing vast resources to winning or creating events.

Events management knowledge frameworks, such as the International EMBOK Model (2006), include knowledge domains encompassing functional areas (classes), phases, processes and core values. The core values of creativity, strategic thinking, continuous improvement, ethics and integration are the values that must permeate all decisions throughout events management regarding every event element, phase and process. Events thinking, according to Rutherford Silvers (2004), is 'the ability to view and align an individual event project's needs and methods within the entirety of an event business's short- and long-term goals and objectives in order to maintain a focus on the larger issues and impacts that should be factored into plans and tactics'. The discussion hereunder will relate the key events knowledge domains (administration, design, operations, risk, sponsorship and marketing) to strategic management.

EVENTS AND ADMINISTRATION

The administration knowledge domain deals primarily with the proper and strategic allocation, direction and control of the resources used in an event project. Since resources are considered finite, by definition, it is imperative that they be acquired, developed and utilized in the most efficient and effective manner to benefit an event project and limit its risk (Rutherford Silvers, 2004). People engage in planning activities every day of their lives (Wanklin, 2010). Planning what one would like to achieve is usually carried out through a rational and deliberate set of actions ranging from day-to-day living, working and leisure, to numerous technical activities such as financial planning, economic planning, human resource planning, events planning, etc. Planning can also vary according to levels of detail, ranging from local events to mega-national or international events. Having an events plan helps in coordinating various activities in order to achieve a particular vision. Operational planning was discussed in greater detail in Chapter 5.

Unless events organizations strategically plan and coordinate the events they are responsible for, the events will not take place when they are intended or required to occur. In addition, the ongoing management and sustained quality of an event or events will not easily be maintained if a well thought out plan is not in place and continually reviewed (Wanklin, 2010).

The main person usually responsible for the coordination of the events programming and implementation process is a project manager (or, if it is a mega-event, several project managers could be involved). The major intention of project management is to meet certain agreed targets, within budgets and within the timeframes that have been stipulated by the events organizer. Project management was discussed in greater detail in Chapter 5.

EVENTS AND DESIGN

The 'design knowledge domain for events management focuses on the artistic interpretation and expression of the goals and objectives of the events project and its experiential dimensions emphasises' (Rutherford Silvers, 2004, Internet). The elements developed within each functional area combine to create the events experience encounter that will either be enjoyed or endured, with some options considered 'risky' by their very nature or by design (Rutherford Silvers, 2004).

Berridge and Quick (2010) emphasize that the activity of design for events management embraces actions that are purposeful, systematic and creative. In this view, design should then be considered a critical tool for events management as it relates directly to developing the events concept and the events experience. Furthermore, it enables the events manager to envision and implement the event. Events managers should therefore see themselves as not simply logistical and organizational problem solvers but as 'experiential engineers', who are able to piece together the overall picture of the event. Remember, events environments are produced on the basis that the majority of those attending will receive a fulfilling experience, no matter what type of event it is or what purpose it serves. Therefore events managers should regard themselves as 'packaging and managing an experience' from start to finish and imagine all aspects and details of that experience (Berridge and Quick, 2010). Events design is discussed in further detail in Chapter 5.

Box 10.7. Fan parks get local flavour for 2010.

The fan parks were built in and around the stadiums, in host cities outside the World Cup zone (townships), in non-host cities inside South Africa, in the Southern African Development Community, across the African continent and in the 32 countries participating in the event. These fan parks ensured that as many people as possible were able to view the matches and get a better idea of what South Africa is about.

Soccer fans feasted on traditional Cape Town food at the city's fan park and public viewing areas.

This is despite the fact that Cape Town's fan park on the Grand Parade was an exclusion zone (a FIFA-protected area where those who are not rights holders are prohibited from advertising or selling branded goods).

Shammel Ho-Kim, the city's fan park and public viewing area coordinator, said the 2010 Fan Fest on the Grand Parade 'definitely' had a Cape Town flavour.

It was indicated although none of the products of FIFA affiliates' competitors, such as Pepsi, could be sold. Capetonians and visitors could be assured that local Cape Town food was on sale.

'Rotis, boerewors (barbeque sausage) rolls etcetera will be sold to ensure our local flavours are represented,' said Ho-Kim. 'In addition, local arts and crafts will also be sold.

'The Fan Fest will have a distinctly Cape Town and African flavour.'

Source: Independent Online (2009a)

EVENTS AND MARKETING

The marketing knowledge domain for events management addresses the functions that facilitate events business development, cultivate economic and political support, and shape the image and value of the events project. The nature of the event as an 'experience' necessitates a thorough understanding of the unique buyer–seller relationship associated with this intangible product (Rutherford Silvers, 2004). Events marketers, according to Carmouche *et al.* (2010), need to consider how the event's goals and objectives will be strategically achieved in relation to attracting attendees to the event. Events are designed and planned for people and they have to be sold and communicated to the intended target audiences. Although events are diverse in their objectives, type, size and scale, all events need a means of informing, persuading and attracting potential markets. Increasingly, events are being used to increase the sale of goods and services, to promote good causes and generally as an important marketing communications tool. One of the reasons for the growth of events is that they allow face-to-face communication with an organization's target market. Within the strategic planning process of the event, marketing plans need to be developed to cover all aspects of the event, from pre-event research through to measuring the effectiveness of the marketing tools and communication channels. This chapter covers the key role of marketing and communication strategies through the stages of the event. This was discussed in greater depth in Chapter 7.

Box 10.8. TCEB pushes on with five strategies: 'Recovering and stimulating the MICE industry in Thailand 2009'.

The Thailand Convention and Exhibition Bureau (TCEB) implemented five new strategies to revive and stimulate Thailand's Meetings, Incentives, Conferences, Exhibitions (MICE) industry. As part of its highly integrated marketing and PR strategy, and a substantial injection of government funds to support special promotional packages, TCEB has brought together the public and private sectors to work together to address the challenges facing the MICE sector. This initiative aimed to build confidence in Thailand as a MICE destination in Asia.

The *first strategy* – an ambitious and integrated marketing strategy – is based upon three main components:

1. First, to build confidence and motivation among local and international MICE operators (known as 'Sentimental Marketing').

2. The second element – known as 'Experiential marketing' – provides opportunities for representatives of target groups to have a first-hand experience of Thailand.

3. The third element is known as the 'Government and Private Sector Collaboration Trade Show and Road Show.' The goal is to demonstrate TCEB's unified approach and close working relationship between the public and private sectors, and the strength of the government's backing for the MICE sector.

TCEB's *second strategy* is to stimulate the inbound market through the QUICK WIN promotional campaign. For the meetings and incentives market, they have extended TCEB's existing 'Meetings Plus' campaign, which consists of two high-value packages: the availability of the 'Free Third Night' package for delegates at events longer than 3 days, and the 'Hospitality Package,' which provides subsidies for receptions and banquets.

Turning to conventions, TCEB has developed a special campaign called 'Bring More, Enjoy More' by which agents and associations that bring a group of 20 or more delegates to attend conventions in Thailand will receive special privileges. These privileges include marketing support of baht50,000–120,000, and hospitality packages of up to baht30,000–60,000.

Targeting exhibitions, TCEB has developed and launched its 'Beyond Exhibition' campaign, offering attractive incentives to both exhibitors and visitors. The 'Triple-E' package provides accommodation subsidy for a free fourth night, and trade associations are eligible for the '100-A-Head' package, through which exhibitors are able to receive US$100 per person in marketing support if they are able to attract a group of at least 15 people. The '100-A-Head' package is offered exclusively for ASEAN countries and China and India.

(Continued)

Box 10.8. Continued.

The *third strategy* – the 360° communication strategy – is an integrated approach using all key media channels. This is supported by a referral strategy: online testimonials by respected opinion leaders are especially important in building confidence among target groups, since research shows that MICE visitors are increasingly reliant on the Internet as a primary source of information.

The *fourth strategy* – stimulating the domestic MICE market – focuses on promoting and developing four key provinces as MICE destinations. TCEB has launched the 'Meet in Thailand Prosperous Thailand' programme to encourage both public and private sectors to hold their meetings and seminars in Thailand.

The *fifth strategy* – a comprehensive crisis management strategy – is a coordinated plan, involving all concerned agencies. This includes establishment of the TCEB Call Centre and contact centres located at airports. Moreover, TCEB is working to elevate safety and security standards in the MICE industry to comply with Industrial Standard 22300 – MICE Security Management System, or MSMS.

Source: eTurboNews, Inc. (2009)

Events and operations

The operations knowledge domain for events management concentrates on the:

> people, products, and services that will be brought together on-site to produce the events project, as well as the roles, responsibilities, applications, and manoeuvres associated with each. Impeccable coordination is required in order to manage this symphony (or cacophony) of logistical and functional requirements and expectations.
>
> (Rutherford Silvers, 2004, Internet)

This was discussed further in Chapter 5.

Dealing with the future is an essential activity in the operation and management of SMEEs, regardless of size. The origination, planning and delivery of events are a complex task involving many different contributors, including authorities, contractors, public services, attendees and other stakeholders, according to Bromley and Moss (2010). The success of an event is determined by organization, planning and cooperation, and as events can gain high levels of media attention, it is extremely important that events managers, both those internal and external of a venue, ensure that due consideration has been given to operational and logistical elements of the event. These were discussed in greater detail in Chapter 5.

Box 10.9. Cape Town contingency plan for 2010.

FIFA included contingency measures in its host city transport operations plan in case the City of Cape Town's public transport plan was not ready in time for the World Cup.

In its September update of the plan, FIFA noted that the May 2010 deadline to have the Integrated Rapid Transit (IRT) system running is 'very tight and the possibility that this service may not be available for the event poses a considerable risk to the planning of the event transport services'.

(Continued)

Box 10.9. Continued.

The extent of the top-up transport services that were needed for the event depended on how much of the IRT would be ready. The first phase of the IRT was scaled down because of escalating costs. The project, estimated to cost R1.3 billion a year ago, now cost the city R4.3 billion.

Some of the University of Cape Town's Jamie Shuttle Service buses, which were not in use because the event coincides with university holidays, were used for the event's park and ride services.

The completion of the revised Phase1A of the IRT 'within time and budget constraints' has been identified as one of the risk factors of the city's 2010 transport plan.

An estimated 175,000 extra commuters were expected daily at peak times during the event. The city discussed extending the hours of other forms of transport in areas that would not be serviced by the first phase of the IRT.

FIFA said that transport during the World Cup would be concentrated in the city centre, Green Point Stadium precinct and Cape Town International Airport. Transport operations for the event were coordinated from the new Transport Management Centre at Goodwood and the operational cost of managing transport during the event was R80 million.

In a report submitted to the city's transport portfolio committee, Peter Sole of the transport, roads and storm water department said the city had to negotiate with landowners for the use of about 32,000 parking bays.

Most of the games played at the Cape Town Stadium had an 8.30 pm kick-off.

Source: Independent Online (2009b)

EVENTS AND RISK

The risk knowledge domain for events management deals with the protective obligations, opportunities and legalities traditionally associated with any event enterprise, including an event project. These areas are inextricably linked with every choice made and all activities conducted, and are increasingly mandated by stakeholders ranging from regulatory authorities to discriminating events consumers (Rutherford Silvers, 2004). Managing risks, emphasizes Ninow (2010), is a systemic process, whereby there is a gathering of information to assist with the identification of risks and future uncertainties, which affect our legal liability and exposure to loss or harm. This identification process includes examining impacts and consequences on the organization, its reputation, individuals, other people and property. Hazards and unsafe acts are threats to our endeavour and need to be analysed and dealt with. It is generically accepted that risks should be eliminated and avoided as far as possible and reduction and mitigation strategies introduced to minimize probability and severity of risks occurring wherever we can. The protection and safety of people and property is paramount in the context of events and a meeting, recognizing that some incident can occur is part of the process of managing risk.

Box 10.10. Sport safety bill sets the World Cup stage, South Africa.

World Cup host cities and municipalities that fail to comply with provisions in the Safety at Sports and Recreational Events Bill will have to go back to the drawing board if the bill is enacted.

The bill lays down new legislation as a precursor to the staging of large-crowd sports events. It came about as a result of the final findings and recommendations of the Ngoepe Commission of Inquiry into the 2001 Ellis Park disaster, in which 43 spectators were killed.

The new legislation will lead to regulations that affect all bodies that stage events, including municipal and local government institutions, controlling sports bodies and private organizations.

The bill also lays down a regime covering how municipalities should deal with and be responsible for major sports and recreational events, and provides an authority to register and allow any event to take place.

Sports authorities and Parliament's sports portfolio committee are pushing for the bill to be enacted before the World Cup.

Host cities and municipalities that have not followed due process as called for by the bill could have their 2010 events scrapped.

It deals with issues such as security, crowd control, communications and access to stadiums by both vehicles and spectators.

If enacted, the legislation will apply to events staged throughout the country – at fan parks, public viewing areas and for public outdoor broadcasts.

Lesley de Reuck, Cape Town's 2010 operations director, said the city had incorporated the bill and its draft regulations to the city's contingency and operational safety and security risk management strategy for 2010.

'The city will also do so with any other official public events or functions that will be hosted during the tournament,' said De Reuck.

The Western Cape provincial government also recently went on a whistle-stop road show to the province's 15 municipal districts to inform officials of the new bill.

Source: Independent Online (2009c)

SUMMARY

The chapter has explored the business planning and strategic process as it applies to the events industry. The elements of the strategic management process including strategic analysis, strategic formulation and strategic implementation have been reviewed. The chapter has acknowledged the differences between SMEEs and large events organizations when applying strategic management concepts and theories. This has been illustrated through a range of case studies encompassing corporate enterprises through to smaller events operators in both the private and public sector. The chapter has discussed the dynamic and complex nature of the external environment and the formulation of strategies in this context. Business planning is of paramount importance if events operators are to be aware of emerging opportunities and threats that are to influence their strategic decision making.

FURTHER RESEARCH

The Events Management Body of Knowledge (EMBOK)
http://www.embok.org/staticpages/index.php?page=international_embok_model

Event Project Management System
http://www-personal.usyd.edu.au/~wotoole/CDROM/

REVIEW QUESTIONS

1. Select either an SMEE or a large events business. Conduct a macro- and micro-environmental analysis of the business. Differentiate between those factors that are opportunities or threats to the events business.

2. Based upon what you have read throughout this chapter, what strategies would you consider the events business should pursue?

3. Evaluate the level of risk involved in implementing the strategy on the functional aspects of the events business.

REFERENCES

Ansoff, I. (1968) *Corporate Strategy*. McGraw-Hill, Maidenhead, UK.

Antoniou, A. (2008) Influences of core cultural values on the strategic values on the strategic behaviour of SME owner-managers: the case of small to medium sized hotel enterprises on the island of Cyprus, *International Journal of Management Cases* 10, 488–494.

Athanassiou, N., Crittenden, W.F., Kelly, L.M. and Marquez, P. (2002) Founder centrality effects on the Mexican family firms' top management group: firm culture, strategic vision and goals, and firm performance, *Journal of World Business* 37, 139–150.

Berridge, G. and Quick, L. (2010) Design management of events. In: Tassiopoulos, D. (ed.) *Events Management – a Developmental and Managerial Approach*. Juta (Pty) Ltd, Cape Town.

Bolton, B. and Thompson, J. (2004) *Entrepreneurs: Talent, Temperament, Technique*, 2nd edn. Elsevier, Amsterdam.

Bridge, J. and Peel, M.J. (1999) Research note: a study of computer usage and strategic planning for SME sector. *International Small Business Journal* 17, 82–87.

Bromley, M. and Moss, C. (2010) Events operations management. In Tassiopoulos, D. (ed.) *Events Management – a Developmental and Managerial Approach*. Juta (Pty) Ltd, Cape Town.

Carmouche, R., Shukla, N. and Anthonisz, A. (2010) Event marketing and communication strategy. In: Tassiopoulos, D. (ed.) *Events Management – a Developmental and Managerial Approach*. Juta (Pty) Ltd, Cape Town.

Chell, E. (2001) *Entrepreneurship: Globalisation, Innovation and Development*. Thomson Learning, London.

Dale, C. (2000) The UK tour operating industry: a competitive analysis. *Journal of Vacation Marketing* 6, 357–367.

Dale, C. (2009) Business planning and strategy. In: Robinson, P. (ed.) (2009) *Operations Management in the Travel Industry*. CAB International, Wallingford, UK.

eFestivals (2009) Reading's Heavenly Planet festival has been cancelled: recession and poor ticket sales blamed for its failure. Available at: http://www.efestivals.co.uk/news/09/090317a.shtml (accessed 29 January 2010).

eTurboNews, Inc. (2009) TCEB pushes on with 5 strategies: 'Recovering and stimulating the MICE industry in Thailand 2009'. Available at: http://www.eturbonews.com/9179/tceb-pushes-5-strategies-recovering-and-stimulating-mice-industry (accessed 29 January 2010).

Grant, R.M. (2008) *Contemporary Strategy Analysis*, 6th edn. Blackwell, Oxford.

Hannaford, V. (2008) BBC: Live Earth India cancelled, Organisers pull event after attacks in Mumbai. Available at: http://www.bbc.co.uk/6music/news/20081129_LiveEarthIndia.shtml (accessed 29 January 2010).

Henry, A. (2008) *Understanding Strategic Management*. Oxford University Press, Oxford.

Independent Online (2009a) Fan parks get local flavour for 2010. Available at: http://www.iol.co.za/index.php?set_id=1&click_id=180&art_id=vn20090928123622506C338574 (accessed 29 January 2010).

Independent Online (2009b) Cape Town contingency plan for 2010. Available at: http://www.iol.co.za/index.php?set_id=6&click_id=4&art_id=vn20091109045454364C431061 (accessed 29 January 2010).

Independent Online (2009c) Sport safety bill sets the World Cup stage, http://www.iol.co.za/index.php?set_id=6&click_id=2871&art_id=vn20091014125544591C389743 (accessed 29 January 2010).

International EMBOK Model (2006) Available at: http://www.embok.org/staticpages/index.php?page=international_embok_model (accessed 29 January 2010).

Johnson, G., Scholes, K. and Whittington, R. (2008) *Exploring Corporate Strategy*, 8th edn. Prentice Hall, London.

Kirby, D.A. (2003) *Entrepreneurship*. McGraw Hill Education, London.

Kiriri, P.N. (2005) Small and medium enterprises planning: evidence from Australia. Conference Proceedings of the ICSB, Washington DC, 15–18 June [Online]. Available at: http://www.sbaer.uca.edu/research/icsb/2005/title.pdf (accessed 12 May 2006).

Lussier, R.N., Sonfield, M.C., Frazer, J.D., Greene, F.D. and Corman, J. (1998) The entrepreneurial strategy matrix and business performance: an empirical analysis. Proceedings of the 1998 SBIDA Conference, Santa Fe, New Mexico, 4–7 February. Available at: http://www.sbaer.uca.edu/research/sbida/1998/pdf/toc.pdf (accessed 12 November 2004).

Lynch, R. (2006) *Corporate Strategy*, 4th edn. Financial Times Prentice Hall, Harlow, UK.

Minzberg, H. and Waters, J.A. (1985) Of strategies, deliberate or emergent. *Strategic Management Journal* 6, 257–272.

Ninow, E. (2010) Events risk and safety management. In: Tassiopoulos, D. (ed.) *Events Management – a Developmental and Managerial Approach*. Juta (Pty) Ltd, Cape Town.

North East England (2009) Strategy: Festivals and Events Strategy Available at: http://www.tourism-northeast.co.uk/pages/strategy (accessed 29 January 2010).

O'Toole, W.J. (2010) Events strategic development. In: Tassiopoulos, D. (ed.) *Events Management – a Developmental and Managerial Approach*. Juta (Pty) Ltd, Cape Town.

Porter, M.E. (1980) *Competitive Strategy: Techniques for Analyzing Industries and Competitors*. Free Press, New York.

Porter, M.E. (1985) *Competitive Advantage*. Free Press, New York.

Rutherford Silvers, J. (2004) Updated EMBOK Structure as a Risk Management Framework for Events. Available at: http://www.juliasilvers.com/embok/EMBOK_structure_update.htm#HumanResources (accessed 29 January 2010).

SA Tourism & DEAT (2002) Towards a national event strategy for South Africa: final report (October). SA Government (Department of Environmental Affairs and Tourism and South African Tourism), Pretoria.

Schindehutte, M. and Morris, M.H. (2001) Understanding strategic adaptation in small firms. *International Journal of Entrepreneurial Behaviour and Research* 7, 84–107.

Sexton, D.L. and van Auken, P.M. (1982) Prevalence of strategic planning in small business. *Journal of Small Business Management* July, 20–26.

Tassiopoulos, D (ed.) (2010a) *Events Management – a Developmental and Managerial Approach*. Juta (Pty) Ltd, Cape Town.

Tassiopoulos, D. (2010b) An investigation into the co-producers of preferred strategic behaviour in small, micro and medium tourism enterprises in South Africa. Unpublished dissertation for the Degree Doctor of Philosophy, University of Stellenbosch, Graduate School of Business.

Thompson, J.L. (2001) *Strategic Management*, 4th edn. Thomson Learning, London.

Thomson, J.L. (1999) A strategic perspective of entrepreneurship. *International Journal of Entrepreneurial Behaviour and Research* 5, 279–296.

Ticketmaster (2009) Available at: http://www.ticketmaster.co.uk/ (accessed 29 January 2010).

Topping, A. (2009) Ibiza's recession-hit dance scene fights to tempt clubbers back, http://www.guardian.co.uk/travel/2009/may/31/ibiza-music-recession-summit (accessed 29 January 2010).

Van Wyk, J.A. and Tassiopoulos, D. (2009) Policy, politics and events: a case study of South Africa's 2010 FIFA World Cup™: managing international sports events in sustainable political context. Paper presented at the *6th International Conference for Consumer Behaviour and Retailing Research*, Vorarlberg University of Applied Sciences, Dornbirn, Austria, 16–18 April.

Wanklin, T. (2010) Events planning and co-ordination. In: Tassiopoulos, D. (ed.) *Events Management – a Developmental and Managerial Approach*. Juta (Pty) Ltd, Cape Town.

chapter 11

Event Legacy

Geoff Dickson

OBJECTIVES OF THE CHAPTER

This chapter discusses the concept of legacy, or the long-term benefits of an event to a host community. The emergence of legacy thinking is associated with triple bottom line approaches to organizational performance, corporate social responsibility (CSR) and sustainability. This chapter helps to explain why governments invest in hallmark and mega-events and the pivotal role that leveraging plays in legacy creation.

This chapter will:

- explain the concept of event legacy, and differentiate it from event impact;
- explain the different legacy types commonly pursued by hallmark and mega-events; and
- identify examples of event legacy best practice.

INTRODUCTION

To comprehend the nature and dimensions of an events legacy, it useful to consider three well-established management concepts – CSR, sustainable development and the multiple constituency approach to organizational effectiveness. The classic approach to CSR is that organizations need only focus on activities leading to improved financial performance. More recent approaches to CSR hold that economic sustainability is a necessary but ultimately insufficient measure of an organization's effectiveness. Sustainable development refers to 'development which meets the needs of the present without compromising the ability of future generations to meet their own needs' (World Commission on Environment and Development, 1987).

Sustainable development is a fundamental objective of the European Union. Sustainable development requires the integration of short- and longer-term objectives. Social, economic and environmental issues are viewed as inseparable and interdependent factors underpinning human progress. Social, economic and environmental criteria represent a triple bottom line. Sustainable development requires organizations to address society's problems and to maximize benefits and reduce/eliminate disbenefits to their stakeholders. A stakeholder is 'any group or individual who is affected by or can affect the achievement of an organization's objectives' (Freeman, 1984, p. 46). The multiple constituency (i.e. stakeholder) approach to organizational effectiveness posits that effectiveness is the ability to satisfy multiple strategic constituencies both within and outside the organization. Within this approach, events are 'intersections of particular influence loops, each embracing a constituency biased toward assessment of the organisation's activities in terms of its own exchange with the loop' (Connolly *et al.*, 1980, p. 215). An event has a CSR to provide positive benefits for all its stakeholders. A successful event needs to be more than just 'operationally excellent'. Events should always seek ways of contributing to the 'big picture'.

STRATEGIC EVALUATION

With the rise of government investment and the increasing professionalization and bureaucratization of the events industry, there has been a corresponding increase in the sophistication of event evaluation. The purpose of strategic evaluation is to determine the quality, value or importance of an entity. The need for evaluation is not unique to the events sector: 'the bottom line for organizations in all sectors is the clear demand to measure outcomes and use both quantitative and qualitative data to tell compelling "performance stories" about how well their strategies have worked' (Love, 2001, p. 438). Within the events industry, and especially for major, hallmark and mega-events, increasing emphasis is placed on the strategic dimension. This strategic dimension emphasizes the long-term community benefits associated with the event. Operational excellence and short-term impacts have been joined by longer-term considerations such as destination branding, creation of business networks and new business investment.

WHAT IS LEGACY?

Event legacy is not the same as event impact. An impact is short term, whereas an event legacy is far more enduring. The traditional, short-term focus on event impacts is not sufficient to justify the significant government investment necessary to stage them.

> One of the biggest infrastructure investment projects is in the 2010 FIFA World Cup. We have, as government and the nation at large, pledged that the World Cup will leave a proud legacy from which our children and our communities will benefit for many years to come.
>
> (Jacob Zuma, President of South Africa – maiden state of the nation address)

Preuss (2007, p. 211) defined an event legacy in the following way:

> Irrespective of the time of production and space, legacy is all planned and unplanned, positive and negative, tangible and intangible structures created for and by an event that remain longer than the event itself.

Legacies can occur at any time and they can vary in length. Legacies may emerge before the event, during or after the event. Legacies can also vary in their duration – a facility will probably exist for many decades, whereas an increase in national pride or community cohesion may only endure for a few months. Legacies can occur anywhere. Legacies will nearly always be at their strongest in the immediate host community of the event (i.e. host city), but the legacies will also reach into other non-local communities.

> The legacy of the Games is not exclusively the property of the former Olympic host cities; rather it should be understood in global and universal terms…
>
> (International Symposium on Legacy of the Olympic Games, 1984–2000)

Event legacies are usually assumed to be exclusively positive. The reality is that event legacies can also be negative. A common, planned legacy of large event is to position the host city and nation as an attractive business centre in order to attract new investment and trade. Prior to the 2004 Olympics, the world's media expressed concern over the progress of construction work on the new Olympic venues. Even thought the facilities were completed in time, the reality is that this uncertainty created doubts as to whether Greece was a good place to do business. Similarly, problems with traffic congestion, security and over-commercialization meant that the Atlanta Olympics 'did not receive the kind of media attention it would ideally have liked' (Essex and Chalkley, 1998, p. 194).

Event organizers might like to claim that all event legacies are planned; there are some that are certainly unplanned (which are more likely to be negative than positive). The expected economic benefits to Albertville following the 1992 Winter Olympics did not materialize (Terret, 2008). The German Nazi party sought to use the 1936 Olympics to demonstrate Aryan superiority. However, the success of Jesse Owens effectively highlighted the physical capacity of people with African ancestry. The 1991 Rugby World Cup is often regarded as a major step in the reconciliation of black and white communities in South Africa. Even though the introduction of affirmative action programmes by South African Rugby Football Union (SARFU) was a condition of African National Congress (ANC) support for the bid, reconciliation was not among the reasons used to justify the bid in the first instance.

Event legacies can be both tangible and intangible. Tangible legacies can include new facilities, urban redevelopment and residential communities, public transportation infrastructure and telecommunication networks. Important invisible legacies include new organizational capacities, new relationships between and among businesses and governments, national pride and improved perceptions of a host city as a tourist destination. These intangible legacies are just as important to achieve as the 'bricks and mortar' legacies.

Not all events will have legacies. This does not mean that events without legacies are not worthwhile. The size and scope of an event's legacy will nearly always be in proportion to the size of the event. The bigger the event, the greater its capacity to provide a legacy. The bigger the event, the greater the geographic spread of its legacy.

LEGACY TYPES

Built environment – urban regeneration

Major events often require significant space and there is always a preference to have the event close to the city centre. Parts of inner city that are derelict or have 'marginal uses' (e.g. industrial sites, old markets, jails, unattractive waterfront land) may be transformed into more useful spaces as part of urban renewal or urban regeneration initiatives (Nel·lo, 1997).

Box 11.1. 1988 World Expo, Brisbane.

The city of Brisbane, Australia hosted the World Expo in 1988. The origins of the event can be traced back to an urban renewal study for Brisbane's inner city. James Maccormick led the study and having previously designed pavilions to house the Australian exhibit at previous Expos, he considered that an Expo would be an appropriate catalyst for his proposed redevelopment. Four years after the 6-month-long event, the site was reopened as South Bank Parklands. Few original Expo buildings remain on the site from the event, but many found use in other public spaces. The Expo site was converted into a combination of parklands, swimming pools, a riverfront promenade and a myriad of entertainment venues. World Expo Park, the Expo's theme park located adjacent to the Expo site, was intended to be a permanent legacy of the Expo at its conclusion. It closed 1 year after the event because of poor patronage. The Brisbane Convention and Exhibition Centre now stands in its place. In terms of urban redevelopment, a key legacy of Expo '88 was the creation of an inner-city lifestyle precinct that attracts over six million visitors per year.

Sources: Various

Built environment – non-sporting (i.e. transport and accommodation)

The need to provide transport and accommodation for the short-term surge of visitors provides a city with increased capacity. The 2010 FIFA World Cup is intended to provide a significant transportation infrastructure legacy for South Africa. In excess of US$15 billion was reportedly spent on upgrades to roads and airports as well as the creation of new rail and bus systems.

> The World Cup in 2010 is a catalyst for the development of our system because we need to meet FIFA requirements. But the huge sum of money we are investing will also ensure a lasting legacy for our people.
>
> (Jeff Radebe, South African Transport Minister)

Hotels and other forms of accommodation are often boosted in anticipation of the influx of visitors. Hotel investors need to take a pragmatic and long-term view of the market because it is unrealistic to recover the significant investment to build the hotel from visitors during the event.

> The London 2012 Olympic and Paralympic Games are providing a valuable stimulus to bringing forward developments that might otherwise have taken many years to get off the ground.
>
> (Sally Chatterjee – Visit London interim CEO)

Built sporting infrastructures

The physical facilities within which the event takes place are perhaps the most tangible feature of an event. Accordingly, governments are prepared to invest significant sums of money to ensure that they are functional for the event, add to the branding of the city and ideally have a use well beyond that of the event itself.

It is important to recognize that in order for built sporting infrastructure to be considered a positive legacy, it needs to have post-event utilization. The key is to avoid constructing 'white

> **Box 11.2. 2009 Atlantic Tall Ships Race.**
>
> The city of Belfast invested heavily in physical infrastructure to host the final leg of the 2009 Atlantic Challenge Tall Ships Race as part of its annual maritime festival. The project, supported by the Northern Ireland Tourist Board, the Department of Social Development, Belfast City Council and Belfast Harbour Commissioners, left a legacy of dedicated mooring facilities for private yachts and cruisers.

elephant' facilities. A white elephant refers to a valuable possession its owner cannot dispose of and whose cost (particularly cost of upkeep) is out of proportion to its usefulness or worth.

> The legacy of Athens has been more than GBP500m spent on maintenance and security of Olympic sites to which public access is now blocked by razor wire. In one, a Romany squatter camp has been established.
>
> (Doug Gillon, The Herald, 2 September 2009, p. 16)

White elephant stadia are less likely to occur if the facility is primarily designed for its long-term purpose and then converted to its short-term event use. In 1996, the Olympic Stadium was designed as a baseball stadium, adapted for its Olympic purposes, and then reverted back its primary purpose as a baseball stadium.

Political development

Successful hosting of international events can improve the reputation of the host and make the host more legitimate. Legitimacy refers to 'the cognitive validation of an entity as desirable, proper and appropriate in a widely shared system of beliefs and norms' (Rao, 1994, p. 441). When reputation and legitimacy coexist, an entity is more likely to be considered a 'player' and the ability to influence decisions becomes easier. Hosting events may provide a long-term boost to a host city/nation's reputation and legitimacy. 'This is an opportunity for Australia and Australians to prove we can hack it in the big time' explained Paul Keating, then Prime Minister of Australia, following the announcement of Sydney as host of the 2000 Olympics.

At an organizational level, sport organizations may acquire greater political influence by hosting events. This influence may extend to influence over member organizations, local, regional or national government, or with the international governing body.

> We bring greater influence to the policymaking table and that influence is enhanced further when we host major events and win medals. Hosting a successful dual European Championships will enhance our place in sport internationally, in our own country and throughout the FEI.
>
> (British Equestrian Federation)

Sport – elite performance

Hosting events also provides for improved performances of the home-team athletes. The 'home ground advantage' has been quantified (UK Sport, 2009). After reviewing 100 World and European Championships events in 14 Olympic sports, the host nation achieved a 25% increase in their results. In 73% of the events studied, the host's performance was higher than their average performance at events that they were not hosting (excluding 'non-competitive hosts').

It is clear that we have the opportunity to gain a competitive advantage through further targeted investment in major events. In an environment where medals are decided by increasingly smaller margins, the potential to achieve such a marked improvement in elite performance is highly significant.

(John Steele – CEO UK Sport)

Explanation of this home ground advantage goes beyond familiarity, reduced travel time and no change of time zones, home crowd support and favourable judging as explanations. Government investment in high-performance programmes often increases when hosting an event. It is considered 'embarrassing' if the home team does not perform according to expectations. In order to ensure success at the 2000 Olympics, the Australian Government invested an additional AUS$140 million above and beyond their normal funding. Canada's 'Own the Podium campaign' for the 2010 Vancouver Winter Olympics sought to capitalize on their 'home snow' advantage. These programmes should not be confused with the event – these programmes are about ensuring performance excellence by the home team participating at the event, rather than an operationally excellent event.

Sport – mass participation

Major events are generally assumed to promote physical activity and participation in sport within the host community. The basic premise is that the event's media profile will serve to inspire those not involved in sport or engaged in sufficient levels of physical activity to change their behaviour.

… [G]rassroots participation would be boosted. An already sports-mad nation would get fitter and healthier.

(London 2012 bid document)

However, evidence supporting the claims that hosting a sport event increases physical activity and sport participation levels are inconclusive. It is estimated that only 4% of Australians who became more physically active after the 2000 Olympics attributed this to the event (Bauman et al., 2001). In terms of sports participation, the Sydney Olympics produced mixed results – seven Olympic sports increased the participation numbers and nine decreased (Veal, 2003). Given the difficulties in measuring sports participation and physical activity longitudinally, the authors were reluctant to attribute any of these changes to the event. It is imperative that if an event is to have any chance of being associated with a positive increase in sports participation, then the event needs to contribute to other policies and initiatives to promote sport participation. Simply hosting a major event is not likely to improve sport participation or physical activity levels.

If hosting an event increases the probability of home team success, does this create an opportunity for events to be justified because of their increased ability to showcase winners? The answer is perhaps best provided by Sport Scotland, which concluded that 'care should be taken when asserting that success on the world stage in sport has an impact on general levels of participation'.

Environment

Events routinely seek to incorporate environmentally sustainable development principles into event planning. The ability of events to negatively affect the environment is clear – events concentrate a large number of people in a relatively small space over a relatively short period. Most event-related environmental sustainability initiatives are designed to: (i) reduce threats to biodiversity; (ii) reduce global warming and ozone layer depletion; (iii) minimize air, water and soil pollution; and (iv) avoid over-consumption of scarce and natural resources.

> Energy consumption, air pollution, emissions of greenhouse gases and ozone-depleting substances, waste disposal, wastes use and impacts on biological diversity are all issues for the sporting world to address.
>
> (United Nations Environment Programme)

Fortunately, environmental sustainability is now institutionalized within the major events sector. That is to say, those environmental considerations are now a 'behavioural norm' for event planners. By failing to conform to the norm, an organization and its managers are at risk of reputation damage and losing their legitimacy. This statement does not imply that these environmental considerations are effective, just that event managers will consider them. Events also provide opportunities for '"experiments in living", path-finding for wider society the technologies that may have important, even critical positive benefits for sustainability if widely adopted' (Collins *et al.*, 2009).

The nine Environmental Guidelines developed by Greenpeace for the Olympic Games are appropriate for events of all sizes:

1. Events should be committed to environmental sustainability. A truly sustainable project ensures that: (i) there is no systematic increase of fossil fuels or synthetic substances in the ecosphere; (ii) there is no depletion of the bases of productivity and biodiversity; and (iii) resources are used fairly and efficiently.

2. Events should take precautionary measures – if there is any doubt regarding the nature of negative impacts, then the risk should not be taken.

3. Events should take a preventative approach. It is cheaper and more effective to prevent environmental damage than to attempt to manage it.

4. Events should take a holistic approach. All potential environmental impacts throughout the full life cycle of the event need to be addressed.

5. Events should set specific and measureable environmental goals.

6. The event should involve community, environmental, social groups and the public in event planning.

7. Events should place the management of environmental issues at a senior level within the organization.

8. Events should conduct environmental reporting and ideally expose themselves to the rigours of independent auditing.

9. The event should explain their environmental initiatives and communicate their expectations and aspirations to staff, suppliers, providers, sponsors and media.

An additional challenge for events is not just to ensure that its short-term impacts are reduced, but that the event provides for an environmental legacy. Perhaps the greatest legacy of an event is its ability to change attitudes and behaviours. Before the 2008 Beijing Olympics, the impact of poor air quality on athletic performances was openly discussed. Factory closures and limiting personal use of motor vehicles to alternate days significantly reduced air pollution to acceptable levels. Despite the short-term success, it is unclear of the event has left a legacy of improved attitudes and behaviours towards the environment.

> It is impossible and will not be allowed should the city go backward in liveability because citizen expectations are already driven up by the Olympics and the demand for further social and economic development.
>
> (Deputy chief Tan Zhimin of the Beijing City Building Headquarter Office for 2008 Olympics)

Social

Events are often portrayed as leaving feelings of goodwill and increased feelings of community. There is potential for sport events to contribute towards increased community participation, community creativity and community wellbeing. In practical terms, these are represented by reducing crime and anti-social behaviour, improving educational attainment, developing healthy and active communities.

This potential can only be translated into real outcomes by integrating these initiatives into wider government, sport, physical activity and community development strategies (Shipway, 2007).

Communitas – an intense community spirit characterized by feelings of great social equality, solidarity and togetherness – and liminality – a situation where normally accepted differences between participants, such as social class, are often de-emphasized or ignored – are two preconditions for social leverage (Chalip, 2006). Social legacies are a contentious issue, especially with regarded their enduring nature and therefore, whether it constitutes an impact or a legacy. For example, research conducted before and after the 2006 FIFA World Cup in Germany identified that national pride in Germany increased to 78% during the event from a pre-event value of 71%. Within months, this score had decreased to 72% suggesting that improvements to national pride were not enduring (Kersting, 2007).

Economic

Economic impact studies seek to measure the change in GDP. Short-term economic impacts can be classified as direct (i.e. money spent by event organizers to prepare and stage the event), indirect (i.e. non-local expenditure in host community), induced (i.e. the ripple effect whereby new money is re-spent) and total (i.e. sum of direct, indirect and induced impacts).

There is considerable evidence that major events have an immediate short-term impact on the economies of the host city and region. However, the methods utilized in these studies are often fraught with limitations. Though noble in their stated intentions they have often become 'instruments for political shenanigans' that are 'commissioned to legitimize a political position rather than to search for economic truth' (Crompton, 2006, p. 67). In an effort to provide the largest possible numbers, a number of methodological tactics can be utilized: including local residents, inappropriate aggregation, inclusion of time-switchers and casuals, abuse of multipliers, ignoring costs borne by the local community, ignoring opportunity costs, ignoring displacement costs, expanding the project scope; exaggerating visitation numbers and inclusion of consumer surplus.

The economic impact of an event is concentrated during the event, when non-local visitation will be at its highest. The Olympics are a short burst. You get some infrastructure, which is great, but there is no long-term impact and for the typical family it does not mean much (Van Blarcom, 2007).

There is some evidence that events provide a legacy of increased inward investment in the region. The promotion of inward investment means to attract businesses to an area from elsewhere in the country and from other countries. When the investor is an international company, it is termed 'foreign direct investment'. In this context, the companies are attracted the improved infrastructure, communication and emerging business opportunities in the community.

A host community may also improve its export earnings. This is achieved by the 'trade fair effect', whereby foreigners shift their interest to the consumption of local products.

Events can also create a tourism legacy. In addition to the short-term influx of people for the event, some events have the ability to increase tourism before and after the event. Some events are able to put a destination 'on the map' and make a known destination seem vibrant and exciting. There is debate as to whether and how this increased awareness and improved brand perceptions translate into increased visitation. Regardless, events are now an integral part of the destination marketing mix for many cities. Destination branding through events is a powerful and proven tool to create greater awareness and visitation for a destination and hence provide economic benefits to the host city.

The ability of events to stimulate new relationships between and among organizations is another economic legacy. For example, it is reasonable to expect that, in the context of a nation-wide mega-event, regional tourism organizations may increase their level of collaboration with each other. This increased collaboration may provide long-term benefits as these organizations revert to business as usual after the event.

The event may also provide the opportunity for the people to acquire new skills and for organizations to acquire new capacities. A positive economic legacy can be attributed to the event if subsequent increases in domestic production can be attributed to these new skills and organizational capacities. Both paid and volunteer employees of an event can acquire new skills, which can be put to use in the years following the event.

> RWC 2011 represents an opportunity to significantly up skill and improve the capabilities of rugby and some other sports administrators operating in New Zealand. The development of a nationwide workforce capable of delivering RWC 2011 will also significantly increase the depth of the rugby administration pool at all levels.
>
> (New Zealand Rugby Union)

LEVERAGING

Event legacies will not simply materialize – they must be pursued. Leveraging refers to 'those activities which need to be undertaken around the event itself … which seek to maximize the long-term benefits from events' (Chalip, 2004, p. 228). The purpose of leveraging is to be 'proactive in planning for the creation of specific event benefits for the host community, and taking strategic measures to make those events sustainable' (O'Brien and Chalip, 2007, p. 320).

The term 'leverage' is used because the event provides a lever (and therefore mechanical advantage) that can make goal attainment easier. Leveraging is not an activity undertaken by the event itself. Rather, the events stakeholders undertake leveraging activities. The event can be viewed as providing a platform from which other organizations can launch their own leveraging activities. Events that adopt a 'build it and they will come' attitude will not realize all of the potential impacts and legacies. Legacy planning should commence as soon as possible in the event planning process. This ensures that the event becomes a tool to attain the desired legacies. It is still relatively common to see a search to identify possible legacies well after organization of the event has begun.

LEGACY HYPERBOLE

There is no shortage of public relations spin, government distortion regarding positive legacies. There are clear incentives for impressions of positive legacies to be created. Positive legacies provide evidence of benefits to the community, justify the public expenditure and encourage other cities to bid for future events. It is important that critical thinking skills are applied to legacy arguments. A healthy scepticism is likely to ensure that legacy aspirations and legacy realities are not confused.

Box 11.3. 2009 Kaohsiung World Games.

The Triple Bottom Line (TBL) is an approach to evaluating the sustainability of mega-events post-event. The original concept was developed by John Elkington in the 1980s to demonstrate how organizations can create or destroy economic, social and environmental values (Elkington, 1999). It was later broadened for TBL reporting or sustainability reporting (Sherwood *et al.*, 2005). A consequence of such a view is that it requires analysis of broad issues with economic, social and environmental dimensions.

Kaohsiung is the second largest city in southern Taiwan and was symbolic of the 1980s and 1990s Taiwanese economic boom, but its de-industrialization is similar to that of 1970s and 1980s Western European economies that have experienced a transition to high-tech and service-dominated sectors. The government has sought to boost the economy through leisure and consumption-oriented development. This includes rejuvenating derelict districts, building mass rapid transport systems, waterfront development, re-imaging the city and hosting mega-events. For international political reasons, the World Games was the first mega-event held in Taiwan. The World Games are a multisport event held the year after the Olympics. The sports are predominantly non-Olympic sports.

This evaluation of sustainability took place during the event development. Using a TBL framework, it was possible to identify relevant issues at a point when intervention by the organizers could improve sustainability.

1. Sustainable economy

(i) *Changing consumer habits*: this research highlighted that changing consumer habits was not fully considered at the outset of the 2009 World Games.

(ii) *Investment*: a key justification for hosting sports mega-event is that public investment in infrastructure and venues, and private investment in hotels and tourism facilities leads to long-term positive economic impacts. Tourists will visit future events using the new facilities and an improved host city image is projected to the world and potential tourists. However, local enterprises were not fully involved in planning the Games or potential international business opportunities.

(iii) *Employment*: contrary to local residents' expectations, neither event organizers nor urban planners made commitments to jobs for host residents. There were no effective strategies to ensure the long-term sustainability of employment opportunities.

2. Sustainable society

(i) *Community and housing*: the main considerations for constructing new facilities were transportation and land availability, and meeting International Federations Standard (IFS). An issue for social equality and inclusion was the relocation of some local populations but the tight preparation schedule for the Games meant a failure in communication about potential impacts on local people.

(ii) *Combating social exclusion*: sports mega-events can help social sustainability by including potentially disadvantaged groups in sports participation. There was little consideration of this by the organizers and no explicit consideration of the needs of women or disabled in Games-themed projects.

(iii) *Sustainable development in event policies*: the Kaohsiung 2009 World Games had no holistic policy for sustainable development. Application of the TBL Framework identified this gap with Kaohsiung City Sustainable Development Network (KCSDN) potentially able to bridge gaps between policy and implementation.

(continued)

Box 11.3. Continued.

(iv) *Community-wide participation and socially sustainability*: the inclusion of 'host communities' in planning processes is essential for the success and sustainability of a mega-event (Frey *et al.*, 2007; Leonardsen, 2007). The TBL Framework found only limited host resident empowerment in decision-making and consultation.

3. Sustainable environment

(i) *The protection of natural resources and cultural heritage*: it was identified that a sports mega-event helps protect natural resources and cultural heritage, but with the National Sports Park, there was no long-term conservation plan.

(ii) *Sports facilities and landscapes*: for the Kaohsiung Games, there was no robust planning to protect and enhance the built environment or landscape infrastructure post-event.

(iii) *Transport*: sports mega-events present transport challenges with major environmental implications. Applying the framework approach indicated that the Kaohsiung Games did not have strategies to reduce private transport in the event zones during the Games and no strategy to encourage public transport use.

(iv) *Water management*: the Kaohsiung 2009 World Games involved refurbishment of the Lotus Lake but there was no monitoring planned and hence no evaluation possible.

(v) *Waste management*: a mega-event involves generating large volumes of waste and pollutants. The TBL Framework analysis indicated a lack of strategy and monitoring with little attempt to set or meet recycling targets.

(vi) *Biodiversity*: application of the framework showed the Kaohsiung Games had no biodiversity action plan to ensure the quality of biodiversity to be maintained before, during and after the Games.

Source: Ian D. Rotherham, David Egan and Shang Chun Ma, Sheffield Hallam University

SUMMARY

An event legacy refers to all the planned and unplanned, positive and negative, tangible and intangible structures created for and by an event that remain longer than the event itself. There is no limit to where or when these structures may occur. The specific nature of the legacy is related to the type of event – different events will create different legacies. However, all legacies can be classified as to whether they are social, cultural, economic and environmental in nature. There was perhaps a time when events could be pursued without much thought given to their legacy. However, as soon as events received government investment, they became vulnerable to government influence. This forced event owners to position their events as catalysts for the achievement of outcomes beyond that of an operationally excellent event that was enjoyed by all and managed to meet financial investments. It is now widely accepted that events can be leveraged to provide sustained benefits to the host community.

FURTHER RESEARCH

Leveraging:

Chalip, L. (2004) Beyond impact: a general model for host community event leverage. In: Ritchie, B. and Adair, D. (eds) *Sport Tourism: Interrelationships, Impacts and Issues*. Channel View Publications, Clevedon, UK.

Limitations and potential misuse of economic impact studies:

Crompton, J.L. (2006) Economic impact studies: Instruments for political shenanigans? *Journal of Travel Research* 45, 67–82.

Legacies:

Gratton, C. and Preuss, H. (2008) Maximizing Olympic impacts by building up legacies. *International Journal of the History of Sport* 25, 1922–1938.

Toohey, K. (2008) The Sydney Olympics: striving for legacies – overcoming short-term disappointments and long-term deficiencies. *International Journal of the History of Sport* 25, 1953–1971.

Websites:

http://www.sports-city.org/sports_legacy.php
http://www.agreenerfestival.com

REVIEW QUESTIONS

1. Reflect on an event and identify legacies that can be classified as: (i) planned, intangible, and positive; (ii) unplanned, intangible, and negative; and (iii) planned, tangible, and negative.

2. What limits or conditions, if any, would you place on the following statement? 'An event has a CSR to provide positive benefits for its stakeholders.'

3. Why are major event legacies more capable than impacts to justify the considerable public investments necessary to stage them?

4. How does an operationally excellent event contribute to the event legacies?

5. What factors have led to the expectation that events create legacies?

6. Is there an inherent conflict between the provision of new physical facilities and environmental sustainability?

REFERENCES

Bauman, A., Ford, I. and Armstrong, T. (2001) *Trends in Population Levels of Reported Physical Activity in Australia 1997, 1999 and 2000.* Australian Sports Commission, Canberra.

Chalip, L. (2004) Beyond impact: a general model for host community event leverage. In: Ritchie, B. and Adair, D. (eds) *Sport Tourism: Interrelationships, Impacts and Issues.* Channel View Publications, Clevedon, UK.

Chalip, L. (2006) Towards social leverage of sports events. *Journal of Sport and Tourism* 11, 109–127.

Collins, A., Jones, C. and Munday, M. (2009) Assessing the environmental impacts of mega sporting events: two options? *Tourism Management* 30, 828–837.

Connolly, T., Conlon, E.J. and Deutsch, S.J. (1980) Organizational effectiveness: a multiple-constituency approach. *Academy of Management Review* 5, 211–217.

Crompton, J.L. (2006) Economic impact studies: instruments for political shenanigans? *Journal of Travel Research* 45, 67–82.

Elkington, J. (1999) *Cannibals with Forks: The Triple Bottom Line of 21st Century Business.* Capstone, Oxford.

Essex, S. and Chalkley, B. (1998) Olympic Games: catalyst of urban change. *Leisure Studies* 17, 187–206.

Freeman, R.E. (1984) *Strategic Management: a Stakeholder Approach.* Pitman, Boston, Massachusetts.

Frey, M., Iraldo, F. and Melis, M. (2007) The impact of wide-scale sport events on local development: an assessment of the XXth Torino Olympics through the sustainability report. Paper presented at RSA, Region in Focus? International Conference, Lisbon, Portugal.

Kersting, N. (2007) Sport and national identity: a comparison of the 2006 and 2010 FIFA World Cups. *Politikon* 34, 277–293.

Leonardsen, D. (2007) Planning of mega events: experiences and lessons. *Planning Theory & Practice* 8, 11–30.

Love, A.J. (2001) The future of evaluation: catching rocks with cauldrons. *American Journal of Evaluation* 22, 437–444.

Nel·lo, O. (1997) The Olympic Games as a tool for urban renewal: the experience of Barcelona '92 Olympic Village. In: de Moragas, M., Llinés, M. and Kidd, B. (eds) *Olympic Villages: a Hundred Years of Urban Planning and Shared Experiences*. International Olympic Committee, Lausanne, pp. 91–96.

O'Brien, D. and Chalip, L. (2007) Sport events and strategic leveraging: pushing towards the triple bottom line. In: Woodside, A. and Martin, D. (eds) *Tourism Management: Analysis, Behaviour and Strategy*. CAB International, Wallingford, UK, pp. 318–338.

Preuss, H. (2007) The conceptualisation and measurement of mega sport event legacies. *Journal of Sport and Tourism* 12, 207–227.

Rao, H. (1994) The social construction of reputation: certification contests, legitimation, and the survival of organizations in the American automobile industry: 1895–1912. *Strategic Management Journal* 15, 29–44.

Sherwood, P., Jago, L. and Deery, M. (2005) Triple Bottom Line evaluation of special events: does the rhetoric reflect reporting? Paper presented at Third International Events Management Conference, Sydney.

Shipway, R. (2007) Sustainable legacies for the 2012 Olympic Games. *Journal of the Royal Society for the Promotion of Health* 127, 119–124.

Terret, T. (2008) The Albertville Winter Olympics: unexpected legacies – failed expectations for regional economic development. *International Journal of the History of Sport* 25, 1903–1921.

UK Sport (2009) Home Advantage: the Performance Benefits of Hosting Major Sporting Events. UK Sport. Available at: http://www.uksport.gov.uk/docLib/What-we-do/Events/Home-Advantage.pdf (accessed 22 March 2010)

Van Blarcom, B. (2007) Assessing the economic impact of sport/recreation/cultural events/facilities. Available at: http://www.avesta.ns.ca/assets/pdfs_ppts/impacts_guide.pdf (accessed 11 June 2010).

Veal, A.J. (2003) Tracking change: leisure participation and policy in Australia, 1985–2002. *Annals of Leisure Research* 6, 245–277.

World Commission on Environment and Development (1987) *Our Common Future*. Oxford University Press, Oxford.

Closing Remarks: the Future of Events

Debra Wale, Peter Robinson and Geoff Dickson

The concluding chapter will summarize and review the key discussions from the book while also considering current and future developments within the events industry.

The first part of the book introduced and contextualized events by examining their political and cultural influences, historically and in the present global climate. It has taken the reader into the world of event planning, bringing the event idea through its stages of development and providing definitions of concepts to aid event planning. The second part has explained and provided a set of tools for event operations management, providing clarification through practical examples and event case studies. The final section has provided a strategic treatment of critical and contemporary issues challenging the events industry, with emphasis given to the appreciation of the need to manage the political, economic and social environment to achieve a sustainable events legacy.

FUTURE CHALLENGES AND TRENDS

In addition to the challenge of satisfying a range of stakeholder expectations, the following issues are emerging as key drivers in operational events management:

- Environmental management.
- Managing the impact of the global economic fluctuations.
- Managing skills shortages and deficiencies.
- Managing the consumption of alcohol.
- Managing in (and after) crisis situations.
- Managing the rapid advances in technology.
- Managing the impacts of a global power shift to the markets of India, China, South America and Africa (Rushe, 2009).

So, what are the key messages for the future of events? It is certainly likely that the industry will continue to grow and develop to meet event customers' changing expectations and needs. Within the UK, the entertainment sectors (music and theatre) have recorded the best industry growth, with statistics from Mintel (2009a) indicating an 8% year-on-year growth for music festivals and concerts, and a 4% growth for theatre, museums and galleries. This is attributed to the growth in UK inbound tourism as a consequence of the global economic downturn; the UK became a draw to tourists because of the pound's weaker position against international currencies. This provides an example of how global economic fluctuations can positively affect the events industry, at least in the UK. Conversely, negative impacts have resulted in reduced spending and cancelled business. The events industry will need to transform itself in response to environmental change. Adapting to meet the changing needs of the event consumer with their reduced spending power is only one of the challenges.

The events industry has been impacted mainly through the theme of austerity where it became unfashionable to spend, particularly on corporate entertainment. McVeigh and Wainwright (2009) report on the impact that the recession has had on the events industry, explaining that 'the mood of austerity, combined with public anger against bankers, has created a climate where frivolity is feared' and resulted in a downsizing of corporate Christmas parties with the associated impact on the industry realized by booking cancellations. The consequence for event organizations and their venues is decreased revenue. Lloyds TSB, for example, replaced their annual star-studded extravaganza with a modest small-scale alternative.

> For two years running, Lloyds TSB rewarded its top employees with a *Stars in Their Eyes* party, with guests sipping champagne on a flotilla of Thames riverboats to the O2 arena, to be met by chef Gordon Ramsay, who organised the menu. Senior executives took part in a singing competition, followed by performances by the Sugababes and McFly.
>
> (McVeigh and Wainwright, 2009)

Cutbacks in the industry have not only come from seasonal business. Hospitality has been downsized for meetings, cheaper alternatives sought for weddings, and other celebrations and football clubs have had to increase marketing activity to target a wider family audience.

As well as the pressures to downplay frivolity, celebrity culture has also helped to change and influence consumer trends and behaviour, and this has helped to reduce spend on events. Events will change to reflect changing cultural influences and the frugal fashion endorsed by celebrities eager to get snapped demonstrating their respect for the environment.

Conspicuous non-consumption: being frugal and sustainable has become a fashion statement, It comes from a need to be seen as better than other people. It's not about living modestly and being in tune with the environment.

> Two years ago people boasted about how much they'd paid for something: 'It's Harvey Nichols, they only had one.' Now you'll flaunt your eco credentials by boasting about how little you paid for something: 'I got it in a sale/at a clothing swap/charity shop/made it myself.'
>
> (Watson, 2009)

Lavish celebrity weddings are downsizing and this behaviour is being replicated throughout the industry with cheaper alternatives being sought by the general public. The industry is challenged to adapt their offering to match this frugal fashion. This behaviour has wider implications for the events industry with cheaper event alternatives being sought by all.

Environmental impacts are set to continue to shape the events industry, and even the best planner cannot predict the worst threats.

There has been consistent if not increased terrorist activity in recent years. Given their profile, events are often targeted. The Olympics is a perfect example; it can be no coincidence that the timing of the terrorist attacks on London, which brought the capital to a standstill on 7 July 2005, was the day after London was confirmed as the host city for the 2012 Olympic Games. The events sector is no better or worse than the world it inhabits and it is difficult to envisage a set of circumstances whereby the events sector becomes isolated from humankind's inhumanity against their fellows.

The use of events to assist in the branding of the host city is well recognized. Events can provide a tourism legacy, which will live on for years after the event has been staged. It may well be the case in the future that cities will pursue events, but not with any real intent to acquire hosting rights. Rather, the destination will leverage its bid for the event without incurring any of the risks and financial investment associated with actually hosting the event.

Events will continue to intersect with politics. Recent efforts to take events to developing nations – India and the 2010 Commonwealth Games, South Africa and the 2010 FIFA World Cup, and Brazil and the 2016 Olympics – were all political decisions. They were political decisions in the sense that they highlight an events sector complex, akin to the well-recognized military industrial complex (Byrne, 2010). The events sector complex refers to the policy relationships between governments, event owners and industrial support they obtain from the commercial sector (i.e. sponsors, broadcasters). The complexity and intensity of relationships within this complex will increase.

NEW TECHNOLOGIES

New technologies continue to revolutionize the world of events, the recession has provided a vehicle for technological development and innovation with lower costs and carbon neutrality being used to drive popularity and secure its usage in the events industry.

A recent report from the CBI, The Shape of Business – The Next 10 Years, said that the recession would be a catalyst for a decade of business change, dramatically reordering everything from corporate ethics to the workforce (Ford, 2009). The economic impacts of the 2009 global financial crisis have yet to fully impact on the events industry. The events industry relies heavily on the tourism industry for attendance at a range of events and a number of factors including the increase in flight costs have left event planners considering alternative solutions to cut costs and keep events sectors alive. Technology has been a considerable and lasting driver for change in the events industry. Technologies include virtual events used for educational purposes, e.g. tourist attractions providing virtual field trips for students to experience events. Virtual conferencing has developed to include virtual conference centres and a number of paid for products compete for the virtual conferencing market. The equipment is increasingly sophisticated, providing users with a high-quality, secure network, and as systems are refined the conferencing experience is increasingly life-like (Keegan, 2008). Free and popular unsecured conferencing alternatives include Skype and DimDim Webinar.

The benefits of virtual conferencing are being sold as a greener alternative to traditional conferencing, which is being criticized for its heavy burden on the planet and the increasing carbon footprint of delegates (mainly through business travel).

Three-dimensional technology has had a revival because of advances in high-definition technology and computer-generated imagery. Major sports tournaments are being broadcast to audiences in cinemas, allowing sports fans to congregate for the event experience.

This is expected to be the year [2010] when 3D establishes itself. Sky intends to launch a 3D cinema channel and is considering creating one for sport. FIFA has said this year's World Cup in South Africa will be captured in stereoscopic 3D with up to 25 matches shot with special rigs.

(Rees, 2010)

Social networking has had a revolution in the 'Noughties', enabling consumers to post their comments as the action happens and immediately impact on the event experience, providing a public platform to drive the industry forward in meeting customer expectations. YouTube gives consumers an opportunity to post and view user event content, providing a virtual event environment and legacy. Wark (2009) suggests that consumers isolated in computer-dependant environments will seek the event experience in search of real life stimulation: 'One of the ironies of digitalization is that the more we are connected, the more we become isolated … digital isolation will lead to hunger for shared experiences'.

Reflecting then on the notion that many event operators may struggle over coming years with environmental influences and global changes, it should be noted that at the opposite end of the scale, exciting new opportunities are developing. Richard Branson's company Virgin Galactic has been developing commercial space travel for the last 5 years. In 2009, Branson unveiled *Enterprise*, its first mothership, which will begin delivering passengers into sub-orbit in 2012 (Becker, 2009). It is rumoured that Spandau Ballet will bring a new dimension to the concept 'in-flight entertainment' when they become the first band to play in space, in a performance during 5 minutes of weightlessness outside the earth's atmosphere (Becker, 2009; Mintel, 2009b).

In summary then, the events industry faces exciting yet challenging times ahead. Broadly speaking, three types of events will dominate the 21st century event landscape: (i) local, carbon-neutral, sustainable events; (ii) global, mega-events; and (iii) virtual events utilizing new and emerging technologies. As the industry continues to grow and be shaped by external influences and changing customer needs, so will the shape and scope of operations management.

Research in the sector will continue to analyse performance and propose new systems, models and approaches for operations management in events and related management disciplines, the very seed from which this book grew, and will become increasingly important.

REFERENCES

Becker, K. (2009) Virgin Galactic signs Spandau Ballet to perform in space. Available at: http://www.gadling.com/2009/12/15/virgin-galactic-signs-spandau-ballet-to-play-aboard-first-space/ (accessed 29 January 2010).

Byrne, E.F. (2010). The U.S. military-industrial complex is circumstantially unethical. *Journal of Business Ethics*, 1–13.

Ford, E. (2009) Businesses that don't look to the future run the risk of falling victim to changing environmental, economic or technological trends. *The Sunday Times* [online] 19 January 2010. Available at: http://business.timesonline.co.uk/tol/business/related_reports/mapping_british_business/article6994111.ece (accessed 29 January 2010).

Keegan, V. (2008) Soon, all meetings will be virtual. *The Guardian*, Thursday 8 May 2008. Available at: http://www.guardian.co.uk/technology/2008/may/08/telecoms.videoconferencing (accessed 29 January 2010).

McVeigh, K. and Wainwright, M. (2009) Hide the champers, remove that hat: City firms forced to party in secret. *Guardian* [online], 27 November 2009. Available at: http://www.guardian.co.uk/uk/2009/nov/27/city-firms-party-in-secret (accessed 29 January 2010).

Mintel (2009a) Leisure Industry Overview – UK – December 2009. Available at: http://academic.mintel.com/sinatra/oxygen_academic/search_results/show&/display/id=479850/display/id=500561 (accessed 29 January 2010).

Mintel (2009b) 80's Pop Stars to be the First Band to Perform in Space. Available at: http://academic.mintel.com/sinatra/oxygen_academic/search_results/show&/display/id=479850/display/id=500561 (accessed 29 January 2010).

Rees, P. (2010) England's Six Nations game against Wales to be broadcast live in 3D. *Guardian* [online], Tuesday 12 January 2010. Available at: http://www.guardian.co.uk/sport/2010/jan/12/3d-england-rugby-ireland-wales (accessed 29 January 2010).

Rushe, D (2009) Hurtling to a scary future: The world is changing at an unprecedented rate and the value of forecasting is at a premium. *The Times* [online], 28 December 2009. Available at: http://business.timesonline.co.uk/tol/business/article6973967.ece (accessed 29 January 2010).

Wark, P. (2010) What took place in 2010. *The Times* [online], 25 January 2010. Available at: http://women.timesonline.co.uk/tol/life_and_style/women/the_way_we_live/article6966348.ece (accessed 29 January 2010).

Watson, R. (2009) Futurist Richard Watson's predictions for 2010. 31 December 2009. Available at: http://www.speakerscorner.co.uk/file/6104dc183a0d6bbdc8d4f48fca5d8916/richard-watson futuristspeakerpeoplefuturetrend-spottertrends20092010expectations.html (accessed 29 January 2010).

Index

Page numbers in **bold** refer to figures, tables and boxes.